GW01402799

Ebony Books

Presents

David Simon's

How to Unlock Your Family's Genius

A book on family and education

published in 2009

ISBN 978 0 9559 190 0 8

Printed in the UK

For my family, here and beyond

Thanks to Dr. B Goring,
Dr. L Simon-Bleasdille
N Akpom-Simon, J Salmon
& the Ancestors.

Thanks also to the various master teachers,
specialists, authors and elders
who have patiently taught
and/or influenced me to write this book.

CONTENTS

INTRODUCTION

The genius of Black people is largely unrepresented in our schools and homes, but the evidence of this is in our mere survival; as Bob Marley sang, '*We are the Black Survivors*'. In surviving, we have to remember we once thrived; we thrived in ancient Egypt where we built pyramids; we thrived in ancient Ghana with our treasures of gold; we thrived in Mali, Songhay and Benin as we made magnificent bronze heads; our writers and scholars thrived in the great libraries of Timbuktu; our craftsmen and women thrived in ancient Zimbabwe as master masons and architects; we thrived in Black China in philosophy, in Black India as we sat in the lotus position and meditated upon the wonders of mathematics. Even under the recent oppression with the European arrival in Africa, we managed, under inhumane conditions to survive in cane fields, in tobacco plantations and create Santeria in Cuba and Candomble in Brazil: communal systems that maintained a relationship with the Creator. Whether we thrived or survived, family and community were central and central to family and community is our relationship and acknowledgement that *Nature* is the Great Teacher.

To address the current crisis that today's Black communities find themselves in all over the world, we have to once again build families, and communities, based on an education system informed by this Great Teacher; meaning, that we have to put in place an education system that develops the natural genius of Black people, an education system built on the philosophy of self-love, self-reliance and self-determination.

What is family? What is community? The English dictionary says, 'a group of people with common ancestry or deriving from a common stock; a group of people living under one roof; especially a set of two or more adults living together and raising children'. Is this an accurate description of a family; and does the family have the freedom, the skills and knowledge, to survive or thrive? Again, the English Dictionary defines community as: 'a group of people living in a particular area; a group of individuals with some common characteristics; a body of people or nations having a common history or common interests.' The miseducation of black African people means that this common unity is obscure. So, trying to mobilise the family, trying to mobilise the community is a difficult task. Yet, the spirit of the Blacks has not been broken. We saw in the great leadership of Toussaint L'Ouverture the ability to organise, to defeat Napoleon's armies; we saw in the spirit of Marcus Garvey the ability to organise millions of Black people right around the world; we have seen in the work of Wangari Maathai, and her Green Belt Movement, the ability to organise mostly rural African women and start one of the greatest and largest environmental movements in the world. Perhaps it is time that we all start to organise a great education movement; one that is not classroom based, but community based; that draws out from humanity's true potential, an education movement that pays as much attention to the immaterial as to the material; one where everyone who is trained has a role, a system that is not institutionally dominant. Our heroes and heroines named above used their energy, ingenuity, cultural resources and self belief to create movements and revolutions. We need to do the same.

How to Unlock Your Family's Genius

As with *How to Unlock Your Child's Genius*, the first in the genius series, this book is based on my twenty-one years of running Ebony Education which consists of Saturday Schools, family learning centres, parenting classes, a publishing house, a theatre-in-education company, and teacher training projects in West Africa and the Caribbean. We have worked with thousands of African-Caribbean families, as well as families from other communities. I have also had the pleasure of working as a teacher, a learning specialist and to be deputy Head of a basic education department, whilst somehow running a theatre company and staging productions all over the country. These experiences have made me study education with a slightly unconventional approach, but one that I believe has given me a much greater insight into how education and art can be used to empower communities, that are marginalised and oppressed.

There are many crises within the family, which impact on a child's school performance, impact on the break down of relationships, and impact on employment and vice versa. Bad news from the mass media blights the Black community: high rates of mental health issues amongst Blacks, school exclusions, high prison rates, teenage pregnancies, children killing children, break-up of relationships are what is broadcast to us. Bearing this in mind, it is almost a rare joy to see children play, to see families gather and celebrate success, and there are success stories in the Black community! There is a way out from the mess; a way forward, that sees the community mobilised; a realistic, and practical strategy that starts in the Self, that starts in the family, in the home, with small, but strategic steps that will make fundamental changes to the quality, opportunities and experiences of Black people. Our working definition of genius is 'extraordinary abilities matched to social responsibility.' To be responsible is to start with self-love. So, let us do what the Wangari Maathai, 2004 Nobel Prize winner and the rural women of Kenya did; let us, with love, plant a seed in our homes, in our communities and watch our children, the parents, the grandparents, all grow, and realise our true greatness.

Stage 1

The Foundation

Themes of inquiry:

- to inquire into a natural education system that empowers the family
- to inquire into the genius-resources of the Black community
- to inquire into the educational achievements of the Black community
- to inquire into the attack on the Black famisly and the response to these attacks

African Family Symbol of Inquiry

Hwemudua is the symbol of examination. This symbol demands that we examine our lives so that we can achieve perfection. Our inquiry into a new education system based on family will lead us to this human perfection.

Theo's Diary

Heard Amma calling me again. That means the dreams are going to start. I'm not scared anymore.

Had another dream. Am I going mad like the Dr Seamus thinks? Grandma doesn't think so. She says I'm a genius, and I should drink some bush-tea and take some aloe vera at night, especially when the moon is full. But the dreams keep coming. Scared to tell mum. She'll just curse in Jamaican. Don't want to upset her more. Heard her crying last night. Wish dad would come back.

Dreamt about dad. That he gave me all his stamp collection, and maps, and old books.

Mum took me to the museum again. Think it had something to do with my bad school report. I shouted at her when we got home, 'You're not home-schooling me again!' She shouted back; said I was going to grow up like dad. Stayed up in my room. Fell asleep then woke up, as mum's lips and tears touched my cheeks. Had another dream. Found myself in the garden and built a time machine with bits from the old lawn mower that Dad never got around to fix; an old computer, hair dryer and the old washing machine that the council said they're going to collect. Dream ended. Mum woke me up for school.

Wednesday

Got detention again. Did well in maths test. Said I won't be allowed to go on the school trip. Mum's going to be real angry.

Saw Dad on the street. Outside the council place. Said he'd been in another meeting. He was with a lot of white people with name tags and smiles. Said he'd phone me tonight, but I'm still waiting.

Made my gang official. We're to be known as 'The Revolutionaries', just like in Dad's old books. We all took on names; Malcolm X, Lumumba, Toussaint, Garvey, Sobukwe and Biko. Everyone's real excited. Told them to keep it secret, because that's how revolutionaries work. Taught everyone the Revolutionary salute, secret handshake, signs and showed them the Abeng horn that I'm going to blow when the revolution really starts.

The Beginning

These are the diary entries of a young Black boy entering adolescence. We do not often read these kinds of thoughts for statistics of Black children have them as faceless data. Newspapers only report on them when there is a crime or tragedy. These are the thoughts of Theo who now lives in a broken home. His spirit is troubled but no one knows how to heal him or give him the opportunity to heal himself and understand why Amma, this ageless Black woman of his dreams, insists in reaching out to him. In some ways Theo's family is typical, in some ways not. His parents have parted. School life does not suit or understand his learning style and pace, and culturally he is dying in this education system. Yvonne, Theo's mother agrees for his meetings with the education psychologist to continue, though she had had it stopped temporarily because of the damage it was doing to Theo.

This book is about a family, who, having fallen apart, go on a journey and it is a book about the community that this family live in discovering, ways in which it might rebuild itself using the talent within. We need to put in place an alternative family education that is linked to true community development and that requires an understanding of many disciplines: history, sociology, educational psychology, neuroscience, culture, business, empowerment and art. I am an independent black educationalist and have been for some twenty-one years; each week counselling parents, buying resources, teaching children, managing staff; spending long lonely nights in what I consider innovative curriculum development; researching how children and adults learn and how they are motivated. I read, I discuss, I write endless lesson plans, schemes of work; attend conferences and listen to frustrated parents pouring out their hearts about their children's education. I am part of the supplementary school movement in Britain, the only black grassroots education movement of its kind that has seen thousands of supplementary schools emerge, some for only a few months, others for years and decades.

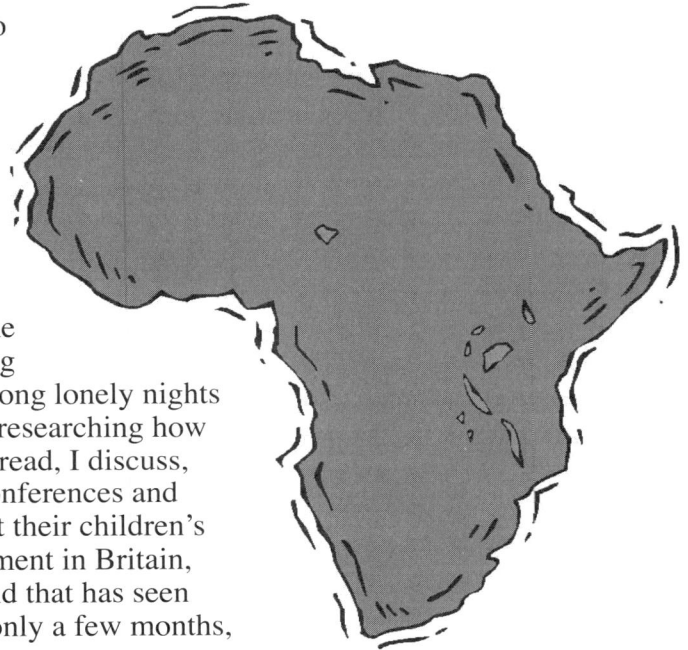

So, this is my journey. I never intended to become an educationalist. I was/am a writer of novels, poetry and plays; many of which have been popular, but the work of education keeps dragging me back. In truth, it is spiritual work, for when you work with any learner, child or adult, you have to develop ways to prise out their genius, especially if it has locked up for years. It is not only that we need more variety to our education system, but we need one that has family at its centre. This therefore implies that if family is central, then community development is the aim. There can be no more education for servitude, which is what the present system amounts to, whether the teacher is conscious of this or not. We have to plant the Tree of Knowledge back in the everyday lives of Black people (and all other people). This great task is not simply the job of one person, or one organisation but the job of millions of people worldwide. We all have a role; we see children all around us, and whilst great rain forests are being ruthlessly cut down, I do my part for the environment in this book and plant an African tree of Knowledge here, so that it can take root, and once again we can live with self-determination, dignity and excellence.

It is a sunny day in south London; a lazy Sunday that is almost idle except for the play of children whose mischief is the only thing that flutters a few leaves on a surprisingly barren tree. This is how things are all over the Black Diaspora and the continent; the African Tree of Knowledge is not being nurtured. Now, five hundred years after the first slave ships we try and grow tulips, marigolds, chrysthamiums, white roses rather than cultivate our own tree. Our tree is bare, naked in the modern world for all those to humiliate it. Dogs come and urinate at the base of its trunk; occasionally people have picnics there, whilst lovers will sometimes scandalise the tree's shade. Few can remember the great significance of this tree, perhaps only the moon whose light insists on still giving it its glory of old. Yet, the Tree has roots, roots that stretch deep into the earth from where it grew from a seed. Its potential is still magnificent. We all have this magnificent potential, but there are so few who know the great science of how to work the land, know how to enrich the soil, know how to plant trees. We start again. What resources do we have to make this tree grow into magnificence?

The Pyschology of Self-Determination

Self-love, self-reliance and self-determination are big tasks, but these are the most important things that can be taught in the home and striven towards. We have the skills and knowledge. We can build a home. We can design the home in our cultural tradition. We can devise ways to ensure that the home is powered by a new form of environmental energy. We can ensure that a business emerges from this home. We can ensure that the adults of the house set up apprenticeships for the children to learn the family business. We must be certain that this home creates family wealth that will help the rest of the community, and the community supports the family. All efforts must guarantee that the adults of the home run the susu, that will help others to build their houses. Of course, there may be troubles in the family from time to time, so we have to ensure the family have those wise enough to help them, and when the adults of the family get old, will they have accumulated enough wisdom to help the young, as they build their home in the improved tradition of the first family. We must ensure that the families that follow build schools, colleges and universities on the same principles that they have built their homes, cooperative economics. We have to ensure that those who now have their houses, because of the susu and wisdom of the first house, pour libation in honour of the family that built the original home. Those who now have houses must keep teaching the children that they live in good houses because of the *sacrifice* of the first family. If we believe in the power of the home, the strength of the family then let us begin to build!

Building a Family

Some would say, there seems to be less knowledge of courtship, of rituals around sexual practice and the cycles it should follow; there seems less knowledge of fatherhood, motherhood and the protocols and responsibilities around marriage. John S Mbiti in *Introduction to African Religion* writes:

> *We have seen that according to the African views of marriage, its main purpose is to produce children. Children are greatly valued in African life…If the wife is barren, then she and her husband may arrange for him to have another wife so that children are born into the family. If the problem lies with the husband, then a close relative or friend is asked or allowed to sleep with the wife in order that she may bear children for the family.*

This emphasis on family, on community implies social responsibilities, which also implies community involvement. In Western culture marriage is often something for just two people; a private affair, as is divorce. However, the impact of separation, especially on children is extensive and has a wide impact on society. I have noticed that when someone has one or two relationship break-ups, they then seem open to the idea of arranged marriage or at least the involvement of a third party. There is a belated acknowledgement that marriage is not just about two people; that consideration has to be given to family wealth, family history, family health as well as to romance. Is it wrong for others to play an advisory role; to look at the whole social impact that the marriage might have and for them to consult their elders, their ancestors and God. Or should we all turn to speed dating, online dating, singles parties etc. These might well have a place, but it is clear, as we will see in this book, that family is not just about romance.

About Family

Niara Sudarkasa outlines the two models of families: one being based around blood ties (consanguity) and the other being based around ties created by spouses (conjugality). In the Western world families built around the nuclear (conjugality) family system have tended to be the dominant one, whereas, in Africa, the dominant family structure has been the one centred around blood ties or kinship ties (consanguity). In her article Black Families she writes:

> *African families, on the other hand, have traditionally been organised around consanguineal cores formed by adult siblings of the same sex or by larger same sex- segments of patri – or matrilineages. The groups which formed around these consanguineally related core members included their spouses and children, perhaps some of their divorced siblings of the opposite sex. This co-resident extended family occupied a group of adjoining or contiguous dwellings known as a compound. (p91)*

So the African family consisted of compound-families with their sophisticated and complex relationships, protocols and rituals which meant that they were, to an extent, self-reliant and self-determining, but above all, wealth creating communities; micro states. Amos Wilson, in *Blueprint for Black Power*, says, the family is:

> *..a primary organisation, a fundamental generator or source of power where the human and non-human capital resources of its members are pooled and shared as means of achieving its vital goal. (p57)*

These family arrangements ensured the family wealth (use and trusteeship of land), family health and family prosperity. They were, and in some cases still are self-generating communities. Key to all of this was the family learning system and the early exposure of children to this, not least the exposure that African children had to family governance and systems of socialisation. Issues concerning adultery, divorce, theft, etc., did happen in the traditional African family but the family-compound system meant there was a social security structure in place to ensure that children were not abandoned. Divorcees still had a compound home to live in and in many cases the family of the bride received financial and material compensation for the ending of the marriage.

When we look at marital arrangements in traditional African communities we find that polygamy was common, with the husband and the first wife having considerable power in the organising of the compound. I am not either recommending or denouncing this marital arrangement but simply noting its existence. I do not mean to paint a romantic picture of family in Africa but I do want to portray its strengths as a social organisation, even though this marital structure, might, in some cases not be suited to all present day situations. However, co-wives were entitled to proper wifehood and had their own living space, kitchen and store space. In the design of the whole compound we find that it is based on scaling symmetry and recursive self-organising patterns, which is natural in Nature and, for the African, in systems of governance. This recursive self-generating village (logarithmic spirals) planning and architectural design patterns, also found in human DNA and many of the Ghanian Adrinka symbols, is seen in Africa's oldest and most popular board game, Oware (Ghana) or Ayo (Nigeria).

How to Unlock Your Family's Genius

Again John S Mbiti gives us further insight into the African family when he writes:

> *For African peoples the family includes children, parents,grandparents, and other relatives such as brothers, sisters,cousins and so on All relatives have duties and responsibilities towards one another. Everyone knows how he is related to other people in the clan and the neighbourhood. The idea of family also extends to include the departed, as well as those who are about to be born. This family concept spreads vertically and horizontally.(p115)*

However, we are dealing with the modern Black family which, in the West is experiencing increased single female households, marital break-ups; pressures from high unemployment, educational underachievement of the children and high incidence of mental health issues. It is clear therefore that we need to strengthen the family by adopting many of the features of the compound- family, which does not have to be based on blood ties but could be based on friendship and/or love. Whether we look at the African-Caribbean communities in the Caribbean or England, or the African-American community, or even Africa itself, you see families in trouble in all areas; families unable to defend themselves from attacks in all directions. So let us become the self-generating compound-family and begin to generate our wealth; generate schemes to ensure our health, generate our manhood and womanhood, and our school for the children of our modern compound family.

How to Recognise Your Family

This might seem odd but for those of us living in the West that puts so much pressure on families, many of us do not have a working model of what is family. Some might see it as just those living in the same house, or just blood brothers and sisters, or the inclusion of uncles and aunts and nieces and nephews. For us now, the Black family does not have the physical compound but many of the strengths of this compound system need to be reinstated, such as, family governance, the creation and inheritance of family wealth, the control of family health, the ownership/trusteeship of family land, and the social security of the family compound system. Families in the West and in Africa, where the Western model of nuclear family is becoming more obvious, the actual recognition of family and the role that family members play, or could play is obscure. So, the recognition of your family needs to be deliberately stated. Who are my family? I used to do an exercise with the children at the Saturday Schools of making them draw their family trees. This became very unpopular and many parents complained because some children had very little contact with their father's side of the family, and some did not know their fathers. So we can see that issues around family are immediately problematic. However, children especially need to recognise who their family is. Issues of shame, anger and ignorance have to be addressed. An exercise that I have done with families when taking family learning classes has been to ask the families to draw their family. This produces amazing results and allows for a discussion about family and its different generations. Also, this exercise allows:

- Families to talk about previous generations

- Families to look at family photographs and family memorabilia and see who their family is/was

- Families to appreciate and give thanks to the efforts of previous generations for the sacrifices they made which have led to greater opportunities for the next generation

- Families to learn from the past mistakes of previous generations

How to Strengthen Your Family

This whole book is about strengthening family, but we can start by outlining a few key activities that we should do.

- Inquire through research into what is family and the different family structures and their successfulness.

- Share this inquiry with other family members if possible.

- Look at the family health patterns and take qualified advice to address it through diet and lifestyle e.g., diabetes and high blood pressure.

- Organise a family event and invite family and friends to the gathering; in this way you allow for families to socialise and support one another.

- Reconnect with family members if both parties are agreeable to it

- End family feuds, sometimes by not arguing about the issue that caused the feud, but by an invitation to a social gathering.

Family and Therapy

It is 1987, Spring. But this spring betrays old nursery rhymes for there are no showers, only hints of sunshine and my own naïve optimism at having put up a sign on a dilapidated youth club which reads: 'Ebony Supplementary Saturday School'. Many had reservations about the project, but I was determined. By the spring of 1988, thanks to the local black pirate stations and my own guerrilla marketing, my Saturday School was full and I had moved to bigger premises. Many children, like Theo, have been brought to me; usually by the mother, bewildered and desperate; ushering in their confused child, hoping that I might give some kind of quick fix to their child's educational underachievement. It was that year that Theo's parents walked into the school, carrying a case file that was also weighted by shame. Yet, there was hope in their demeanour; an air of defiance accompanied their entrance.

I expected them to say the usual, that their son needed support, that they weren't happy with his progress in school but their stuttered beginning was different. It called for me to listen to them carefully and to look into the slightly shy eyes of Theo, who gazed at the ground as his parents spoke.

"…You see he hears her, but he can't explain what she wants. At first we thought he was hallucinating. Then the school got involved, and that made things worst…" Their story continued, becoming background muttering as I looked in the files that they brought and at the mystery surrounding this small child. A few seconds passed before I caught myself again and heard the father's tale of how Theo had arrived at Ebony. "…But she keeps calling him."

"Who's she?" I enquired, trying to appear as if I had been following the story with absolute care. "Amma," almost half shouted the mother; irritated that I had asked and missed a previous detail. "Amma, the first woman of the earth!" Perhaps my gaze gave away that I was now looking hard at the parents, to see if they weren't some crack pots. This prompted them to provide me with more details. Apparently, when Theo was in class he would sometimes shyly ask his teacher about history; different epochs in history, perhaps even wanting to know some secret that the history books didn't speak about. According to the puzzle that the parents pieced together, Theo, though a bright child, became moody, introspective and sometimes disobedient. His school, which was in no way innovative, reacted in the usual way by labelling his behaviour disruptive.

How to Unlock Your Family's Genius

Although I conducted a quite thorough initial parent interview I was still unclear about 'this woman', unclear as to how I could help and to the so-called behavioural issue. Fortunately, while the parents left still unsure as to whether I was the right person to support their child's learning, they provided his case file for me to further investigate. So this is Theo's case, our typical case that we are to use as our inquiry into what is happening to family and the family learning system needed to achieve community success.

The Ancient Africentric Education Curriculum: Sharing Good Practice

Evidence of our family learning systems can be found in the architecture, literature, mathematics and astrology of ancient Egypt (Kamit) but most of all in the quality of people that it produced who would create a successful civilisation that would last so long, 3500 years. We know that every temple had vast libraries, the best known of the African libraries being Alexandria (Greek name given to African library), and learning centres like Ipet-Isut (Temple of Amun at Karnak).

Architecture

Buildings in Kamit (ancient Egypt), both wooden and stone, displayed great knowledge, history and wisdom, and were built in harmonic proportions, whilst also being orientated to celestial bodies. This achievement was based on knowledge of mathematics. The first great building to be constructed from stone was The Great Step Pyramid of Saqqara (2630 B.C.E.), designed by Imhotep for King Zoser. We also find that the pyramids, like The Great Pyramid of Giza, were aligned true north, an achievement which indicates that the builders mastered the knowledge of geography, geodesy, astronomy and geometry. The Great Pyramid of Khufu was constructed with 2,300,000 stones, each weighing two and a half tons. Unfortunately, Theo, when he went to the British museum on a school trip knew little of this and so didn't pay much attention to the evidence of his people's great achievement. Occasionally he glanced at a statue, wondering why it represented someone so calm, so at peace, so at home on their throne. If he could have re-visited Kamit, he would have seen boys his age studying in school-temples, being prepared for great leadership: a system of education that would use all means to develop the mind-body intelligence to its greatest heights.

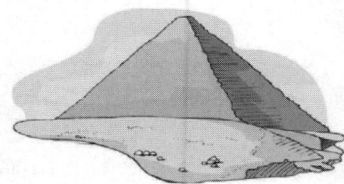

Literature

The Pert Em Heru (Coming Forth By Day) is one of the oldest religious book in the world and tells of the journey of the scribe Ani. This book was never mentioned to Theo. He studied the Bible, and didn't realise that many of its stories, psalms and concepts came from this even older Black African book.

Mathematics

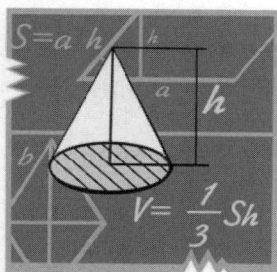

Two documents, plus architectural evidence, provide us with the mathematical education that Black Egypt had that enabled them to produce thousands of engineers, architects, technicians and astronomers to achieve their magnificent buildings and astrological calculations. The first is the Rhind Mathematical Papyrus (1900 B.C.E.). The papyrus consists of over eighty mathematical problems and solutions. The problems focus on the square root (Pythagorean Theorem), area of a circle, rectangle, triangle and trapezium. In school, as Theo sat at his desk, he would struggle with similar calculations. Why was it that a child thousands of years ago could do these calculations, yet in the modern world, the child would not only struggle with these problems, but would have numerous assessments performed on them to say why they were almost incapable of such feats.

The second mathematical document is the Moscow mathematical papyrus. Cheikh Anta Diop in, Civilization or Barbarism (1981), quoting V.V. Struve and T. Eric Peet that the Egyptians knew the exact volume of a truncated pyramid and area of a sphere. Diop, speaking about the plagiarism of Archimedes writes:

> The other 'borrowings' in which he indulged himself during and after his trip to Egypt, without even citing his sources of his inspiration, show clearly that he was perfectly conscious of his sin, and that hereby he was being faithful to a Greek
> tradition of plagiarism that went back to Thales, Pythagoras, Plato, Eudoxus, Oenopides, Aristotle, etc., which the testimonies of Herodotus and Diodorus of Sicily reveal to us in part. (p242)

But no one told Theo this. He learnt about Pythagoras. In his maths book there was an old picture of a white man, who he was told was very clever. In his science lessons he learnt about Archimedes and he can remember learning something about Plato and Aristotle. Unfortunately Theo didn't learn anything about Imhotep, the astronomer, philosopher, poet, architect and physician. So we can see that there are things that puzzle Theo; systems that not only hold him back but make him angry, make him confused and makes him feel vulnerable. There were things that he wanted to talk to his father about, but his father was not simply gone, he seemed to have found another love, his world of liberal politics and all he left Theo with were memories and his old books on revolution.

We have looked at the young boy called Theo, a portrait of a pupil searching for himself during his adolescence, whilst also negotiating a system of education that would label him a failure. Yet, there was an adventure in Theo that the school could never see, an adventure that could teach him. During these years of running Ebony and of teaching children like Theo, I would concoct adventures to rescue him from the education system, even though this fantasy was confined to my imagination. It was as much therapy for me, as for anyone who might one day read it and that one day has come.

The Three Mile Radius

If you were to examine the three mile radius around any urban school, and look beyond the trees that line the roads; the local parks, cafes and wine bars; if you look into the derelict shop fronts or little alleys off the main road or outside the local British Rail station, you'll see drug addicts and drunks and those with mental illnesses sleeping rough or begging or stealing.

Then there is the more subtle attack on children and childhood that we need to look at. Children are being stalked; advertisers want to sell them junk food; violence is sold to them through computer games; pornographic magazines are placed on the same shelving or space as children's sweets that rot their teeth. Children are given a credit card with little or no financial literacy training. I have seen drug dealers waiting outside schools, their flash cars parked a little way off. Some children are surrounded by hopelessness; they have been targeted to consume brands with their parent's money and once they become workers they will continue robotically. They have been programmed. If they were to one day become the unemployed then they will want what they cannot afford, but the pressures to have will continue. The advertisers of cars, porn magazines, junk food, alcohol and the rest will continue to target them. These children of the three mile radius might steal to have something; and they will steal, rob and curse in the three mile radius.

The teachers who teach in the school of the three mile radius, do not live there and their children do not go to school in the three mile radius. Many also want out. Staffroom talk is of the mountains of paperwork, or early retirement or leaving the profession. They drive through and when they arrive at work they deliver a curriculum that they do not believe; that has little relevance to many of the pupils. The Ofsted school inspectors do not live in this three mile radius nor do many of the education officials, who we trust to improve standards.
In the staffrooms, teachers of schools that are surrounded by the complex three mile radius, in an attempt to explain the underachievement of their school, blame the community, where the attack on childhood and family is so unrelenting. Often, they do not understand the world of their pupils or their family; nor

do those who put together the curriculum that the children follow each day. Blame has a function in the teaching profession; it allows for the attack on someone else; without any self appraisal. However, if we look carefully, we find that teachers underachieve too. My experience is that many, deep down, want a different system. They don't want a system where children are like battery hens. If we look even more carefully, we find that the relationship that the school has with the local community, is that it denies its resources to an already excluded community. On weekends, the school is locked up. It should be open to the community who want to run community events, but they are excluded. The 'vision' of the education authorities cannot include a real role for the community; at best, they will have some auxiliary role, some minor subservient role. The whole education profession, the school and college and university, has a defence mechanism of blame supported by a plethora of assessments, which label and categorise the learner. This is where the real bullying takes place. This inability to learn about self results in the school system being intransient, stubborn, bullish and unable to engage with its learners if the learners do not look like and speak like them. All this impacts on family, so families must take action.

Action Research: Research Leading to Family Action

Throughout this book the reader is encouraged to engage in action research on the various themes that we will explore with an aim to become more knowledgeable about issues affecting their home, family and community so that they can take informed and strategic action to improve their circumstances. I therefore want us to look at action research as a method of inquiry, as a way to investigate what is going on in our communities.

Action research is designed to empower students, parents and teachers, and is in contrast to traditional research in that it is not expert led. It can be said to be a method of inquiry that encourages self-reflection at grassroots level, allowing the individual or organisation to gain a greater understanding of their practice which they can now improve upon. The German psychologist Kurt Lewin, ('Action Research and Minority Problems in 1946), is credited with coining the term 'action research' and its small spiral step approach. This spiral step approach is as follows:

1. **Identify general or initial idea**
2. **Reconnaissance/fieldwork**
3. **Planning**
4. **Take action**
5. **Evaluate**
6. **Amend plan**
7. **Take new action based on amended plan**

We can see from the above steps that action research is useful to us at this early stage in making us aware, that it is our responsibility to undertake research for ourselves and it raises our awareness of being conscious of problem-solving. The Black-African community has to adopt a research methodology that addresses historic disempowering features that might undermine research. For example, when so much of oppression has focused on self-hate, low value of Black culture etc., then the research follows patterns that does not address the part played by this self-hating mindset. This means that our research/inquiry has to be spiritual as well.

Already you would have seen that in addition to the above method I am also using Adinkra symbols (which appear at the beginning of each section) to help our inquiry as they remind us of the themes and the approach that our inquiry should take. These symbols were developed by the Ashante people of Ghana and their origin is said to go back to the 17th century, and may well go back to the Ivory Coast. There are said to be nearly one hundred Adinkra symbols which are used in Ghanaian society as gold weights, in jewellery design, stool decoration, textile design and architecture. The meaning associated with each symbol is multilayered and they are of further use to us in supporting our reflective learning, in reminding us of our intellectual tradition and in giving further insight into the many topics we will cover in the book.

Stage	Themes	Possible Research Material
1	Resources and health	• Education: school reports; national reports; books on education; newspaper articles; recorded anecdotes; dvds, documentaries, films. • Health: medical records; newspaper articles; books on community health; books and articles on natural healthcare, raw food diets. • Business/wealth: books, articles and reports on business; notes on spending trends; notes on wealth ownership

An Africentric Approach

Afrocentricity seeks to do many things but mainly it seeks to celebrate the achievements of Black African people; it seeks to confront the Eurocentric approach to scholarship, history and education and it seeks to place the achievements of the Nile Valley civilisation (ancient Egypt or Kamit) at the centre of its whole methodology and theory. Key to this whole movement are the works of George G. M James (The Stolen Legacy) W.E.B Dubois, Marcus Garvey, Aime Cesaire, Leopold Sedar Senghor and Molefi Asante. For our purposes in this book we can say that our Africentric approach is to place the African (Black) family at the centre of the whole inquiry and seek to understand and develop a practical way of working with families that addresses our most pressing needs. Africentricity allows the practitioner to celebrate self; to say this is who I am and this is the science of learning that my people have developed. All too often we are instructed to work in multiculturalism, which, as a noun might be fine; but where is its science, its heritage? It simply ignores the inequalities that operate in society and the practitioner simply ends up accommodating others, whilst in a hidden state of self-denial.

What I have presented so far has made me reflect on education and family, and now I want to share with you writings that have come out of this reflection

Writings of a Educationalist

On Leadership

> *To put the world in order we must first put the nation in order; to put the nation in order , we must put the family in order; to put the family in order we must cultivate our personal life; and to cultivate our personal life, we must first set our hearts right.*
>
> **CONFUCIUS (Chinese philosopher/teacher)**

To School Or Not To School:
Homeschooling in the Black Community

"To a very great degree, school is a place wherechildren learn to be stupid"

How Children Fail by John Holt

How to Unlock Your Family's Genius

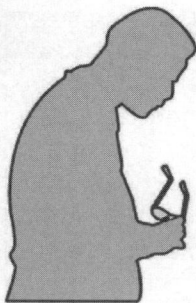

Why are African-Americans and the Black community in England turning to homeschooling faster than any other group? Why are 90% of these homeschools run by women? Why has homeschooling become one of the ten fastest growing trends in the US? And why are homeschooled children in some cases two years ahead of their counterparts in the State school system? But before we ask these questions we should investigate this phenomenon and the various factors that have caused over 150,000 African-Americans to turn their homes into schools, and a growing number in Africa, the UK and the rest of the Diaspora. Perhaps we should be bolder still and ask if the homeschool model is a viable option for more black families all over the world to consider.

About twenty years ago or so a member of a homeschool organisation called, *Education Otherwise*, came to see me at one of our Saturday schools. It was a cordial meeting, where she told me of an interesting study that she had carried out which revealed the political power structure that exists in schools which is never overtly mentioned. It was simply this: for some weeks she studied where the parents waited for their children in the playground. Her study revealed that the white middle-class parents stood closest to the doors that led into the school. Then came the white working class parents who stood in the middle, and finally the black parents who stood at the sides and back of the playground. A simple study that revealed the power structure within the school and wider society. Yet, at that time I was unaware of homeschoolings roots within the black community, dismissing it as a white middle class option and that the users of my Saturday schools wouldn't have the resources to make this an option. This was a mistake on my part. I, like many others, thought that homeschooling was simply when a family educated their child at home with one or more of the parents taking on the role of the teacher. Is this all there is to it? Wouldn't the child suffer from not socialising with other children? These questions demand research and not simple answers.

In Britain there are about 150,000 homeschooling children and in American it is said to be 1.5 million. Modern homeschooling is greatly influenced by the Austrian educationalist, Rudolf Steiner (1861 – 1925) with his philosophy of holistic child development. The four main motives that lead families to home-educate their children are:

- To instill/support religious values and beliefs

- Academic concerns with the school system

- The need to have a family life that integrates schooling

- Dissatisfaction with the State school system

Research conducted at Durham University (Rothermel, 2002) gives us a further insight into homeschooling:

- In National Literacy Project 80.4% of home-educated children scored in the top 16% band.

- Homeschooling allows parents to act as parents and educators

- Homeschooling allows families to develop non-academic intelligence in the children

- Homeschooling encourages family learning by allowing the parents to learn with their children

- Fathers were more involved in the education of homeschooled children than in school based families

- Homeschooling allowed children to use their own natural learning style

- Homeschool allowed for the curriculum to be negotiated between parent and child

- Homeschool children mixed more with people of different ages

With the black community we might add the desire to have their children experience an Africentric curriculum.

As one black homeschooling parent told me once: 'I just couldn't keep sending my child to school to fail.'

Homeschoolers have the law on their side, both in the UK and US. Under the Education Act 1996, section 7, the parents have the right to provide their children with their own full time education. The law only requires the families to go through a deregistration process whereby the parents give the LEA written notification that their child is receiving alternative education.

A closer look at the phenomenon of homeschooling shows that many parents are wanting to protect their child's childhood which they see as being under attack, from a system that is increasingly labelling children as having special needs requirements. In any one classroom you will find children labelled with, attention deficit hyperactivity disorder ADHD, dyslexia, obesity, child depression, mild autism and behavioural problems. Many parents will question the intervention prescribed by the experts who advocate the use of Ritalin (America uses 90% of the worlds Ritalin) for ADHD. The parent reads or sees teen pregnancy, child shootings, youths with guns, gangs in schools and terrible underachievement. The school authorities bring in the educational psychologists, the police and other specialists. There are more and more interventions in school as the system breaks down. The children are more diagnosed, tested, branded, categorised, labelled, confined/restricted and socially packaged to be thrown out into society. In the US, industrialists like Rockerfeller and Carnegie funded educational institutions so as to help create a compliant workforce. They gave more money to schooling than the government. School, as John Taylor Gatto (New York teacher of the Year, 1990) informs us, did not start because the authorities wanted to help children. Children were taken from their families and marched to school whether the parents wanted it or not.

Today children are still being marched to a place that the community little understands. Do any of us really hear the soul of the black child crying, or any child for that matter? The parents do! Children are rarely asked what they want. Often, the school system is disappointing to child and parent and teacher. It hides behind jargon that neither child nor parent, and sometimes teachers, can understand. It protects its right to educate with professional bodies, unions, reports and a massive and corresponding bureaucracy that gets bigger as does the failure rate. The child ends up fearing authority (as apposed to learning to respect and understand authority), which school was partly designed to do. Also, when it comes to the child protection policies in many ways these policies do not protect the child enough when we still have advertising directed at the pre-teen market, when advertisers use sex to sell products and services to children. There are few safe spaces for children generally, and even fewer safe places for the Black child. A homeschool might well have been created just to ensure a safe place for the child to develop, but the homeschool philosophy needs revamping.

So for many children childhood is becoming more confusing and more dangerous. The parent who earns a living in a material world buys their child a bigger TV, a new DVD player, a new mobile phone, new trainers/sneakers. The children simply consume junk. They watch it, they eat it and they eventually aspire to be people who are really consumer junkies. Junk is also what they will get in the classroom. For the African-American homeschooler there may be the added dilemma of opting out of school when a generation earlier, during the civil rights movement of the 1960s, their parents had fought so hard for the right to send their children to desegregated schools.

In her book *No Logo*, Naomi Klein has a chapter aptly named, *The Branding of Learning*. She writes:

"They (advertisers) are fighting for their brands to become not the add-on but the subject of education, not an elective but the core curriculum." She goes on to explain how in-class advertising and credit card invitations are now stalking the child; schools are giving vending rights to corporations that produce junk food, junk advertising. The school will/has become the place for logo promotion, brand extension opportunities, and curriculum manipulation. Yet, despite this, our school children and graduates may achieve some academic success but probably will not understand why Grandma is obese, why Grandpa has high-blood pressure, why Uncle Joe has had a stroke in his forties and why young cousin Sheila is pregnant at thirteen. The type of education that the Black child receives in school is not linked to community development/empowerment, which means community awareness. The homeschool, with its direct links to the economics of the home, its stronger cultural base gives a functional purpose to education; it gives the Black community an opportunity to create an education system that also acts as a defence mechanism against this absolute onslaught on childhood and the very sanity of the child and family.

However, the traditional white middle-class homeschool model, though useful, is not the answer. The homeschool in the black community has to have a support network; the community library, resource centre, science labs, cultural centre and online support, similar to one that we run at Ebony Education (www.ebonyeducation.com). Such a system is not only possible but is happening all over the country. Since writing *How to Unlock Your Child's Genius*, I have been contacted by several Black groups; some homeschoolers, and others who have set up reading clubs, youth clubs, after school clubs. These are parents who have taken up the initiative when they have seen how their children have underachieved. These projects have been planned. Sadly, this is not always the case, for the Black child who has been excluded there is no time for planning. In the last year alone we have had many families come to us whose children have been permanently excluded and in some cases the parent(s) have been unable to get them into any school. There are cases where the children are at home by themselves. At Ebony we offer homework, a little counselling, and an online service. It is not enough. We as a community can do more. Only three weeks ago a mother came with a thirteen year old son and said, "I've been to school after school but no one will take him. He just sits at home. I'm so worried." The solution to this and many other cases is turning our homes into education centres. Home school is really part of family learning, and it was this national system of family learning, with its system of multiple teachers and non-institutional educators, that saw Black people make their highest achievement. If we do not take collective action, we will be leaving our children to the cruel education of the street, where they will find some kind of respect from their peers, camaraderie, protection and excitement.

We have great examples of Blacks founding schools, colleges and universities (Booker.T. Washington and Mary McLeod Bethune). Did we not build great universities in Timbuctu; did not the freed slaves found schools in the US before mass education in America. Did not the black Moors of Spain in the middle ages build the first schools and music academies in Europe? A closer study of systems of education devised by Black people themselves will reveal a blend of home education, family learning, vocational education (trade guilds), apprenticeships and temple-colleges/universities (Karnack).

Chancellor Williams, in *The Destruction of Black Civilisation (1974)* summarises the traditional/modern education system of African people which modern educational consultants like, Dryden and Vos, in their book *The Learning Revolution (1993)*, are more or less advocating. I now present a summary:

Age	Education Content	Education Type
Primary Education (5 – 11 years)	• Learn through play • Household responsibilities • Storytelling • Mental arithmetic	• Homeschooling • Family Learning
12/13 – 19 years	• Civic responsibilities • Financial literacy • Warfare • Competitive Sports • Boyhood to Manhood • Girlhood to Womanhood	• Family learning • Institutional learning • Apprenticeship/vocational
19 – 28 years	• Community Work • Political • Military Work	• Industrial Guilds • Institutional

Then why can't we, with all the resources that surround us build a homeschool/family learning system if we really care about the NEXT GENERATION?

In her wonderful book, *Smart Moves*, Dr Carla Hannaford, having studied educational systems around the world can find none better than that in Africa. Using a sub-heading, *A First World Learning Plan from Africa*, to support learning and brain development, she writes:

A. A rich sensory environment full of sound, touch, smell and visual stimuli.
B. Lots of movement and the ability to freely explore one's own body in space.
C. Security and basic needs gratification that fosters full exploration of the physical environment.
D. Parents or other adults available as listeners, consultants and interactive participants in each child's growth.
E. Plenty of time and practice for pattern recognition – of sensory-motor patterns, language patterns, rhythm and music patterns, and human relationship patterns.
F. The establishment of responsibilities, boundaries, and respect for self and others.
G. Encouragement of imagination, art, music, communication and interactive play.

Such an education system has to have family learning placed centrally. There can be no real learning without family. The homeschool is a great introduction to the education system that we, the Africans need to put in place for our children and our community. This is the journey that Yvonne tried to take when she homeschooled Theo, and it is a journey that we must all investigate.

Notes on Building Family

Our family history, our family tree is our family capital; invaluable resources that we have to take time and care to understand and utilise in continuing to build family.

Our family tree is a 'tree'; that is, our metaphor in understanding how to nurture family. A tree needs light to grow, for photosynthesis to take place, and in looking for that 'light' in your family tree you will find a character or some individuals that built and stabilised your family tree. These are your family heroes, who represent family resilience and this resilience is knowledge; invaluable capital which you have to study and contemplate and learn from. Theo's grandmother has so much to offer but in the modern family grandparents are not valued as they should; their usefulness is looked upon in terms of economics. It is the small things that they bring to the home that are really big learning tools. The stories of past generations: who did what, who said what; these lend themselves to family pride, family oral history and remind the present generation of their traditions.

From this contemplation comes an understanding of the 'miracles' that have taken place in your family tree. You may come from a people that have undergone many traumas but your family miraculously survived. Evidence of this survival are the fruits that your family tree has produced. You are one of those fruits.

With this realisation that you are part of the 'family harvest' that has come from your family tree, you will begin to perceive your legacy which owes much to many great matriarchs, many a great patriarchs, who, in building family had to display courage, patience and skills as entrepreneurs.

Building family demands that we take lessons from our family tree and perhaps move away from this 'great man/woman' type of history that schools and the media feed us. In our family tree we will see collectives, characteristics, patterns of behaviour that are lessons for life.

Family Wisdom
On Parenting

- Talk and listen to your child/children as often as you can.

- Inspire them with deserved praise, gratitude and encouragement.

- Develop routines within the home for conversation and togetherness e.g., meal times and family meetings.

- Take time to realise the resources you have in the home and beyond to support your parenting.

- Realise that both you and your children make mistakes from time to time so don't be too hard on yourself or them.

- When you are making the family a meal, remember to sprinkle a little forgiveness in there.

- Don't be too busy and deny your child and your partner some love.

- Learning does not only come from books so play and laugh a little with your family.

- Learn from parents that you admire and who have happy children and families.

- Remember that asking for help is all part of being the hero/ heroine.

Stage 2

Healing and History

Themes of inquiry:

- **Helping and healing the family**
- **The power and function of memory**
- **The natural learning style of the Black family**

Sankofa – learning from the past

The **Sankofa** symbol reminds us of the importance of learning from the past whilst moving forward. This symbol reminds us to always be moving forward whilst returning to our roots. In our inquiry the Sankofa symbol reminds us of our great system of education based on family and the need to reintroduce it to the community. However, accompanying this rediscovery is a need to recognise that healing is part of our learning journey.

Theo's Diary

Just after I got detention I heard Amma calling. Often she comes when it rains, or I'm upset like when Dad doesn't phone. Couldn't wait to sleep. She keeps telling me that she's the first woman, the first human on the earth and knows all its secrets.

Today I had to see Dr Seamus, the psycho. As usual asked me questions about Amma, but he doesn't understand. Told him about the Sankofa bird she brought and the golden eggs that was in the bird's mouth but he just didn't get it. Not like Ade, and Marcus. But I know the only reason they keep making me see him isn't because I have special needs, it's because of my gang. They're scared of my revolution. They're scared of Malcolm X, Garvey, Biko, Sobukwe, Lumumba and Toussaint. Names from my dad's old books on revolution.

Thursday

Me, Biko and Garvey had to go to Ms Maudsley's office, the Headteacher. We all got a warning. 'Anymore graffiti with Black is Beautiful and Long Live Biko on the walls,' she said, 'then you will get excluded.' Dr Seamus came into the office, told Marcus and Ade to leave, and asked me about Amma. I stood proud like Paul Bogle before they hanged him. I had a little piece of paper in my pocket and read some words of Malcolm X: Revolution by any means necessary!, I shouted. Dr Seamus snatched it from me. 'Stop with your Blackness!' he bellowed. 'Oh Gerald,' shouted Ms Maudsley as she went to pick up his glasses that had flown off his long pointed nose. One thing I can say about Dr Seamus, is that he always blushes when Mrs Maudsley walks into the room. He even sometimes fixes his pink tie and tries to smile, believing he's some kind of Hollywood heartthrob. Ms Maudsley then said she was going to send a letter home to my mum. They both looked at me, and stared. 'Are you and Ade and Marcus a gang Theo?' she asked. I took a deep breath, pulled my shoulders back. 'We're just family,' I replied and then walked out of the office.

At break-time, when I walked back into the playground, all my comrades were waiting for me. I knew I had to act like a real leader, so I looked them straight in the eye and said: 'Men, our revolution has started. We will take over the school. We will make it ours. We will have lessons that mean something to us. We will have pictures on the wall of our heroes. We will teach ourselves. We will throw Dr Seamus and all his special needs reports out of the window, and we'll tell our parents to come into the school more often, even my dad!' My voice began to break so I stopped speaking.

How we must all come into the world of education

…because there is the spirit of tree within a tree, therefore its flowers blossom fragrantly, it turns green, its branches and leaves flourish; this is called the marvel.

The Book of Five Rings-Miyamoto Mushashi

The education case file on Theo started 8 million years ago in East Africa; a small Black woman who slept amongst the long grass, under the naked moon, the tropical silence of mosquitoes, and the still lingering hum of God's first mantra, to which an African goddess danced with cowrie shells round her ankles and neck. It started at the time the scientists call The Big Bang. It was this black woman that first suckled humanity; who, alone gave birth to the joys and sorrows of life. She was the most intelligent human ever to have lived. A ll humanity sprang from her desire for life, yet no one can trace her beginning. In the Omo Valley in Ethiopia they found one of her children; bones of a human they would call homo sapiens, and named this African woman 'Lucy' (who they believed lived 150,000 years ago), after a Beatles song. Before her there was the skeletal remains of another Black woman, another daughter of the first one in Hadar in Ethiopia (Australoithecus 1.18 million years ago), and before her there was another. No archaeologist can trace the beginnings of the Black race, or this Black woman but this child, Theo claimed that he heard her. It was she that started the whole thing. After some time, his parents became convinced that he was telling the truth; that he heard this woman, this being, this ancestor, this mother of all, Amma, crying as she roamed the earth hunched from the weight of her primordial legacy of pain. What was this pain? It was this boy, Theo, who heard her wail, who heard her praying. It wasn't always like this. Once she had given birth to humanity she, in beautiful grass skirt, became proud of her children; the children of the Nile, of Ta Seti. Amma's journey, which is now being carried on by Theo, is to be free and for this to happen he has to rid himself of the trauma of enslavement; re-discover a natural way of learning that is suited to his genius and perhaps then, and only then, this case file might be closed but first, he, inspired by Amma, must go on a journey with his family.

A Community Response to the Miseducation of Theo

We might blame others or we can take positive action. We can castigate the Theos in our community or we can listen not to their angry shouts, but to the quiet in their sleep and there we will hear their dreams. What is the dream of Theo and other children like him? As a teacher I realised that I never really knew because I was too bogged down in delivering a curriculum, and the administration around the curriculum. But there are times when an incident will allow you a moments thought. Often, with so-called disruptive children, there will be a time when their mask of disobedience slips, when, as a teacher you are not caught up in your own irritation; you are forced to look into the child's heart, and what you see is their soul's desire to be at peace.

There are options for Theo's mother, just like there are options for the Black community around the world to set up an education system that will address issues of disempowerment, including pride in oneself, culture and collective responsibility.

How to Build a Saturday School

Step 1

1. Research into the need and feasibility of such a project/business
2. Assess the evidence of such a project/business by looking at data, reports and anecdotal evidence
3. Put together a business plan however basic.
4. Put together a team of people to help regardless of their qualifications as commitment is what will really count in the long run.
5. Try and raise the start up finance.
6. Visualise the project/business being successful

Step 2

Legal Requirements and Good Practice

- Look into public and employer liability insurance
- Criminal Bureau Checks should be conducted on all staff
- The necessary governing policies should be in place like Child Protection policy, Health and Safety Policy and Constitution
- Take advice on your legal status e.g., charity, co-operative or community interest company (c.i.c).
- An effective and proactive management committee should be established with minutes taken at all meetings.

Step 3

Curriculum Development and Resources

- The main curriculum should focus on 'basic skills' which might include English, Mathematics, science and a cultural programme (and or Mother Tongue lessons) with special projects that the assessments show the community needs.
- Regular curriculum development staff meetings with pupil involvement to develop teaching materials and assess pupil learning.
- Establish a reading club in the school to address low reading levels.
- Have regular staff training and team building meetings or excursions.
- Have parent training workshops showing parents how they can support their child's/children's learning.
- Take time to look at a variety of resources and visit schools and have presentations on how resources are used.
- Link the curriculum to the community's needs and culture

Step 4

Curriculum Development and Resources

- All management committee members should have clear roles and responsibilities
- Annual AGMs.
- A clear school mission statement.
- A basic development/strategic plan should be drawn up and acted upon.
- Constantly investigate leadership models that suit your school's cultural set-up.

Step 5

Teaching and Learning

- There should be both formal and informal lesson observations and teachers given honest and supportive feedback.
- Teachers should be encouraged to have peer assessment in lesson observations.
- A variety of learning styles should be used; that is, visual, auditory, Kinaesthetic and tactile, all embedded with cultural empowerment.
- Whilst personalised learning is very much in vogue there should also be emphasis on group learning with discussions and practical investigations.
- Thinking skills should be embedded in all subjects and real life situations addressed where possible.
- Encourage pupil peer assessment.

The setting up of the Saturday school is only the first step in the establishment of a family learning centre that might also include, a homework club, youth club and parenting courses. This community centredness makes the learning environment more learner and teacher friendly, giving all ownership of the learning experience, as opposed to the classroom environment where the learner is alienated in an atmosphere of almost perpetual reprimands and the experiencing or witnessing of punishments. Perhaps this is what Theo has experienced.

Theo's Learning State

School Strategies in Dealing with Theo's Case

School Strategy	Specialist Support	Teacher Attitude	Theo's attitude/ Lifestyle change
Threats of exclusion	Interview with Educational psychologist	Low expectation of Theo	Becomes disinterested In education

The Physical and Emotional state of Theo

Breathing Pattern	Brain	Emotional State	Confidence/ Self-esteem
Upper chest breathing; Shallow, leading to tension	Lacks oxygen; Negative thinking From brain stem instead of higher brain	Suppressed anxiety. High levels of stress, mild depression	Low; compensates by mixing with boys who have been excluded and rebel against the school through misbehaviour and fantasy.

The Statistics (UK)

- Only 31% of Black African boys and 23% of Black Caribbean boys achieve the bench mark of 5A* - C GCSEs, compared to the national average of 40%.
- Black Caribbean boys are three times more likely to be excluded from school than the average.
- Young Black people are more likely to participate in higher education.
- Black African and Caribbean students are significantly less likely to attend an 'old' (pre 1992) University than the average and more likely to drop out or achieve a low grade for their degree. (Reach report, 2007).
- The Commission for Racial Equality's report into racism in prisons found that in 2003 there were 6000 black people on undergraduate courses and 10,000 black people in prison in England.

My visits to America, the Caribbean and Africa show that they have similar statistics or increasingly similar patterns of failure emerging.

A Snap Shot of Theo's Early Miseducation

His school was just off Hither Green Lane,
shrouded by tall trees that kept secrets and green solace. Back then, Theo would leave his mother's hand and run to the school gates, dodging other parents and children. He was eager, to enter into some kind of learning that had not quite been explained to him. In his first term, in the playground he would experience bullying, the loss of friendships and he could cope with that, but there were things that his soul could not cope with. The first was the fairytale. There would be a good witch, and bad witch, a princess, a prince, a king, and queen, a castle and a magical Kingdom. But he was not part of this magical world for he could not see himself in the prince. Each day he would be given a book to read in class or take home. The school reading scheme was based on stories about pirates; swashbuckling pirates that fought over gold bullion, silver, rum, ships and treasure chests: stories set in exotic places, but Theo could never relate to these stories even though he would find himself caught up in the fantasies. The black witch, the boy with brown hair made him feel something was wrong, but Theo liked to play, to act out his fantasies. When the Christmas school play came along, his hand went up first to take part, but he would not be in the star role, in fact, he wouldn't have any role at all, except a very minor non-speaking one. The parents, Sebastian and Yvonne, still have the photographs, the old VHS video tapes, and in them Theo appears to be smiling, but

the old cameras seemed to photograph his sadness. By Year 5, Theo found himself not being invited to the parties of the other children. It broke his heart when a child who he thought was his best friend, didn't hand him a party invitation. His parents said he played quietly in his room. In the playground that he used to run through, middle class parents would congregate; they knew how to manipulate the Headteacher, and where the power of the school lay. Theo's parents clearly did not. They naively thought that school presented children with an even playing field.

Profile of a Local Black Hero Who Tried to Save Theo

Her name was Grace, a very slight young woman, who had not long qualified as a teacher, and in some ways had run to the school gates with her newly obtained teaching certificate, in the hope that she might change lives; give opportunities to those that had few. At university she had read Paulo Freire's *Pedagogy of the Oppressed*, and now truly believed in education for social justice. Enthusiasm lit her classroom. Her preparation for each lesson was both creative and meticulous. Her training made her believe in individualism, in the individual education plans, different learning styles, and in the belief that her school was delivering multicultural education. She was a young woman with great dreams for her career progression and for the children she would teach.

The Staffroom of Betrayal

It was when she entered the staffroom that she first felt a little odd; realised that there wasn't this great welcome, that she noticed that something inside of the other teachers had been destroyed, leaving them bitter, and a little resentful to optimism. This wasn't true of all, but many. When she listened to the other white staff members talking about Black children she knew something was wrong. As time went by, as she sat in the corner of the staffroom drinking her tea and overheard talk of another exclusion, she knew they were talking about a brown skinned child. The cold statistics that she had read about at university, were now real children, some of whom she taught. There was the rebel in her, that was rooted in the Maroon spirit of her parents, so she began to challenge how the school treated Theo, and other Black pupils and white ones from the local estate. She over heard the educational psychologist and the headteacher discuss Theo's case so she spoke out again. She saw which children were repeatedly in trouble, so she spoke out. She saw which teachers were getting promoted, which were favoured, which were bullied, so she spoke out some more. Now, she didn't even go to the staffroom. She ate her sandwiches by herself, as she marked the children's books and stared thoughtfully into her herbal tea. Occasionally the Headteacher came to her and said, 'We've noticed that you seldom come into the staffroom anymore, is something wrong?' Grace, now losing a little weight, searched for support. There were a few other black teachers at the school, all of whom had been there far longer than her. She approached them, explained what was happening to Theo, but these teachers had long thrown in the towel, and some hadn't even known there was a towel to throw in. The last thing they wanted to do was to be seen organising with other Blacks, or to highlight any race issues in the school. Now desperate, she ran to her union. She talked, they listened. She protested, they listened. She threatened, they listened. She left the union office and didn't hear from them again.

Slowly, Grace realised how political and controlled her school was. Hate was making her cynical, though she fought against it. She began to read books like Amos Wilson's, *Awakening the Genius of the Black Child*, in search of answers to the destruction of Theo. Some of the parents who didn't like her Afri-centric appearance, complained about her teaching. Grace underestimated their power. It was power that she realised that she should have studied at university. The education system she was in, the system that was destroying Theo's potential, was about power and control. But now her health was suffering. She was unable to sleep; her periods were heavy and she began to have headaches, slight panic attacks and would often cry herself to sleep at night. Suddenly she realises that she can't help Theo. She is fighting for her career. She realises that she has been betrayed by the school, by the silence of other Black staff, by her union. Like Theo, she is alone, believing she has no family.

The White Working Class Hero

Joe had rich ginger hair, and his mind was ablaze with ideas on making all children in this large school achieve. He had come from the north, from a family in a mining area, though they weren't miners themselves. His father was a teacher. Now he was one too at Comprehensive School for Boys, the school that Theo attended. Joe had been brought up on socialist literature, and his mother's no-nonsense ideals that made him an effective and popular teacher. He had come across Theo standing outside the Headteacher's office; seen his slouch and frown with his hands in his pocket. Questions in the staffroom followed, before Joe understood what was happening with Theo, and these enquiries led him to Grace. "This Theo, why's he always outside the Head's office?" Thirty minutes later, a few cups of coffee, and they were still talking. Conversations on Theo became regular. Joe wanted to get more involved, believing that his ideas on teaching could work on Theo. One day he approached Grace and said:

"I know you mean well but it's 'bout class. This whole school's 'bout how to educate the masses for servitude. Don't ask questions; don't think, don't aspire and just take the job that we give yah!" Oddly enough Grace was surprised and a little inspired at his bitterness. He gave dates and times when the working class were betrayed by their leaders or the ruling classes. Grace became less friendly, suddenly realising that he hadn't really understood what she had been saying during their conversations. "Theo is bright, but how can a school that never reviews its practices teach him? How can a school that doesn't understand his community prepare him for the world?"

"You focus on race too much. Class and poverty is what's keeping him back. In a few years when Theo faces the world, he'll face a world that'll exploit his labour; use it and abuse it. It's 'bout class!" Suddenly there was a distance between them. They weren't two newly qualified teachers anymore, but strangers. She got up and walked out of the quietening staffroom.

Betrayal of Grace

In a way Theo's case offered Grace her last opportunity to salvage something from the teaching profession, to give her career meaning and purpose. Every opportunity that presented itself she would seek out Theo, offer him words of friendship; watch the worry in his gait, and just as worryingly, his association with the 'bad boys', who, in his mind he called family. In a desperate attempt to gain support, Grace tried to set up a Black Staff Group. Black staff, though at the bottom of the pile, refused to join: they didn't want to offend their white colleagues, and her militancy had made them feel both guilt, shame and anger, because deep down they knew they should organise to deal with the inequalities and the everyday joylessness of so many pupils in the school. This group of Black staff, would turn on Grace betraying their own deep anguish and confusion. They snarled and ripped her apart with rumours about her sexuality, with rumours about her and Joe, and even rumours about her and Theo. Grace was alone. Theo could see her weakness. He wanted to tell her about Amma, and bring Grace into his family.

How to Respond to the Miseducation of Black Children

Theo's story has been pieced together from thousands of cases that have been brought to me. The media often portray the Black boy with little emotions; simply as dysfunctional, but I, along with the parents, have had to see the real depth, the real hurt these children and young people experience. A few days ago a parent rang me on the phone. She sounded like a strong Black woman, and told me she wanted advice about her child who had been excluded. Half way through the conversation she broke down in tears, telling me of the actual incident in which a teacher shouted at her boy, saying: *'Get that animal out of my class!'* This is not unusual. Parents like her will bring their child to me, and hundreds of other Saturday schools, and there I will find a complex individual, needing more support, understanding and time from his or her family. I will find a child almost living in their own secret world, because no one has prepared programmes, or opportunities or life changing experiences for them. The families around them, often not realising it, are thinking and operating selfishly. About ten years ago, a friend of mine who runs his own school for mainly Black children in north London, asked me to be a judge in a debating contest between the children. The event was packed out with parents, uncles, aunts and even grandparents all eagerly awaiting the contest. Each of the children spoke very well, but there were two who were outstanding and this was obvious to everyone. However, when we were asked to mark the children, feeling that the two boys were deserving of first prize, I deliberately manipulated my marks so that the two best children tied for first place. When the results were announced, I heard cursing from all directions from one of the joint-winners family. Phrases like, 'dem t'ief us; dem fix everyt'ing; me bwoy should have won!' was heard. Suddenly, an elderly woman, who I assumed was the grandmother of the boy who was objecting to the results, came over to me and 'cut-her-eye' in my direction. Before I left it actually looked like a fight was going to start. It was an example of adults taking no responsibility for *all* the children; not realising that if all the children succeeded then the community succeeds.

Family Intervention on Education

In order for families to be in control of the education the family members will receive, there has to be an understanding of what might be called the learning cycle, and the particular learning needs of a community fighting to create opportunities for themselves to realise their full potential.

I have found that very often the parents of the Black child have failed to put in place strategic measures to lessen the damage that the school system has inflicted on the child. They have failed to make their homes into learning centres, from which community learning centres will emerge. The measures that should have been taken are:

- Before a child is born there needs to be preparation in terms of its living space, early education and environment
- As fifty percent of learning takes place from 0 – 8 years there must be a carefully designed educational programme that incorporates play (varied) and accelerated learning in the early years
- The arrival of the child will put pressures on the relationship if the parents are together at the time of birth. These pressures might be financial, emotional and physical
- The whole family (extended family) should be prepared for the arrival of the child and take a role, both formal and informal, in the child's upbringing.
- Identify three learning mentors for your child: one for academic support, one for cultural support and one for social/ emotional support
- Have e-learning resources, DVD and film education in place to enhance their learning
- It is advisable that your child grows up in an atmosphere where family learning is the norm. Undertake family learning projects like learning about Kwanzaa, or learning a language or even a music project.

The Learning Revolution

Theo was supposed to have been part of the learning revolution. Educationalists around the world, in learning seminars, conferences, books and on the internet talk about this great learning revolution, of being a global citizen, in a global economy. According to these experts there would be a revolution in:

- how to learn
- how to think
- mind-body intelligence
- diets for learning
- music for learning
- learning styles
- family learning
- neuroscience
- teacher retraining
- digital technology for learning

Theo wanted to be part of this revolution. His father always told him, 'Prepare for revolution.' He would shout with a glass of rum in his hand: '..de revolution will not be televised.' For Theo's dad, there was a different type of revolution. A learning revolution yes, but one that Black leaders like Toussaint L'Ouverture, Marcus Garvey, Patrice Lumumba, Robert Sobukwe, Paul Bogle, Claudia Jones, Sojourner Truth and Malcolm X and others had talked about: the revolution in Black consciousness. Theo sensed that there was another revolution waiting. So he kept sneaking into his dad's old study and reading the books, cutting out photographs of these great heroes; listening to old cassettes of them speaking. This was the study that Yvonne, his mum, said she was going to clear out and have redecorated, but he knew she wouldn't, that deep inside she wanted Sebastian, his dad, to come back. Theo, like thousands of black children around the world, had been part of a debate in meetings that Sebastian used to attend before he cut off his locks on Africentric education.

In his book *Towards Black Community Development (1993)*, Manu Ampim lists the six components of the Africentric Movement as:

- Classical African (Kamitic) studies
- The study of melanin and its properties
- Africentric rites of passage programs
- Africentric/multicultural curriculum initiatives
- Spiritual/ religious revivals in traditional African systems
- Black books movement

This movement had little impact in 'mainstream' education, but it was one that educationalists in the Black community grappled to find ways to implant it in the learning institutions where their children languished.

Theo knew a little about the Black consciousness movement from his visits to his father's study and the books and the pictures that he kept there, but his consciousness was only truly excited by Amma. Theo, a shy boy in some turmoil, sat in class wanting an adventure, wanting the woman to lead him to something wonderful, strange and exotic. I thought about Theo a lot, increasingly knowing that the adventure he needed was needed by a million other children, many in worse circumstances than Theo. It was after I looked through his case file again that, in my imagination, I too began to hear voices of a little story, a story for the Theos of the world. What I began to perceive was that Theo's subconscious was seeking a journey. The evidence was becoming clearer and clearer to me. Amma from the Omo Valley, had come back to help Theo, and the rest of us, start a revolution in the way we learn. If we look way back into the case file of Theo; not the case file of the school but the case file for all Black children all over the world, to a time when the family curriculum was the foundation upon which the greatest civilisation ever created was built, then we find minds that naturally inquired into life, minds that were naturally spiritual. We should scrutinise this system, and look carefully at its people, architecture, mathematics, astrology and writing, but we can't forget about Theo and his family living today, and we have to decide if the school or the home or both is going to teach him about this old but modern system of learning. Here is what happens when the family leaves it to the school to teach something so important as history, to a child searching for truth, wondering about his identity, seeking mentors for his manhood, and wanting love, wanting a family.

How to Unlock Your Family's Genius

Stage Two

Period	Historical Significance/Accomplishments
Primary Education (5 – 11 years)	• Use of 1,460 astronomical calendar • Nubian civilisation emerges • Nubian Kingdom of Ta-Seti in existence (3400 B.C.E)
In School	• Theo studies about the ancient Greeks
Dynasties 1 – 2 (3150 – 2649 B.C.E.) Old Kingdom	• King Narmer unifies Upper and Lower Egypt. (2630) • Memphis is established as new state capital
In School	• Theo studies about the Greeks and falls asleep • Theo gets detention
Dynasties 3 – 6 (2649 – 2150 B.C.E.) Old Kingdom	• Step pyramid and Saqqara complex built by Zoser • Great pyramids built at Giza and Dahsur • Pyramid text inscribed in tomb of King Unas
In School	• Theo studies the Romans • Theo learns about Hannibal. Hannibal is portrayed as white even though he was born in Carthage (Africa) • History teacher forgets to tell class of the significance Played by African soldiers, generals and Carthage as one of the centres of the Rome empire
Intermediate Period (2150 – 2040 B.C. E.)	• Enters a period of political decline
In School	• **Theo accidentally farts in class** • **Theo gets detention** • **Theo comes top in history test. No praise from teacher**
Dynasties 11 – 12 (2040 – 1763 B.C.E.)	• Kamit (Black Egypt) unified by Mentuhotep II • Capital relocated to Waset (Thebes/Luxor) • Senworset establishes a colony in Greece • Senworset founds the city of Athens
In School	• Class continue to study Roman Empire • Septimus Severus is mentioned. No mention that he is a black African emperor • School text book show all Romans as white • Theo yawns in class and gets a warning
Dynasties 13 – 17 Second Intermediate Period (1783 -1550 B.C.E.)	• Hykos invaders bring destruction to Kamit

In School	• Theo starts drawing cartoons of Black revolutionaries from his imagination
Dynasties 18 – 20 (1550 – 1170 B.C. E.) New Kingdom	• Hykos defeated by King Ahmose who reunites Kamit • Hatshepsut rules Kamit as first female pharaoh • Amenhotep III (Ahkenaton) introduces belief in one god • Tutankhamen takes the throne in Kamit • Set I constructs a great tomb in the Valley of the Kings • Ramases II takes the throne and rules for 67 years. • Nubian queen Nafertari rules by his side
In School	• Theo gets detention • Teachers speculate as to whether Black history is helping children like Theo • Grace objects and is spoken to by her Headteacher
Dynasties 18 – 20 (1550 – 1170)	• King Ahmose reunites Kamit by defeating the Hyksos • Thutmose I expands the rule of Kamit • Hatshepsut becomes first female pharaoh • Akhenaton introduces concept of one God • Tutankhamen takes the throne • Ramases II rules for 67 years with Queen Nefertari
In School	• Theo is taught about the Victorians (no mention of Oludah Equiano the black Victorian activist) • Theo begins to seek another type of education that has direct relevance to his life
Third intermediate Period (1070 – 750 B.C.E.)	• Kamit declines
In School	• Grace becomes alarmed at the increasing poor academic performance of Theo • Theo's parents try and get him a learning mentor
Dynasty 25 (750 – 675 B.C.E)	• Piankhi, King of Nubia, conquers upper and lower Kamit. • Shabaka unifies all of Kamit • Taharqa invades Spain and Palestine • Assyrians conquer Lower and Upper Kamit • Nubian Kings establish central government in Upper Kamit until conquered by Assyrians
Dynasty 27 (525 – 404B.C.E.)	• Kamit invaded by Cambyses
Dynasty 28 (404 – 399 B.C.E.	• Persians are expelled from Kamit
Dynasty 30 (380 - 343 B.C.E.)	• Last time native born Kamitic kings will rule
In School	• Theo has formed his own gang

So far we have looked at Theo the pupil, Yvonne his mother, Sebastian his father and Grace, Theo's teacher, and what they all have in common is that they are stressed; they are all fighting to find sense, meaning and any kind of purpose in a system that lets all of them down. None can build meaningful relationships with the other in such a hostile environment. Each, in their own way is looking for answers, and we are fortunate for we are using them in our inquiry. If we stop for awhile we can see that they all need some kind of help, or healing; things we used to find in a family.

Family Health Plan

So stage two of our inquiry looks at the healing of a child, and home, and possibly community. We find a family who is in trouble, not only with their child's education, but in realising the resources that they have, which are many, but the genius within them lies dormant. Yvonne does some voluntary work; she reads a lot, keeps a good home, but is confused. Apparently, she grew up in the rural part of Jamaica, steeped in the wisdom of her grandmother, who, if a family tree could be made, she would find that she was Yoruba, and one of the great 'centres' of wisdom in Africa is the oracle of Ifa. She did not know it, but if she could have gone to a genuine priest, he would have told her to take care of her health; not only with herbs and the gifts of plants, and fruits, and vegetables and the secret medicinal truths, of what her old grandmother called, 'dem ground provision, and dem healing way.' No, not only this, but joy; a smile to cheer her; some sweetness and t'ing' as the old people who visited her grandmother's veranda would say. Back home, she would have used some aloe vera or boiled some bush, or bark, or taken some soup, but she had now come to rely on the chemist, as opposed to Nature, and the herbal apprenticeship that her grandmother gave her, in her yard and local forest. What intervention does this family need, indeed the community need, to heal itself? Below is a small health plan, a family health plan to help families like Yvonne's: hardworking and vulnerable.

How to Raise Your Family's Health Awareness

Intelligent Food

To have a healthy brain, you need a healthy diet. The brain makes up only 2% of body weight but uses 20% of the body's energy. It has over 100 billion brain cells which each has around 20,000 connections (dendrites). The lower brain (reptilian brain) controls the instincts like breathing and heart beat whilst your central brain (limbic) controls your emotions. The upper brain controls (cortex) controls your ability to think, speak, reason and create, and the cerebellum (memory muscle) stores memories of things you have done in the past. So the wonderful brain, needs wonderful food which can keep it going, to perform marvellous functions.

In *New Optimum Nutrition for the Mind*, Patrick Holford advises that we:

- Balance your glucose, which is the fuel for the brain
- Take the right amount of essential fats which determine the health of the brain cells
- Take the right amount of phospholipids which supports the brains memory capacity
- Take the right amount of amino acids that act as the brain's messengers
- Take the right amount of nutrients that include minerals and vitamins

Food Types	Function & Examples
Glucose	We digest carbohydrates and break it down into glucose. The glucose is then used by the brain. Eg., corn, beans, nuts, seeds, whole grains, lentils, fresh fruit, vegetables.
Essential Fats	• Saturated and monosaturated fats • Cholesterol • Omega-3 Omega-6 • The omega fats cannot be made in the body and so have to be taken in through the diet. Eg., Omega-3 – flax oil, pumpkin oil, fish oil. Omega-6 – corn oil, sunflower oil, sesame oil, pumpkin oil, evening primrose oil, borage oil (GLA)
Phospholipids Help in the brain cell structure; they improve mood and mental performance.	Eg., fish, lecithin
Amino Acids *Building blocks of protein*	The eight 'essential' proteins that people need to eat out of the 23 proteins. Grains/pulses: quinoa, tofu, corn, brown rice, chick peas & lentils. Fish/meat: cod, salmon, sardines & eggs Nuts/seeds: sunflower seeds, cashew & almond nuts Vegetables: beans, broccoli & spinach
Essential Fats	• Eat five to seven fresh servings of fruit and vegetables each day. • Eat nuts, seeds, beans • Fish • Supplement your diet with multivitamins and minerals

Your family's health can only be at its optimum if you are getting the correct nutrients, plus sleep, water, exercise and relaxation.

It is important that families know the mineral content of the food they eat, and that mineral content is dependent on the quality of the soil, and the quality of the soil is dependent on whether traditional agricultural methods are being used, or whether 'modern' farming with its pesticides, herbicides and insecticides are being used. Perhaps Amma is aware of the wealth of Africa's land. It's said that 90% of the worlds natural resources are in Africa, but the relationship that the Western world has established with Africa through violence, has robbed the wealth and therefore the health of families. Perhaps it is more than the minerals in the food that Amma is trying to make the new generation of Africans defend. Perhaps she has seen the amount of diamonds, copper, gold and oil being mined and drilled and wants more for the people bent over these weeping exotic crops destined for the West.

What are Vitamins?	Organic substances necessary for life
What do vitamins do?	Vitamins regulate the body's metabolism through enzyme systems
What are nutrients?	Carbohydrates, fats, minerals, vitamins and protein
How do Nutrients Work?	Nutrients work through digestion

So that you are aware of the minerals that various foods provide, here is a brief chart indicating the mineral content of foods that you and your family should be enjoying as part of your daily meals. You will see from the information below that a wide variety of organic food is essential to maintain body function and brain chemistry. So relying on taste to determine what foods you should eat is dangerous especially if you are conditioned to junk food.

Mineral	Function	Food Source
Iron	Part of the haemoglobin composition which provides oxygen to the cells. Iron (and calcium) is often deficient in women.	Carrots, tomatoes, lettuce, leeks, radishes, spinach, beans, whole-grain cereals, berry fruits, raisins, figs, liver
Calcuium	Helps in teeth and bone formation and health and the clotting of blood. The most prominent mineral in the body. Vitamin D needed for its absorbtion.	Beetroot, carrots, cress, celery, cucumber, cauliflower, figs, onions, mushrooms, tomatoes, eggs, cheese & wheat bran.
Sodium	Present is in all tissues and is present as sodium chloride.	Apples, beetroot, carrots, cucumber, cauliflower, celery, cabbage, prunes & figs.
Sulphur	Purifies the system	Cabbage, cauliflower, cress, celery, nettles, onions, parsnips, turnips & oranges.

Iodine	Helps balance secretions of thyroid gland. Approximately two-thirds of the body's iodine is located in the thyroid gland.	Artichokes, cabbage, carrots, beans, kelp, lettuce and tomatoes.
Magnesium	Essential for calcium and Vit-C metabolism. Also known as an Anti-stress mineral.	Almond, corn, lemon, grapefruit, nuts, seeds and dark green vegetables.
Potassium	Assists liver and healing	Cabbage, cauliflower, beans, dill, prunes, rhubarb, pears & strawberries.
Phosphorus	Essential for energy & important for bone, hair and teeth	Barley, cabbage, celery, cucumber, cauliflower, lettuce, spinach & watercress.

The body also needs antioxidants to protect itself from free-radicals which are loose oxygen that can damage neighbouring cells. Below are a good source of antioxidants.

Carrots (Vitamin A) Antioxidant Food Source	**Whole Wheat Flour** (Vitamin B 5) Antioxidant Food Source
Oranges (Vitamin C) Antioxidant Food Source	**Wheat Germ** (Vitamin E) Antioxidant Food Source
Spinach (Iron) Antioxidant Food Source	**Lettuce** (Manganese) Antioxidant Food Source
Mangoes (Vitamin A & C) Antioxidant Food Source	**Lemon** (Vitamin A & C) Antioxidant Food Source

Melon (Vitamin A & C) Antioxidant Food Source	**Beans** (Vitamin E) Antioxidant Food Source
Tomatoes (Vitamin A & C) Antioxidant Food	**Strawberries** (Vitamin A & C) Antioxidant Food

Balancing the Body

In looking at family health we have to consider food balance in terms of acid and alkaline foods, food which, if too acid can lead to health problems. This balance is scientifically measured on a pH scale of 1 to 14, 7 being the neutral. All the body's regulatory systems work to keep this balance and when the body is too acid then it is vulnerable to disease. By eating the right foods you can maintain this balance, thereby stopping the body itself from having to struggle with an acid environment and therefore producing toxins.

Like the earth, your body consists of 70% water and this water must be in a mild alkalizing condition. Below is a brief summary of the balancing effects of common foods.

Source	Balancing Effect
Vegetables & Sprouted vegetables	Provides vitamins, minerals and micronutrients
Grasses (wheat grass, barley grass, oat grass, lemon grass, kamut grass)	Rich in vitamins and minerals
Prebiotics (special foods that probiotics eat)	Natural sources are asparagus, beetroots, chicory and garlic
Raw & Fresh foods (vegetables and some fruits: avocado, tomato and bell peppers)	70 – 80% of your food should be raw. Raw food has more active enzymes than cooked foods. Fresh food is preferable for when something is picked the nutrients begin to decrease.
Water	5 to 8 glasses of purified water should be drunk each day.

Family Meals and Family Cohesion

- Family meals should take place at regular times and be in a relaxed atmosphere
- Healthy meals should be planned, which will mean that planned shopping should have been completed first
- If your budget allows there should be a variety of healthy foods, and on occasions, from different parts of the world (although, local food is environmentally better and more nutritious).
- Any televisions that are in the eating area should be turned off and positive conversations encouraged
- Food education and good table manners should be instilled in all the family

Family Health: Supplements, Water, Sleep & Movement

Below are some supplements that should be taken regularly by families:

- A multivitamin and mineral should be taken daily (depending on quality of food)
- Vitamin C should be taken daily (depending on quality of food)
- B Complex
- Vitamin D (through exposure to sunlight)
- Sleep (adults 8-9 hours, children 10 – 11 hours per day)

Emotional Goodness

Below are some reminders of the need for the family to take in some emotional goodness which might seem obvious, but as a father and someone who has worked with families for over twenty years, these reminders should not be taken lightly:

- Laughter and smiles
- Praise and encouragement
- Individual and group play
- Service to others
- Sharing and understanding
- Simplify your life
- Silence and reflection

It was as the relationship between Yvonne and Sebastian began to break down that these simple things stopped. Instead, their lives became more complicated and stressed. Neither could see that a way out of their problems might be to re-establish the basics: friendship, trust, laughter and support.

Movement and Learning

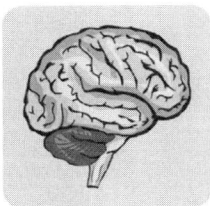

Movement is key to learning as it develops gross motor skills, that is, the ability to use the large muscles of our body, and fine motor skills, that is, the use of the smaller muscles of our bodies for writing or handling a knife and fork. The good diet mentioned above coupled with play will determine muscle tone, muscle strength, quality and co-ordination of movements, range of movements and in particular, movements that go from one side of the body to the other; often referred to as crossing the midline. This crossing the midline is key to Brain Gym, developed by Dr Dennison who worked with remedial children in America, developing 26 movements to support learning. Such movement programmes raise the awareness of sensory integration: the movement sense (vestibular system) and special awareness sense (proprioception) which are interlinked to cognitive development.

Family Tree

The popularity of tracing your ancestry was partly created by Alex Haley (1921 – 1992) who traced his ancestry back to Kunta Kinte who was captured as a slave from the village of Juffure in Gambia in 1767. From the publication of Haley's book, *Roots* (1976) and the successful airing of two television series shortly afterwards in 1977, many others have also thought to trace their roots. This has been made easier with the science of DNA and the tracing of genetic genealogy, allowing someone to trace their ancestry for several generations.

How to Make Your Family Tree

1.   Write down your own name and those of your parents underneath. Underneath that write down their parents (your grandparents) and carry on like this as far as you recall. (See diagram below). On each individual member that you wish to trace their details you should collect information on:

   a. Their correct name
   b. Date of birth
   c. Education
   d. Religion
   e. Date of marriage
   f. Name of spouse
   g. Date and place of birth and marriage of children

Try and make detailed and referenced notes on all members.

2.   Seek out relatives, friends of the family who can give you information about previous generations. Once you have gone back to your great grandparents, stop and seek out documents that might give you further information about your ancestors.

3.   Contact remote family to see what information they might have. Often, the elders are more than happy to give information about family, and you should compare what you have found out so far with their information. If you can try and get photographs, old letters; visit the family cemetery if there is one, this will bring you closer to understanding your ancestors. It also might be an idea to have a digital recording machine if the person interviewed feels comfortable with that.

4.   Having researched enough oral family history and family anecdotal evidence, you might now want to obtain information from official sources like birth and death certificates to verify the information that you already have. This type of information can be obtained from marriage and death registry, electoral registers, newspaper obituaries, governor papers, national archives, records of residence and land ownership and census records.

5.   You might wish to register with online genealogy websites for further information.

6.   The next step is to try and write down alongside each family member their characteristics and qualities. As you begin to do this you begin to piece together a family tree rich in culture, wisdom and a picture of your family that have sacrificed so much in order for you to be reading this book right now. Give thanks and perhaps pour libation (see end of book).

Writings of an Educationalist

A Black leader on Leadership

You don't have to see the whole staircase, just to take the first step.

DR MARTIN LUTHER KING
(Leader of the Civil Rights Movement in America)

I came into teaching by accident. Prior to 1987 I was running a theatre company, Beat Theatre company; putting on small scale fringe theatre productions on a shoestring budget, but I was happy; it was what I wanted to do, and yet as time went on I felt unfulfilled. Each production became a little more boring than the last; tedious rehearsals, the squabbles amongst the cast; praying for good reviews after each first night performance. I did not know it at the time, but my work in theatre; the years I spent developing my writing craft; studying literature from all parts of the world; reading poetry, plays, novels and biographies were part of my training to become an educationalist. In 1985 when I did come into education, I brought my theatre training with me. In the classroom I saw both tragedy and comedy; I saw children who, despite their hardships, still had humour, still had ambition. I first worked with children who had been abused. They were difficult because the system didn't really cater for them; there were few options other than formal school, or a slightly less formalised learning, so these children would keep disappearing; running away to somewhere they thought they were safe. When they returned we would find that this 'safe' place was where they were abused again; and those that did not return, more often than not ended up in a children's secure unit after committing some hideous crime. This was my baptism into education. It was on the North Peckham Estate, a rough area to some, but for thousands their home, where they lived with little resources and a few opportunities. As I was setting up Ebony Education at the time, I visited some local schools, and other education institutions; looking at what I was told were models of good practice, yet the institutions seemed alien to the local people. Most did not know how to engage with the education system and the system definitely did not know how to engage with them. There was little trust between the education body and the people, and those in power bore no reflection on the community they claimed to serve. I was fully aware that virtually each child I was working with would more than likely spend some of their adult time in prison. This already seemed to be their lot. I read case file after case file; attending case conferences with grim faced police officers, social workers, educational psychiatrists, teachers and others, there, seated to discuss the future of a child they hardly knew outside of the case notes. One day, in February, I was given the case file of a fifteen year old boy who had not been to school for years; went from foster home to foster home, and was now involved in petty crime. His name was Joey. When I met him, having been told that I was to be his teacher, he said little as he secretly sussed me out; determining whether I was trustworthy or not. Everything about him was hidden; his world was the world of local gangs, petty criminals and police. He was a Black boy, medium height and very dark; with eyes that told his sad story. His mood changed from day to day which hinted that he might be on drugs. His clothes were expensive; he knew how to obtain money and spent it on dressing himself up. As a teacher one of the first things that I do is try and gain the trust of the pupil; but he was so suspicions of adults that this strategy couldn't even be attempted in the usual way. But this young man was fascinating; he was a character that I had wished I had created in one of my plays. He used his

charm to work the system; to coax his key worker, to get this or that. I later learnt that he was of West African background, though he carried himself as if he was of Caribbean heritage. I began to see the desperate actor within him. It was around May, I had to get some teaching resources to work with him, when he suddenly decided that I was part of the system that he hated. I walked into the classroom. He said something, which I dismissed with a shrug or perhaps silence. He took offence, this time getting in my way and squaring up to me. Another teacher passing by, seeing that there was going to be a confrontation, told him to leave the room, instead suddenly he threw a punch at me, which missed. For a few moments he fought me and the other teacher, until he was forced to run out of the class. Days later I was still shaken. 'Was it my fault?' I'd ask myself. I never saw him again. His anger lingered with me for months. I would see this same anger in not only black teenage boys but in their white counterparts who I also worked with. Race ideology had fooled them into thinking they had power in the white world. They had nothing. Perhaps they would meet in opposing gangs, or in prison, or in a urinated lift on a run down housing estate, or in a crack house. Joey is part of Theo, the star of this book who will allow us to investigate a people looking to rediscover their genius. I didn't understand Joey at the time. I knew something deep within was wrong. I know now that the tree that grew within him was not being nurtured by the community that he belonged to; and that the community had largely forgotten to care for others. Individualism now dominated to an extent. The corrective interventions that the education system put him through, and has put thousands of Black children through (and white working class) is a jungle of ad hoc theories, meaningless strategies that come under the guise of learning support. The greatest damage is, perhaps, that of the Black community who do nothing, except look on and complain. We need to plant 'trees' again; to nurture them, to understand their seasons; again, this is true environmentalism.

Notes on Building Family

The reality for many families, and for Yvonne and Sebastian, are that families are often broken, whether it is due to a marital breakdown or a family feud. To build family we have to explore ways in which we can heal family relationships. The family feud, or family breakdown may seem insurmountable but this is sometimes due to dynamics that few realise is going on. The 'Me', protects itself by saying that it is right, that it has been hurt, that it has taken the right action by being abusive to another person, or not talking to another person and so on. This is its pattern of thought, and this thought further protects itself by wearing several *illusionary masks*: the mask of anger, the mask of blame, the mask of shame and the mask of self-pity. Once these masks are worn for any length of time on a regular basis then behaviour patterns of those involved get more complex, more vindictive, spiteful, hurtful and even cruel. Memory, which is a key tool in healing is used for the wrong purpose, that is, to hold on to the 'Me is right' position.

Coupled with this is the false idea of private relationship, that is, two people in a family like Yvonne and Sebastian, believing that it can work out by itself. What we have to understand is that the family network has been made weak by the lifestyle that both Yvonne and Sebastian have been following in the belief they are living an individualistic and modern life. There has been no cultivation of support from elders, or mentors, or anyone else. They have followed a lifestyle that has deskilled their community and themselves.

Once this stage of masking is now habitual then follows *compensatory* behaviour patterns. Partners in a marital break-up seek to associate themselves with something powerful; whether it is a cultural shift, career change or aspiration, or even being more assertive in regard to their ideology or political view. It is really another mask.

This cycle can only be broken or confronted through compassion, whether the compassion is offered by someone else or the persons themselves, like Yvonne or Sebastian, who might find the strength within them to forgive each other.

The removal of these illusionary masks and the use of memory to remember our true essence is what compassion is concerned with. This continues the *light* which we said our family tree needs, if it is to continue to grow.

Our family tree is full of these flickering lights and the true mission statement of your family tree is to achieve this full illumination. But why, however, is Theo so confused about things? Why is he not aware of this illumination? The truth is no one has, through tradition and culture, explained or trained him in his role in continuing his family objective.

So to heal family pain we need to be compassionate, we need to see the good practice of healing in our family tree and we need to remove these illusionary masks that we put on to make ourselves important and remember that our true essence is to be at peace.

Family Wisdom
On Motherhood

- Mothers need to be mothered too so give her some more love.
- Often great caring mothers need to be reminded to care for themselves.
- In pain, in joy, in reality we all continue to be suckled so let's say thank-you with a gift that you know she'll always want, a smile.
- To learn the art of motherhood is to learn the art of creation.
- Don't give your mother pity; give help and a silent thank-you to the universe for giving you her.
- There will be times when a wife will mother her husband, but remember she is a wife too and needs love.
- When your mother tells you off for doing wrong, thank her for doing right.
- Nature has many styles of motherhood which all come from love.

Stage 3

Family and Africentric Learning

Themes of inquiry:

* How we understand and read the world
* How children with learning difficulties read the world
* How the Black community needs to understand and read its great history

Funtunfunefu – symbol of unity in diversity

Funtunfunefu

This symbol reminds us that although people have different views they can and must be reconciled in order for common goals to be achieved for the benefit of the whole community.

This symbol is at the heart of good African governance, that is, unity in diversity. In our inquiry it reminds us of the common gaol of family, despite family feuds; to build a better world for the next generation and to allow them to realise their full and true potential.

Theo's Diary

We decided to start growing Afro.

Me, Ade and Marcus got called in to see the Head again. Standing there, she kept looking us up and down, then took off her glasses and shook her head. 'I'm so disappointed in you all,' she said. 'Graffitti, Black Power slogans that have caused offence; calling yourselves Biko, Malcolm X, Tupac. What on earth do you think you were celebrating?' she asked us. Well, I couldn't keep quiet. I just let fly. Tell her about how Black History Month is really supposed to be celebrated. Not just stick up two pictures on the wall of Nelson Mandela and Mary Seacole. Next thing I know I started to sing Bob Marley's song, 'Get Up Stand Up', then I opened my eyes and see Ms Maudsley, Marcus, and Ade all looking at me. I felt betrayed. She told the other two to leave. I was in there all alone. She picked up the phone and called Dr Seamus. Someone else answered and she left a message. Later that day I went home with my head low and a letter in my bag to give to mum.

Dad came to the house when I was in bed. This time he took more of his things, but he left his books on revolution that I've been reading, and he had some strange after shave on. Mum mocked his smell then walked to the hallway to get some bills. Heard them argue. They were arguing about money. Dad left and slammed the door. He took the letter. Afterwards mum phoned Auntie Rose. Before I fell asleep I decided not to ask mum to buy me a new bike.

Mum had another argument with the plumber that came to the house. Wanted to charge mum more money than they agreed. He slammed the door like dad. Had cold bath.

Amma came in my dream. Told me to celebrate Black History Month, but when I got to school Ade and Marcus said they didn't want to be called Biko and Tupac anymore. They too got a letter to give to their parents and now they start to look at me funny just like Dr Seamus.

Biko and Tupac are dead.

How to Unlock Your Family's Genius

A Family In Search of a Good School

It is now the year 1989. The dream for the creation of Ebony Education, did not start with me, but with a thin African woman on the island of Carriacou, my great great grandmother on my mother's side who told my great grandmother to tell the children that would come after them that we were Igbo people. It is said, that though we no longer wear facial marks, those with clairvoyant gifts can tell what tribe we are from. Sometimes, for romantic reasons, I like to think that those marks still adorn my lineage; that the schools that she secretly founded in the Caribbean bush as Igbo priestess, I now continue, though with modern technology. Yet, she had more than I do now in 2008. She had a model of her peoples' cosmology, and less fear than the modern Blacks, who, like me, live in the West bombarded with a subliminal psychology of underachievement. In the brutal experience of slavery, there were no good schools. She created them from an obeah wish and the command from the Goddess Yemaya, who had swam across the Atlantic and seen the carnage of spilled dead Africans, had not forgotten her people. This great great grandmother to a nation, had built her school in the bush, away from the curse and rape of her slave master. She taught women the herbs to use for childbirth, she taught her people how to bury their dead, she taught them when to sing before the full moon, she taught them how to prepare unsalted food, she taught them how to make Stone Feast for those lucky enough to have a stone erected when they dropped in the cane fields; she taught them Igbo words of power when the master came drunk and violent to a young slave boy or girl. This was her school. I realised from these childhood stories that my mother gave me beside the fading wick of a paraffin heater that, and my haphazard primary research that the great institutions of black education that had been forged even under brutal slavery, were still in the world, waiting for the blacks to rediscover them. Yet, it was not that simple, for these treasures of education, of African pedagogy, because of propaganda, were as if they lay in swamps surrounded by snakes, for many Blacks, felt ashamed to muddy their hands and apply this knowledge to the plight of their people today. Above all, Black teachers would take only from modern universities, believing that they had the tools to unlock the genius of Black children. To this day, this remains the great deceit. The Black teacher reads Piaget, Steiner and Montessori and others. Yet, they enter the teaching profession naïve, just as the Black parent, and the innocence of the child do. In time these educationalists become memories that rot outside the school gates. If there is a page worth reading, it might be of as historian like E.P.Thompson, who, in *Making of the English Working Class*, tells of how the white working class were broken by the ruling class, and then made to fight in wars to protect the wealth of this same group of propertied people. This history, would be absent from the minds of the teachers, who had believed in this classroom based system; in this traditional role of the teaching profession. Ebony had only been going a year or so when I realised that I was the only one wanting an approach to education outside of the classroom. It would be my meetings with people not within the education profession that would make me walk along Deptford, Catford and Lewisham high streets like a Buddhist monk, contemplating an education system linked to community development.

Some call it Guerrilla Marketing, but for me it was more than a walk; it was a primary research, it was a deep meditation upon the lingering psychological affects of imprisonment/slavery, it was a journey into what the Buddhists call the nature of mind. Each Saturday, after I had visited one of my schools, I would take leaflets and drop them off at local Black hairdressers, barbers, takeaways, restaurants and other outlets where black parents frequented. Saturdays is the day away from work, a day usually spent shopping. How a people shop reveals their economic prowess. Amidst this Saturday rush of market stallholders shouting out their bargains, of buskers, of mad-prophets with religious books, of the homeless begging in a door-front, of roaming police officers, I would increasingly watch Black people, queuing up in shops owned by other communities, almost robot-like giving what little money they had to other people, who, around 4.30pm when the markets closed, would be seen loading up their vans, to drive off with the wealth of a people whose affairs they took little interest in. As time went by I would get to know the proprietors of the black businesses, usually people, who by the very act of starting up their own business, were making a statement and taking action about their children's future welfare. Our conversations were always about the Black shoppers, many of whom would not support the black businesses, or come into the shop; or if they did, curse and complain, as they spent no more than £1.00, leaving miserable-faced as they checked their change. Yet, there was a reason for their bitterness and sometimes cynical approach. It was this. They had witnessed mass crime. Not of actual bullets, but war crimes by cultural assassins deliberately sent into the Black community to create division, create psychic destabilisation, mistrust and self-hate. When a people don't love themselves they cannot prosper. These same shoppers would watch the news, watch the soap opera, watch the sitcom, watch the documentary and see wrongful portrayals of themselves. It made them want to be like the shopkeepers and stallholders they gave their money to. This was why they bought dozens of skin lightners, hair straightners, blonde wigs, and later, they and their men would go for white partners, Asian partners, Arab partners; any partner other than Black African, and then tear the word racism from their dictionary of thought. So one day, seeing this brutal self-hate, I had to ask myself the question: What is Love?

Is love unconditional? Is love when there is no division between observer and observed, therefore for love to be there must be a state of mind where thought itself is obliterated? And what of power? Are the two related: love and power? In Blueprint for Black Power, perhaps the most important book a black teacher, or parent-teacher can read, Amos Wilson says this about power:

"Social organisation amplifies power (p38).

On writing on Chancellor Williams' structural organisation for Blacks he says:

The structural education Chancellor Williams suggested includes the following divisions: economic planning and development; political action; *public education*; community services; youth activities; Afrikan affairs; intelligence and security; and the commission for spiritual assistance." (My emphasis)

How can we teach Power to our children. Again Amos Williams gives us a clue when he writes:

Culture is a social machine, a power grid or system. As a holistic system it is composed of a number of subsystems, power systems in their own right. The family is one such fundamental cultural subsystem….The family is a system where power is customarily and legally exercised.

Black History Month and Kwanzaa provides an opportunity when the Black Community can teach children about Black Power. So let us look at how we can shape these two events to teach our children. Theo's father made the mistake of trying to do things based on individualism. I was told that he wore African shirts, changed his name to an African name, read Pan-African books but went alone because he could not work with anyone else. Individualism is a myth that no other community has used to gain power.

In Search of a Good School

Theo's parents, like all responsible parents, went in search of a good school so that their son could get the best education possible. They looked at school results, spoke to friends, listened to talk on school reputations and browsed through prospectuses that never had pictures in them of children that had brown eyes like Theo's. After a test, for which they had to pay for, Theo entered a private school. It was the start of Theo's father's decline. He had to take on an extra job to pay the private school fees, which made him bitter, for he could only talk about the revolution, but each morning he had to do a part-time cleaning job. Stress, money problems and his Pan-African dreams that his wife could no longer tolerate, put a strain on their marriage. Arguments were heard as Theo did his homework. Each day Theo came home from school a different child; a child who had lost a little something from his soul, a little confidence, and no longer heeded their grandparents words: *'make sure y'make good in life!'* One day, after another argument that could have been about money, or whose turn it was to cook, or why they other didn't hug each other anymore, they decided to take Theo out of private school. The experiment, that so many families engage in was over; traditional teaching, sound discipline, prefects and big money may have gotten their child a few more GCSEs, but something in their child's spirit was dying as he struggled to study Latin, whilst divorced from his own cultural learning.

How to Establish a Good School in Your Community

Your Home School

In *How to Unlock Your Child's Genius (2004)* I outlined an eleven step educational programme for parents on how they can improve their child's education and develop a home school. I showed parents how they can become parent-teachers and further involve the wider community in supporting their child's education. In summary the *How to Unlock Your Child's Genius* programme went as follows:

Stage Three

Topic	Action	Outcome
1. National Curriculum	Know your child's school curriculum and develop your own empowerment curriculum that might focus on life skills.	Parent able to plan Their child's education and understand the assessment procedures.
Diet & Learning	Ensure that your child's diet supports their learning.	Correct brain chemistry
2. Learning Styles	Complete learning styles Questionnaire	Able to apply greater variety to your child's learning.
Know Your Child	Complete questionnaire	Greater understanding of your child.
3. How Your Child Learns	Understand how your lhild learns and teach them how they learn.	Empowers parents and creates self directed learner.
4. Creative learning	Use mind maps and music to stimulate the child's learning.	Whole brain learning takes place.
5. Emotional Literacy	Understanding emotions in learning, the influence of the media and the need for financial literacy	Correct emotions for Learning. Monitoring of the child's media consumption
6. Rites of Passage	Develop rites of passage programmes that addresses community needs.	Child/young person develops skills to equip them in life.

7. Complimentary Therapy & Education	The use of Bach flower remedies and homeopathy to address Emotional issues in children and parents	A stress free learning experience.
8. Education and Culture	Celebrating achievement in a cultural context	A culturally rich learning experience.
9. Thinking Skills	Strategies to deal with racism and class in education	An anti-racist action plan.
10. E-learning	Awareness of online learning environments	Action plan for linking into online learning.
11. World Citizenship	Encourage the child to be aware of global issues like poverty	An awareness of global issues and its effects on fellow citizens.

At present we have a ludicrous situation whereby the parents have no formal training on how to support their child's education; potential educators in the community have no recognised role or venue in which to play a critical role in the learning of children and young people in their community; most trained teachers are not trained to address the central issue of race and class and community engagement. In fact, my experience has shown that some of the most contentious meetings take place at parent evenings. The parent will want to know why their child is not achieving; the school will be defensive, they will blame the family, the community, the special needs demands, and the lack of resources.

In the schooling system, the school educates a child as if human intelligence is solely located in the head/brain. Our body-mind intelligence is dependent upon movement to be properly developed. Movement stimulates neural pathways which are developed through the experience of listening, thinking, imagining; that is, we build our base neural pathways through our sensory experiences. This sensory system begins to develop within two months of conception. The vestibular system (inner ear) which governs our sense of movement and balance is the first to develop. This is why the movement of the foetus and later the new born baby is vital for brain development as it stimulates the brain for new learning. Also, touch is important for learning; so too, visualisation, which develops neural pathways. Theo often gets told off in school for rocking, or wandering off, or fidgeting in order to satisfy this instinctive need of the brain's development. Of course this would not be allowed, so he would become frustrated. The limbic system within the brain is associated with emotions (part of our basic survival system), and this limbic system controls the release of neurotransmitters that can both strengthen and weaken the immune system. The limbic system is also part of our learning mechanism as positive learning requires the emotion of joy. In a state of joyfulness neurotransmitters like GABA, acetylcholine and interferon are produced which improves the learning experience. If the learning experience is perceived as negative then adrenalin is secreted and this produces a negative learning state. Play is vital for learning. How could Theo be joyful when he was being constantly told off in school for not sitting still? Theo's play before he went to school was creative and coupled with vision of his going on to be someone in the world. Within one year of going to school his play changed; his vision of himself changed, for he saw himself as a white hero. There was no vision in this make-belief world other than to beat the baddie. Here began his demise.

Once he out grew his white make-belief hero then he became more lost. So in our home school we must allow for movement.

All through this book there will be the yearning to find an alternative education system; the need to have a space to innovate, to be free from the 'the middle class models of excellence' that have done so much damage, not only to Black children but white working-class children. The burden of running an independent education company are huge; the need for funding to keep teacher child ratio low are immense. When black projects are funded there is immediate control from the establishment, whose main purpose is to control and dominate. Often the funding body will have a Black funding officer, who invariably will have a white line manager, who pulls the strings. In many cases the project will be funded to fail; enough money to start, but not enough to succeed and prosper. In education, the funders will require you to do as they do. Domination means that they want you to do as you are told, and behave as you have been instructed. It means that you must run your company based on these middle-class models. You are then bogged down with endless administration, most of which is of no use to anyone, but they will not fund you for an administrator so you therefore have to divert resources from teaching to paperwork, and your service suffers. Who loses out? The children and the families! So you are forced to realise that self-sufficiency, self-reliance are cornerstones to everything you do. You have to innovate, based on research, based on trial and 'error'. You have to be brave enough to explore the learning style of the Black child and publish. You have to be prepared to stand on a platform and talk about what you truly believe is the way forward, the education of Black people all over the globe. You have to be prepared to do battle with Blacks who cling to the slave mentality; who are paid pennies, in dull mundane jobs that they believe have given them status; you have to do battle with the liberal racist, with the Uncle Tom, with the ignorant, and hardest of all, you have to forgive them, because they, and their children need the education system that you are trying to reveal more than anything else.

Who controls the education of a nation, controls how that nation thinks. Does the nation think critically; question issues around class, race, gender? Or will they just take what's given; greedily manipulate the system to get their child into a 'good' school, and forget about the rest? Will the nation think about those that leave school unable to read or write and who will probably end up in prison, in low paid work, in poor housing, in a mental institution with an accompanying drug problem? Will the nation be able to think honestly about a way of life that destroys the environment and burdens the poorest countries in the world that have least resources to combat environmental damage? Will that nation think critically about war, peace or even love; or will it be fed, and consume, endless hours of sport, entertainment, or news propaganda, telling them that they are the best, the first, the one in the right? Who controls the education system controls the thinking of the people; their outlook on wealth, and perhaps more importantly, their outlook on debt.

Without critical thinking a people, any people, will perish and so what is needed is an education movement that questions everything; empowers the powerless, and gives inspiration. No one organisation can achieve this, but collectively, a group of dedicated people can. The independent Black education company, or project, or Saturday School/family learning centres, or even church or mosque is central to this. So in reading, or writing, we have to teach our children to read the world correctly. To read codes of disempowerment; to read the face of poverty, crime despair and joy. The child cannot learn to read books that do not make them think critically, so reading schemes, reading methods, and curriculum designs have to be devised to make them understand their world. This requires innovation, freedom to innovate; freedom to question, to contemplate and the courage to act. This act, is very much curtailed when those that give you funds wish to maintain the very system that you challenge.

How Our Children Read the World

We have to teach our children to read, not just story books, but read the media and its messages. We have to look at how they read and interpret advertisements; how they read popular media and how they read society. Let us first start at looking at how we can help our children in traditional reading.

Family Learning: reading together

Reading together is a great way to learn together and build family relationships and interests. Below are brief guidelines on reading which are useful in allowing families a deeper understanding of reading methods, remembering that reading has to fulfil other purposes.

Children should have the opportunity to:

1. Read for fun
2. Read out of interest
3. Read books that demonstrates positive cultural identity
4. Read about their history and be presented of acts of courage and achievement
5. Read books that show good reading methods
6. Read fiction and non-fiction books

In addition to this, children should be encouraged and shown how to make their own picture books that address issues of cultural identity, gender, self-esteem and confidence. This means that the word, should be accompanied with a positive picture, for negative imagery impacts tremendously on the child. The making of the book is an important psychological journey. In 1940s, psychologists, Dr Kenneth Clark and his wife Dr. Mamie Phipps conducted a 'Black Doll/White Doll' experiment, where Black children were asked to choose which doll they liked best. The experiment found that 72% of Black children preferred the white dolls. *The Voice Newspaper* (17.9.07), on its front page featured an article by Steve Pope entitled, Which Doll is Bad, highlighting the repeat Black Doll/White Doll tests as part of a documentary for *Colourtelly*. The experiments conducted on 24 children showed 80% of Black children preferring the white doll to the black doll. The article reads:

The interviewer asks the four year old girl, *"Which one do you like?"*

Without hesitation the child picks up the white doll and explains her choice.

"The white doll is the nice doll because she has nice skin."

When asked, *"which doll is the bad doll?"*

The girl again has no doubts. *"The bad doll is theblack doll, because she has black skin… I'm black too, but I don't like myself because I'm black."*

The article goes on to quote one Black boy who answers:

"I want to play with the white doll, because it doesn't have dark bits.."

Bearing the above in mind, when we teach our children to read this psychology of self hate must not be ignored, and must be firmly addressed. The impact for both childhood and adulthood cannot be underestimated.

How to Read and Spell with Phono-Graphix

Phono-Graphix is a method of teaching children how to read. Phono-Graphix was developed by Carmen and Geoffrey McGuninness from 1993 – 1996 in their Orlando reading clinic.

Phono-Graphix uses a logical code to understand the English language

About The English Language

- The English language is made up of 44 sounds
- These 44 sounds are made from 26 letters

The Skills Needed to Use Phono-Graphix

- Blend sounds
- Segment sounds
- Manipulate sounds

Uses

- To teach children to read
- To Support remedial students
- To support ongoing reading

The Main Concept

- Letters are pictures of sounds
- There are sometimes several ways to spell the same sound e.g., o, ow, oe, ough
- Sounds with the same letters may make a different sound in different words e.g., show, brown

How to Read With Synthetic Phonics

Synthetic Phonics was developed/tested in Clackmannanshire in Scotland. Synthetic phonics is similar to Phono-Graphics in that it involves children learning the 44/45 sounds of the English language.

It is based on children segmenting, blending and manipulating these sounds. This system advocates the learning of these sounds before the child starts to read. The system teaches phonics systematically.

It is a system that allows the teachers/parent-teachers to develop reading materials to use at home. It provides the parents with knowledge of the phonic system.

Synthetic Phonic Guidelines

- Assess the child's awareness of sounds
- Segments, blend and manipulate the sounds
- Teaches the spelling process alongside the reading process
- Provide decodable words (then sentence, the text level)
- Doesn't teach words by their whole language shape
- Doesn't teach letter names (except in a song) to avoid confusion
- Varies the pace of the teaching

Enjoyment and Reading

The National Literacy Trust report (Clark and Rumbold, 2006) found that pupils from lower earning families (pupils on school meals) are far less likely to be reading for pleasure. What the research indicates is that enjoyment is central to learning/reading. Further, they have found that:

- Reading for enjoyment amongst boys has declined from 70% to 55% amongst Year 5 pupils.
- The decline in reading for enjoyment was greater in boys than in girls.
- Reading declines as the pupil gets older.

Now that we have looked into reading methods, as a family, choose some interesting books (both fiction and non-fiction) and get reading! Remember, make reading fun and interesting!

The Role of the Parent

There are times when children will need encouragement to read and to be introduced to a variety of books to keep their interest in reading. When reading with children you might need to prompt the child; have a discussion about a character, or the story, or the illustration, or find out other books by the same author. The child should be encouraged to explore the world of books both in the library and on the internet. Eventually the child should have their own little library or their books should form part of the family library and consist of:

1.	**Dictionary**	1.	**Story sacks**
2.	**Thesarus**	2.	**Comics**
3.	**Encyclopaedia**	3.	**Newspapers**
4.	**Atlas**	4.	**Advertising materials**
5.	**Cultural books**	5.	**Song lyrics**
6.	**Reference books**		
7.	**Story books**		
8.	**Poetry books**		

The reading experience can be made even more enjoyable for both child and parent by including the following:

- Sharing the reading; allowing the parent to read to the child and vice versa
- Having a discussion on a moral, social or cultural issue that might arise in the reading
- Questions being asked by both parent and child to prompt discussion, develop thinking skills and expand vocabulary
- Reading with good intonation to develop listening skills
- Allow child to read books well within their reading capability so as to encourage independent reading and build confidence
- Create a comfortable reading space that is inviting and welcoming
- Encourage the taking of water and movement prior to reading for optimum learning

How to Unlock Your Family's Genius

When teaching your child to read, the parent-teacher or teacher should bear in mind that a child's foveal focus (the ability to focus on two dimensional print) does not fully develop until the age of seven, hence in some countries they do not start teaching a child to read until this age. Although it is said that reading is 20% about sight/eye movement and eighty per cent thinking, it is important to still be aware of eye development and issues that might occur in young children. In addition, the socialisation around reading is key. Teenagers, especially boys, do not read as much as girls, but in my experience, if the social environment of the reading is made more culturally appropriate, in terms of youth culture, then the teenagers will more readily engage in reading. Plus, more children now read online than with books and this also a valid form of reading to a point, but the parent-teacher and teacher should also be aware of the health risks of long hours in front of a computer.

Reading provided Sebastian with an opportunity to build closer bonds with Theo, his son; it provided him with the opportunity to build trust, friendship and understanding, but Sebastian never really understood the opportunities that this simple, but all so important task offered.

How Children Write

Closely related to reading is children's writing. One of the ways to help children to write is to allow and encourage them to write what they like writing, which is stories. You can start by using a stimulus of some sort, like a picture, a piece of music, a cut out from a children's magazine. They might want to explore their story by talking about it; saying who are the characters in the story, what do they look like; where is the story set and what will happen in the beginning, in the middle and in the end.

Special Children

Special children have made Ebony a special education organisation, and each time a special child walks through the school gates it demands more of us, it forces us to look deeper into our own humanity and develop new skills, research more and improve our educational provision. For years I have written poetry and have been fortunate enough to have won a few awards; my inspiration is the human act of teaching. I have always wanted to be a great teacher, not solely in the classroom, but wherever I am revealing something to someone else. All my professional career I have pursued two professions, educationalist and writer (novelist and poet) but in truth, they are one. Both teach, but the drama of what you present to the child or your adult audience, is just a little different. You are asking both child and audience to share in your personal revelation, your discovery of what it is to be human. At the time I was working with Theo and his family, a child with autism was brought to me. When I think back to this period for some odd reason I think of a butterfly. This happened once when I got a phone call from a woman who asked me the usual questions about our service. She listened patiently, then, with slight hesitancy in her voice outlined what had been happening to her child: 'He's in a normal school and they provide him with a support worker, but he just sits at the back of the class and doesn't have a clue what's going on, and then he gets frustrated and starts playing up…' At this point her voice began to break up. As a mother she senses that her child has great potential; she knows that the genius of her child is locked away and she simply wants to give her child an opportunity to fully express themselves.

What Causes Autism?

It is not known what causes autism but it is thought to be a neurological disorder. Autism does not normally occur alone. Children with autism might have epilepsy (20% in pre-adolescence and adolescence), impaired vision (one in five children/adults needs glasses), impaired hearing (one in four) and impaired speech. Autism is a very individual disorder.

How Many Children Have Autism?

About 1 in every 1000 children in the UK develop the syndrome of autism. Some experts believe the possible cause to be genetic, fetal damage caused by rubella infection in uteru, allergies, heredity (one in 20), brain damage during pregnancy (caused by the herpes virus infection) or delivery or during the neonatal stage. In the case of Asperger syndrome, about 3-4 children in 1000 are affected. Autism is more prevalent in males and is said to be three times more prevalent in boys than in girls. Asperger syndrome is also more prevalent in males than in females.

Educational Provision for Children with Autism

Autism is thought to be a developmental disorder. Many children in Theo's class have been diagnosed with special needs, yet Theo wants them to be in his gang because he knows they are special; they have the same look in their eye as he does and it is as if Amma speaks to them too.

Children with autism need education and guidance. They often live in a world they do not quite understand and exhibit a triad of impairments which are:

- Communication – language deficiencies in speech, body language, facial expression.
- Imagination – restricted imagination in many areas although high imaginative skills can be exhibited in certain specific areas.
- Social behaviour – many children with autism display social deficiencies before their first birthday. At two to three years of age the child will typically lack reciprocity and the inability to empathise, however positive social behaviour often develops in the school years.

In Autism, Medical and Educational Aspects (1999), Peeters and Gillberg , provide an overview of the medical viewpoint which I now summarise:

1. At times a chaotic inner world
2. Disturbed time concept
3. Mental retardation
4. Epilepsy
5. Visual problems – disturbed eye movements
6. Self destructive behaviour

I have found that the Black child with autism not only has to cope in a world that does not acknowledge their difference but also racism. When parents come to us, depending on the severity of the autism, we might sometimes advise that they seek alternative educational support. Parents would insist that we somehow try and accommodate their child. It is here that they relay the hopelessness of the support their child is receiving in some mainstream school. What has happened over the years has been that I and the staff at Ebony have had to address what Peeters and Gillberg call the five axes of professional training and education and find the unique learning style of these pupils:

- Sound theoretical knowledge of autism
- Training in patient assessment
- Adaptation of the learning environment to accommodate the learner who has autism
- Functional skills (helping the learner with autism apply their knowledge to practical tasks)
- Finding the unique learning style and pace of the learner with autism

As with so much we do at Ebony, one of the first tasks is to raise the awareness of parents to their child's unique learning style/pace and to offer them training in, *How to Unlock Your Child's Genius*, a course based on my book of the same name.

How to Unlock Your Family's Genius

Theo's first experience of autism was when Marcus joined his schooll. Theo said little as the child sat down next to him, but even the slightly withdrawn Theo found the boy's running to the toilet amusing and seemed to instinctively develop a rapport with the child. Their friendship was not through words but the manipulating of symbols and the sharing of interests. Marcus needed someone to help him understand a confusing world, and Theo, with small actions like handing Marcus a pencil or encouraging him to wipe his nose, built a rapport and trust with him. Perhaps it was because they were both outsiders; had both been excluded in someway from mainstream school that they slowly became friends. Marcus progressed well. Occassionally he would become hyperactive. One of the teachers would take his hand and go for a quiet walk in part of the big old school building. He would come back calm. The peace in his eyes would tell me that he had had time to wonder about things. He understood much more than people thought, yet there was this other world that he lived in and perhaps it was this world that Theo managed to spy into. Months passed. Both Theo and Marcus did well. Then suddenly Marcus stopped coming. I was aware of strains in the relationship between the parents, but this was not in my control. It was a pity. We had learnt so much from Marcus, from his parents. That is how things are at Saturday schools. There are little planned exits. When people are in need they come, and when they find things are fine they leave. The consequences were great for Theo. He had lost an ally. In a way I suppose he felt betrayed, having been let down in his schooling so many times.

The only person who could have helped him was Grace. Her romanticism was fading, though her flat was still littered with books that chanted equality, that made an untidy landscape of egalitarianism. Her health had suffered. The Headteacher, egged on by the psychologist who felt she was trespassing upon his professional territory, called Grace into her office. Grace was weak. Weak from migraines, weak from sleepless nights, weak from sudden headaches, weak from so little love from so few. Her hair was falling, the dare of her flamboyant Africentric dress was now a cliché, and her diary that she kept next to her picture of Toni Morrison had not had an entry for weeks, with the exception of a tear that had snuck in. Grace, fiddling with one of the cowrie shells of her earrings, sat before the desk of the Headteacher as the rather stern woman removed her glasses to allow a thought to work its way to her lips.

"Grace, since you've been with us there's been nothing but excellent reports about your attitude, your commitment and your rapport with the pupils. You are a valued member of staff." The Headteacher, whose name was Ms Wilkinson leaned forward, as if to offer Grace the sincerity of her smile. "I'm very fond of you Grace. I know it hasn't been easy, coming into a rather conservative middle class school with its odd traditions, its idiosyncracies, its school caps and hockey sticks, its old houses, its stuffiness: that's what we are and though we are modernising, one has to accept how things are, Grace." Grace was looking out onto the playing fields where, somewhere amongst the children doing their PE was Theo, who, at one time was one of the best but whose attitude made him cross the line last. She swept her locks back a little, allowing them to catch the fresh daylight that seemed to want to sit in on the conversation now that a stubborn cloud had passed. The headteacher continued. "Grace, we are a big team at this school. Old habits take a long time to change. It's been brought to my attention your interest in Theo. A very bright but challenging pupil. There's been a number of measures set up to support him.."
"He doesn't need support." Grace's words were clumsy and a little rude.
"I understand Grace. We all feel passionately about issues facing our pupils, but certain senior members of staff are a little concerned about this black staff group you've recently started. Ms Parks informs me that you've asked her to order some books relating to identity. We have to take things slowly, Grace. We don't want to alienate staff who have been here a very long time; who have helped all children, irrespective of race. I just want you to be a little sensitive to our traditions." Grace strained her eyes a little. She thought she could see Theo in the distance being told off, being sent back to the changing rooms. She turned and looked at the statuesque smile on the face of Ms Wilkinson, noticing the disturbed neatness of her suit, its odd colouring and the painful clip in her hair that couldn't quite keep her thoughts in order. Grace got up and left. She went into the staffroom. Everyone became quiet, especially the guilt of the black staff. Most avoided eye contact with her. She went into the classroom where she was next to teach and waited; waited for the children to enter and the trickle on her cheek to go away.

An Investigation into the Solitary Tear on the Face of Grace

Is Grace typical of all black teachers and lecturers working in the British education system or any other education system that doesn't seek to unlock the genius of teacher and learner? We can summarise her situation as being:

- Isolated and naïve about the education sector she is working in.
- Fellow Black teachers are scared to show any solidarity because they feel that they will hinder the progress of their careers less by ignoring racism and not making the white teaching establishment feel threatened or uncomfortable in any way.
- The few Black teachers who are in senior positions believe that they have been truly granted power by the system and therefore have to show allegiance to the senior management. Psychologically it would crush them if they were to realise that they were a token as it would mean that their whole career has been a sham.
- The Black staff group that Grace has started is ill-informed and powerless and therefore cannot make strategic decisions. It simply becomes a place of complaint.
- Black staff become reluctant to go along to the black staff

Each Saturday, Grace ignored the advice of her family and went on lonely walks, first through Lewisham market, then through the park where she watched the gardeners work the land, hoping that their dig might reveal answers to her anguish that had no name. Once she sat down on the park bench, the rasp of their shovels cutting through her as she thought about school, her career, Theo; then her mind would wonder; disturbed by something seemingly uninteresting like a squirrel, or bird in the prying tree. One such Saturday, after I had finished running the Saturday schools I sat down next to Grace, or someone like Grace, on this bench; yes Grace, our composite character with her head full of loxology, her pride stubborn as the ugly education system was unmasking itself. She wanted companionship, she wanted to burn all her books on Piaget, Steiner, Vygotsky and others who she thought were her heroes, but now she realised that they were her enemies. Suddenly, ignoring my presence, Grace got to her feet and with an audience of these supposedly simple people and animals, began to curse: "You think you can destroy; me, whose mother did break her back cleaning dirty trains, and hoovering offices, and working shifts! Me!" Later that night she would have sex with her boy-friend, sex not for love but to stop herself from crying; and after the sex she would slowly bathe herself, the shower a ritual where she commanded her personal God to rise again. She was not the first black woman to have made this command. Stories from the oral tradition on my mother's side said that it was the personal Gods of Yoruba, Igbo, Ashanti, Hausa, and other tribes that removed the curse from the blood that was spilled amidst the screams in cane fields. This was Grace's professional development; one, that was completely alien to the flip chart, tea and biscuits; she was a warrior-teacher, still suckling from the nipple upon which Nefertari, N'Zinga, Harriet Tubman and Sojourner Truth all fed. I returned to the park bench several times to look for Grace, knowing full well what was going on in her life; but she was not there. All around I could only see the legacy of the gardener's dig; the joy of blooms that made spite after the rasp of tired shovels, now sleeping in sheds. So many good teachers leave the profession; like Grace, broken, not only by the increasing paperwork, but a betrayal of the true role of teacher, which is that of a learner.

Why does each child bring you pain

Pain you thought you put in detention:
You, the darling of old honoured profession.
Your joy once scribbled on the board
Now fails your heritage and conscience

Why is there no children in the playground

Their games echo without soul;
Only hesitant steps to school gates
Their need to learn, and yours, betrayed.

Celebrate your task
Despite each reckless exam;
Understand the vision in their gaze,
And suckle their untutored dreams

So why does each child bring you pain:
When there is so much joy to teach;
There will be no final graduation:
Only the eternal sweetness of their love.

Eventually, Grace left the school, never had time to say goodbye to Theo, and two years after that she left the teaching profession altogether and never entered a classroom again.

Black Education and Black African Systems of Knowledge

The origins of the world's first writing systems start in the Black civilisations of Kamit (3500 BCE Black Egypt) which developed the heiroglphics: Sumer (3300 BCE), which developed the cuneiform script, Indus Kush (2500 BCE) which developed the Indus script, Black China of the Shang dynasty (1200 BCE) that first produced oracle bone inscription. Many books on the history of writing put Sumer as the first civilisation to invent writing and they try to imply that Sumer was non-black whilst also trying to make Kamit (Black Egypt) not as old as it really is. However, the recent dating of the Sphinx indicate that Egypt was not only a Black African civilisation but was established by earlier Black African civilisations in the once fertile and lush Sahara. Perhaps if Grace had been aware of the long tradition of African scholarship she might have been even more inspired and determined to build her career in education and children like Theo might have realised that it is perfectly natural to be a genius.

Anthony T. Browder, in his book *Nile Valley Contributions to Civilisations* (1992) says:

> *Every temple in Kemet had vast libraries equipped with thousands of papyrus scrolls which contained dissertations on law, medicine, philosophy and numerous other subjects…Much has been written about the "Mystery Schools" of the Nile Valley, but one important factor must be remembered: these schools, and the subjects taught within them, were a mystery only to those who were unfamiliar with that system of education. The purpose of education in the Nile Valley was to create a society where the citizens would understand the relationship which existed between themselves and the universe. In the truest sense of the word, the educational centers in the Nile Valley were the first "universities."*

Claudia Zaslavsky, in her book *Africa Counts*, documents some of the sociomathematics of Africa, that is, how mathematics is used in the everyday lives of African people. Starting with ancient Egypt (Kamit) she notes that the flooding of the Nile necessitated the mathematics for the division of the land and crop yields meant that a system of weights and measure had to be facilitated. She goes on to write:

> *Western culture owes a great debt to Egypt and Mesopotamia. The ancient Greeks have been regarded as the fathers of Western civilisation. But many centuries before their time Egyptian priests had developed a complete curriculum for the training of their members. This included philosophy, writing, astronomy, geometry, engineering, and architecture. Indeed, the upper-class Greeks completed their education by studying with Mesopotamian or Egyptian teachers.*

Evidence of a Black African Education System and its Systems of Knowledge

Evidence	Function
Hieroglyphs	Knowledge of advanced science
The Library of Alexandria	National Library
Rhind Mathematical Papyrus	Understand how your lhild learns and teach them how they learn.
(1900B.C.E)	Mathematical text book for
Imhotep	Architect, philosopher, astronomer, poet
Dogon Knowledge of ancient Kamitic science.	Knowledge of advanced science

The Libraries of Timbuktu

Timbuktu, Mali in West Africa, founded in the 11th century was one of the greatest centres of learning in its day. From the fourteenth century onwards its reputation as a centre of learning, where books were valued more than gold, spread throughout the world. Books were both bought and written by local scholars, resulting in great libraries being created and a vast indigenous book production system of African-Arabic texts. During the Songhay empire (1468 – 1591) many African scholars were patronised by royalty and King Askia (1548 – 1583) even founded public libraries.

Leo Africanus, an XV1th century historian wrote on Timbuktu:

> *There are many judges, doctors and clerics here, all receiving good salaries from King Askia Mohammad of the State of Songhay. He pays great respect to men of learning. There is a great demand for books, and more profit is made from the trade in books than from any other line in business.*

Timbuktu had three universities (Sankore University, Jingaray University and Sidi Yahya University) and 180 Quaranic schools. In all there are said to be over 1,000,000 manuscripts still in existence in Mali. This Black African literary tradition is rarely taught in schools. Black children are constantly told they come from a solely oral culture. We can begin to imagine a people with a great heritage in learning, who valued books, who established schools and universities. None of this was told to Theo. He sits at the back of the class, where, whilst many of his friends dream of being a rap artist, he still dreams of being a revolutionary.

The Souls of Black Folk Want to Learn Again

The education of the Blacks was the great debate between great two great Black educators, Booker T. Washington and W.E.B Dubois at the beginning of the twentieth century; a debate that took place amidst lynchings, southern poverty, negro spirituals and the terror of the Klu Klux Klan. This great debate, which still has relevance today, was about what type of education should freed slaves receive. This period was known as the Reconstruction period and ended in 1877, at a time when the Federal government had turned its back on the newly "freed" slaves. Booker T. Washington was born a slave in log cabin in Virginia in 1856, and was later to become the founder and principal of the Tuskegee Institute, a traditional and industrial school for blacks in Alabama. He is often partly remembered for his Atlanta Compromise speech where he advocated a vocational education programme for Blacks rather than an academic one, and he also advised Blacks to give up their fight for political rights on parity with whites. W E B. Dubois was born in 1868, in Great Barrington, Massachusetts and at the age of 35 years he was to write his classic *The Souls of Black Folk* (1903) in which he addressed the burning issue of the education of Black people. He entered this debate hearing the work songs and lingering stench of plantations. Dubois saw the role of education as that of liberator. *In The Education of Black People* (1973) he writes:

> *The man who teaches blacksmithing must be more than a blacksmith. He must be a man of education and culture, acquainted with the whole present technique and business of organisation of modern world and acquainted too with human beings and their possibilities. (p.78).*

When writing on the role and nature of the black education institution, Dubois, in the essay, *The Field and Function of the Negro College*, says:

> *…no matter how much we may dislike the statement the American negro problem is and must be the centre of the university. It has got to be. You are teaching Negroes. There is no pretending that you are teaching Chinese or that you are teaching white Americans..You are teaching American Negroes in 1933 and they are the subject of a caste system in the Republic of the United States of America and their life problem is primarily this problem of caste. In studying the case of Theo we will see if Dubois is today correct in his analysis.*

Black Women, Education & Entrepreneurship

Whilst history has remembered these two men on the subject of black education, an integral part of their story is that of black women educators who founded and taught in schools for Black children. Education for both black slaves and freedmen was viewed with hostility by the white establishment especially set against the landscape of slave rebellions of which the most noted ones took place in 1800 (Gabriel), 1822 (Denmark Vessey), and 1831 (Nat Turner). These schools were founded under extreme conditions, many of them were attacked by the Ku Klux Klan and only opened for four months of the year. Again, history tells us that many schools were supported by white philanthropists, but increasing evidence points to a significant number of schools founded by the black community themselves as documented in *Black Women in White America* (1973).

Black women educators like Susie King Taylor (1848 - ?) born a slave in Savannah Georgia, opened a night school for adults in Liberty County, Georgia. Nannie Helen Boroughs (1883 – 1961) founded the national Training School for women and girls. Mary McLeod Bethune (1875 – 1955) founded the Bethune-Cookman College and was president of the college from 1904 – 1942. Fannie Jackson Coppin (1837-1913) was another black woman educationalist who was born a slave and who went on to become a distinguished principal. She was principal for forty-one years and went on to make a number of innovations, which included industrial education that pre-dated that of Washington's Tuskegee Institute.

Black Education in Europe

The Moors, who ruled Spain for 800 years, brought education and higher learning to Spain and Europe (711 BCE), learning which included agriculture, engineering, architecture, scholarship and education. They built sewer systems, artificial lakes and engaged in shipbuilding. However, in education the Moors made education universal in Spain, building over 70 libraries, seventeen universities and an observatory in Seville. Wayne B. Chandler in his essay, The Moor: Light of Europe's Dark Age informs us of a black African renaissance man called Zaryab, a man talented and trained in both arts and sciences. He was a musician, astronomer, geographer, botanist and introduced the asparagus as a delicacy to Europe. He also went on to found a school of music.

The Moors acquired knowledge that would help Europe to have their Rennaissance. They translated into Arabic Greek and Sanskrit texts. Arabic numerals and arithmetic, which is used today was originally adapted by the Moors from India and brought to Europe. Beatrice Lumpkin and Siham Zitzler in their essay Cairo: Science Academy of the Middle Ages, under a sub-heading entitled African Mathematics write:

> The very word Algebra is an Arabic word, adopted in Europe to describe some of the new mathematics that the Moors had brought into Europe.

The Black teacher, like Grace comes into the teaching profession with no knowledge of this great legacy of black scholarship, heritage and tradition. They believe, as does the Western education system that you can read Piaget, Vygotsky and others and unlock the genius of black children, whose community they know little about and sometimes regard with great suspicion; even coupled with pseudo intelligence theories about Black single parents, rap music, and black 'street' culture. This knowledge is essential for the Black teacher (and the white teacher) as it makes them aware of their responsibility to use education as a tool of liberation; provides models of education that are not simply classroom based but very much embedded in the community from which the children originate, and the investigation of this African education legacy, serves as a tool for the teachers continuing staff development. Here lies a great wealth of good practice.

Poor Grace has no allies. The Black staff are complex stereotypes. They ignore the issues of race and education. They pretend it does not exist because they do not want their white colleagues to feel uncomfortable, but there is a deeper reason; they do not want to confront this Black education history. Psychologically, the black teacher and parent-teacher, have been greatly damaged by having to live in a world, and operate in a white system that only wants white heroism. This complete falsification of history is in every book that the Black teacher has had to read, it is in every advert that they have seen, it is in every essay that they have had to write, it is in every film, play or music they have listened to. Grace is unaware that when she cries at night, hundred and hundreds of other teachers cry too.

Will Theo Go to University?

In both America and Britain there are more Black people in prison than they are in university. Prison education is one of the few ways that those of us in the 'outside' world can support Black prisoners and help them to stop reoffending, and make the most of the opportunities available to them. Yet, great stories have come from prison, stories of men who discovered why they had ended up in prison, questioned the values of society and the incorrect values they held and sought to change their lives and challenge the system that imprisoned them. People like Malcolm X and George Jackson have given us classic stories like (*The Autobiography of Malcolm X and Soledad Brother*); stories of Black men awakening to the true role of their manhood. Over the years I have seen hundreds of students like Theo lost in the education system, and for many the school incarcerated their potential; high percentages of prison inmates have low academic achievement rates or learning difficulties. In these prisons the Black inmates are starved of

How to Unlock Your Family's Genius

light, starved of ultraviolet rays that help produce vitamin D. At night, when once they gazed at the Moon and stars, and wrote hieroglyphs to announce themselves as the worlds first astrologers, they now cry and scream with the curse of creeping mental illness, or yell under the batons of the prison guards. These young people in prison should really be studying the universe. Which of us can offer them support without condemning them first? Who can forgive their crimes, especially if their crimes are against their family, our family? As yet, Theo cannot see into the stench of the prison; cannot see the cues of Black men being fed food not too dissimilar to that 'served' on putrid slave ships.

In *The Science of Melanin: Dispelling The Myths* (1995) Dr T. Owens Moore says:

> *In other words melanin is involved in the transformation of one form of energy into another by coupling together two different physical states (vibrations and electricity).*

We find melanin a central constituent to the intelligence of the body. Areas of the brain with high concentrations of melanin are:

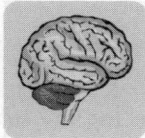

1. Brain stem
2. Substantia nigra
3. Locus coeruleus

Dr Moore informs us that there is a direct link between the vestibular system and neuromelanin; the vestibular system being the first part of the brain to develop and in charge of vision, touch and proprioceptive information about the body's position. Interestingly, Dr Carla Hannaford, in her book *Smart Moves*, when looking into the development of body/mind integration in Africa comments:

> *Of the 10,000 children assessed for learning readiness prior to school entry each year in Kuazulu, the black rural children have consistently scored far superior to the white urban children on all but three of the fifty assessment tests.*

Dr. Hannaford puts this high scoring down to a holistic education system, part of which is to tie the baby to the mother's back which allows the baby's cognition to develop. She writes:

> *From its position on her back the baby is free to turn its head strengthening its neck muscles in order to see and hear the vibrant life going on around it from binocular and binaural perspective. The infant's muscular development is rapid, giving the baby even more command over its sensory-motor input.*

   In science classes Theo learns about photosynthesis. He is given a definition. The teacher tells him that photosynthesis is a chemical process that takes place in the green plants, a process that produces food in the form of glucose ($C_6H_12O_2$). Theo, like all the other black children in the world of education, fail to see any connection between light and their own genius. In his mathematics classes, Theo is taught about number, number as quantity but not as harmony, the harmony which permeates in the universe. He is not taught about the harmony of number that exists in a flower's spiral. In his music classes Theo is taught about great European composers, but he is not taught about the Om sound that permeates the world and was the sound that brought life to this world, that was the sound that was first heard by Amma. He is not taught about the African kora, and its healing harmonies. Theo is blessed with melanin which allows him to operate in eight forms of energy: electrical, light, sound, kinetic, thermal, gravatitional, potential energy, elastic and chemical energy. Occasionally, when Theo is not nonchalantly gazing out of the window, he hears what the teacher is saying and knows something is wrong but is not sure what. He is taught that everything is dead; everything is inanimate, but the educational stories of his grandmother tell him that *the world is animate*. As strange as it might seem, there are those of Theo's heritage that would like to join the lesson; who would like to stand on the podium with the science teacher and point not to the interactive whiteboard, but to the Sirus star system. These teachers are the Dogon masters of Mali, who, taught about duality in the universe, the cosmic womb, the infinity of God, and the relationship between God and man/woman. This is the learning he wants from his family tree, but no one in the school believes that he has a family tree, perhaps, with the exception of his gang to who he brings his dad's old books for them to read and wonder.

Anger Has No Place in Education

For twenty-one years parents have come to me and sought advice on their child's education. Some appear to be calm, some are tearful, some are naïve and some are angry. This anger is easily exploited by those who want to further disempower the family from which the black child has come. In the early days I would go along to a community meeting where there would be talks on black issues: relationships, the state of the Black family, the situation of Black people in psychiatric institutions, diet and health. Always someone would stand up and shout: 'We need our own black schools, more Black teachers', but we have already seen in the case study of Grace how weak the Black teacher is; even if they are in senior management positions they are powerless: they have to deliver a curriculum that they had no input in developing. They have to work in an institution where they have had no input in its design, that keeps them out from real power even if they think they are in a powerful position. They are not organised for power therefore they can never have real power. The senior Black teacher thinks that they have been allowed into T*he Club-of-Power,* a right awarded to them because of their *individual* success. The rhetoric from these community events gets everyone fired up; people shout; people call each other brother and sister. When the sad event comes to an end everyone goes home. Nothing has changed. On Monday morning the Black child goes to the same school. The teacher delivers the same curriculum. The community complains about the sad education system. Is there a place for anger when a people, for their very own survival, have to put in place a global strategy?

Writings of an Educationalist

On Leadership

> *…what is necessary as a prelude to anything else that may come is very strong grass-roots build up of Black consciousness such that Blacks learn to assert themselves and stake their rightful claim.*

STEVE BIKO
(South African Black consciousness leader)

Education of the Blacks: the supplementary school movement

Old black and white television newsreels show the 'first' generation of West Indians arriving on the *SS Empire Windrush* in 1948, carrying 492 Caribbeans seeking an adventure, employment and better opportunities than they could find in their hot homelands. Many dreams danced to their early calypso and mento beats, and central to this was the education of their children. They believed that their children could become doctors, lawyers, teachers and other professional people; people who'd drink from the fountains of the Western intellectual tradition and build, not as cheap labourers, but as equal architects of modern post-war Britain. Yes, a generation of brown people who believed in fair play, the truth of biblical passages and the power of prayer. But the folklore of old coastguards and lighthouse men, said that there was another ship that followed the *SS Empire Windrush*, hidden in the morning mist: according to their pipe smoked tales, seventy-two oarsmen and women rowed quietly, under tired blown sails and made their way to the shores of England, carrying rebel 'pirates' of western thought, sailing like

Stage Three

How to Unlock Your Family's Genius

smugglers of days gone by. It would be many years later, that the journey of this ancestral mythical ship would be understood, for when it came time to hoist the names of supplementary Saturday schools aloft, they would take the names of these men and women who fought for the liberation of mind. Names such as: The Claudia Jones Supplementary Saturday School, the Marcus Garvey Supplementary Saturday School, the Mandela Supplementary Saturday School, the Queen Mother Moore Supplementary Saturday School, the Malcolm X Supplementary Saturday School. It would be then, that those of us who would open these schools, would realise that this ship's cargo was more than gold bullion, it was the black radical tradition that went back to Kamit (Ancient black Egypt), and this radical tradition had to be continued if we were to successfully fight for the education of the Black child.

However, before the black child could walk to school, the roads had to be made safe, for they, the children, were spat at and cursed, in such a way as if to stain their souls. First came the bloody street fights with racist Teddy boys and others; fights with iron bars and knuckle-dusters on street corners, alleys and outside workingmen's clubs. It was never a fair fight. Blows from the government in the form of immigration acts knocked out the naïveté of many of these brown blessed people, who, had listened to the colonial voice from radios and believed in British government officials like Enoch Powell who had recruited them to come and work in Britain, saying that they would be welcomed. By 1958 there were anti-black race riots, and in 1959 Kelso Chochrane, a black carpenter was stabbed to death in north Kensington by a white racist mob, who, like the murderers of Stephen Lawrence many years later, would never be caught. Incidents like these made the blacks realise that they were on their own. If they wanted to go to church, the doors of Christian churches were closed in their face. If they wanted to buy a house, the building society refused them a loan. If they wanted a room to let, *signs of no dogs or coloureds* kept them away. So they formed their own churches in living rooms, community halls; they created their own financial institutions by using susu hands/partners and bought the big old houses in the inner cities. This generation is old now, or dead. They took the blows of early immigrants, and some tilled the soil so that the seeds of independent education could be planted. Despite everything this generation achieved more than realised. Many ended their last days with twisted arthritic fingers from factory work, or lay in old people's homes with wretched back pain, or travelled back to the Caribbean followed by the cursed smell of bedpans that they cleaned for too little pay. Perhaps one day we'll remember them, raise our glasses of rum and water, sprinkling a few flowers on their graves and memories. Perhaps.

By 1960s the hurdles of employment and housing had been overcome to some extent. The typical West Indian family gathered in the evenings around precarious paraffin heaters; women pressed each other's hair at weekends, the children went to Sunday school, the men worked long shifts; families attended dances at the local town hall and Bank holiday coach trips to the seaside, and there was always rice and peas and chicken. But their children were failing in the British education system. The Black child was being classed as educationally sub-normal and sent to special schools. And this failing came amidst wicked immigration Acts of 1962 and 1968, both aimed at limiting immigration. The educational establishment, when occasionally challenged or questioned, used pseudoscience. They blamed black speech. A plethora of theories was put forward: '*Patois undermines the black child's grammar; it causes aggression, it confuses the black child!*' So in this decade of realisation and distrust, the Black community began to open up their own supplementary schools, most running on Saturdays, and providing extra classes for children in English, mathematics and culture. These classes took place in homes, local halls, schools and church rooms. The pioneers were Bini Butuakwa, John LaRose, and Reverend Wilfred Wood who opened the first supplementary schools between 1965 and 1969. It was a struggle and there was opposition and hostility. In 1966 the Afro-Caribbean Self-Help Organisation (ACSHO) opened in Birmingham and established a supplementary school. First, the local education officer claimed that the school taught revolution, then the caretakers' union complained that the school was being let to the Black Power Movement, and amidst all these bizarre accusations, a local headteacher questioned whether the school could offer lessons of any real educational value. It wasn't only the schools that had a battle. Parents too had a struggle. I remember one such case when one cold December, a mother walked into our school with a small round and ungamely child; a little family that were loyal to their local Pentecostal church, and she, the hardworking mother, seemed distraught at the worsening situation of her child's education. The usual interview followed. The mother had a report from her school's educational psychologist. In the months to come we would work with this child, not simply teaching her English and mathematics, but social skills, encouraging her to come out of a shell that she had been put into. It was difficult. We hadn't the specialist skills we have now. We stumbled in our helping of her. This little girl, with her proud plaits and her knock-knees, was by no means our most challenging case but her situation was, for she seemed embroiled in educational bureaucracy. A plethora of letters littered her case file. The mother wanted her to go to a 'normal' school, but the authorities wouldn't have it. It was the headteacher who was intransigent. After a year or so of her attending the Saturday School, during which time the little girl had stopped dribbling and stopped having a runny nose, the mother again went back to the school with a plea in her step and our school report on her daughter, to ask that her child be allowed to attend an 'ordinary' school. Her request was rejected. She was devastated. The church hymns that seemed to accompany her dignified fight for her child seemed to die. We didn't see her again. I like to think that this little family are still together and happy in their home-made church. I like to think that the little girl will share in the optimism of a new day, and be reminded of life's freedom by the playful wind that used to trouble her plaits. I like to think that God sent her to us to strengthen our resolve as educators, to make us less romantic and sentimental; reminding us that we were involved in work that could actually save life. I cannot help but think that we lost this little girl, that she should have remained in our colourful world of learning. It wasn't that the Headteacher won, it was that we were too weak. It's these tiny struggles that pile up on the supplementary school, that make those of us who run these projects, on late Saturday evenings, contemplate the education of the Blacks.

In 1971 Bernard Coard wrote *How the West Indian Child is Made Educationally Sub-Normal in the British School System*. A pamphlet that articulated what was going wrong in the school system, and highlighted the effects of institutional racism on the black child, by pointing out the lack of expectation that the white teacher had of the black child. A year later, another revolutionary called Walter Rodney would write another book with hidden parallels called, How Europe Underdeveloped Africa (1972). It was an equally important book. This time it didn't simply show how the soul of the Black child was being destroyed but how the race of the Blacks was being devastated by the taking of diamonds, iron ore, uranium, oil, lead, zinc and gold from this ancient African soil, making this once great continent economically sub-normal. Both injustices would bring confrontations. In the world of education, the confrontation would be between Black child and teacher, for the Black child would be disciplined and taught within this colonial legacy, and all would pretend that this bloody history was no longer relevant, or had any kind of impact. Yet, the teaching, the curriculum, the discipline, the textbooks, the attitudes and the policies, all stank of this earlier period. Therefore, implicit in the teaching and learning of the black child in the British education system was the indoctrination of white middle class values, that was really at the heart of state education. Tragically, in the classroom, this confrontation would reach a climax. The black child, for so long having sat in this negative learning state, should have felt the blossoms of adolescence, and mapped out their territory of adulthood with a learning mentor to teach them about life. But the years of cultural disrespect, of subtle humiliation, and maybe of weak family support, would result in their rebellion within the school and the school would react by excluding the child.

Between 1973 -1976 the rate of unemployment, for black youth, rose twice as quickly as it did for their white counterparts. The supplementary schools that opened had to further unearth Black heroes, to use history as beacon of Black achievement, and in doing so it reminded the Blacks that they had a radical tradition that had to be part of the black child's education if they were to be honestly prepared for the world. Imhotep, Nefartari, Cuffee and Nanny of the Maroons; the Black Caribs of St Vincent and

How to Unlock Your Family's Genius

Jamaica, Paul Bogle, the Black Victorians like Oludah Equiano and Sancho were part of our tradition. They were men and women who were concerned with education and liberty; their example was also an essential part of the training of the Black teacher. The move for Black History Month that had been born from the American civil rights movement began to take root in Britain. The supplementary movement embraced this history. I, as a young graduate and budding' teacher wanted to know how African gods/ principles permeated their curriculum; how Yemaya and Obatala had been part of their mathematical equations of war. I wanted to know what sweet geometry they used to draw secret maps in the sand to plan raids and ambushes.

1980s was a decade of blood and tears. The riots of the inner cities lit the skies over British prisons that were full of yesterday's underachieving young Black men; their 'teachers' now uniformed guards. It was the decade that saw thirteen black youngsters die in a mysterious fire in Deptford, and which was followed by a march of protest by the Black community. The outlawed Black sailors who had left their ships for awhile marched too. Reports rained down on us like confetti: first the Rampton Report (1981) and then the Swann Report (1985) looked into the issue of Black children underachieving. But it was also a time for those who would fight to organise. Groups like The Camden Black Parents and Teachers Association were established. It was in this decade, in the ripening Spring of '87 that I opened Ebony Supplementary Saturday School, unaware then, that I, young poet and novelist, would serve my apprenticeship as teacher, and later as educationalist in this small project. Now, as I reflect on the decade, and of the maturing Ebony, I realise that it was she that made me into quiet psychologist of my people. The training that supplementary schools offer is, in my opinion, far greater than the teacher training in universities, for its success is centred around the engagement of culture in the child's learning and the honest partnership between parent and school. Here, the Black teacher performs with greater creativity and innovation even though they have limited resources. Here, in these Saturday schools, they are not isolated to become victims of brutal discrimination, as they are in the state school system. So, we can say of the supplementary schools, its essence is unity. This is its uniqueness. It stands tall in a disunited community. Its mere existence is a great lesson plan. When Blacks buy from non-blacks its existence teaches black economic unity. When Blacks kill non-Blacks, its existence teaches cultural unity. When Black men disrespect Black womanhood, its existence teaches respect for the omnipresent feminine principle that permeates the world. What of the weekly running of the supplementary school? It consists of the preparation of teaching materials, the teaching of children, the managing of resources, the counselling of parents, the motivating of students, the writing of reports, designing assignments: work hampered by limited budgets. Is this the supplementary school's great work? Yes. It is the constant investigation into the learning of the Black child that unlocks their genius. This builds camaraderie. There is no stronger bond than that between black women, when the futile love of a man is not there to sabotage this friendship. The supplementary movement has been largely built by these women. Teachers, mothers and volunteers. Black men cannot leave the education of the next generation, and therefore the defence of their community, to women alone. Who will defend these women? How long do we expect Black women to have babies, work, raise boys and teach? Many women who bring their children to our school are single mothers, who often tell me that they want a Black male teacher, hoping that this will not only address any discipline problems, but hoping that the child will take from the Black male teacher's example. They want a role model. Their home has none. We try our best. How long can we as a community sing Marley's song: *No Woman, No Cry*

Ebony Saturday Schools has served the community for twenty-one years now. Six thousand children have used our services in England. It has several branches, its own publishing house, a home tuition service and supports many schools in Africa. Our work has brought us regional and national media attention, and awards (CarAF London Supplementary School of the Year Award 2005 and the London Schools and Black Child Conference Award, 2006), and an even greater vision. If we continue to use the names of the rebels who were teacher-activists, we have to realise that they sought not to copy the system of their oppressors, but to create something that would give dignity to their humanity. This might mean that it's time we dropped the word supplementary from our titles, for are we supplementing something that is already wrong, or are we creating something that is new?

The future of the supplementary movement is uncertain. The schools are diverse. Some seek funding from local government or charities so their future lies in the hands of a funding officer or committee. Some seek to raise money by their own means, and perhaps ensure their independence more. Perhaps the future of the movement lies in the hands of the Black churches that have a loyal clientele, resources, self-reliance and independence to carry on the movement. If they do then they, like us, must be clear as to what education is. Amos Wilson, in his classic book, *Awakening the Natural Genius of the Black Child* (1991) wrote: 'I think it is vital that we understand the major function of education is to help secure the survival of a people…And it's going to require a different kind of education than what is available today.' This different type of education is what has occupied many of the supplementary schools, certainly at Ebony it has been one of our primary focuses. In 2004 I wrote the book *How to Unlock Your Child's Genius* which presented an eleven step holistic educational programme for parents, and showed parents how they can become parent-teachers whilst also improving the learning environment of the home and their community. The book deals with subjects like educational management in the home, diet and learning, e-learning, learning styles, how children learn, thinking skills, financial literacy, education and culture and more. We launched it at the Black Child Conference staged by the Greater London Authority, and within hours of displaying the book we were overwhelmed by its reception. We sold out within a couple of hours, and ten months on we have sold several thousands at workshops, talks, community gatherings and events. Everyone wanted to promote the book. Pirate stations, black churches, youth clubs, teachers and people who hadn't even been active in education before. Its success is tribute the supplementary movement as a whole, for the book has come from this movement and perhaps, could have only come from this grassroots movement.

The supplementary schools must be careful not to restrict themselves to a tiny corner of a city, lost to the wider community and even the community abroad. Earlier this year, one calm Sunday morning, I gave a live radio interview on a community station where the DJ played old reggae classics that in itself, had a scent of mellow herbs. I was asked the usual questions about the book by the slightly languid but genuine host; a Rastaman who'd nod his head to my answers, as if listening to music in an old blues-dance. Towards the end of the interview, the host asked people to phone in to put questions to me. One of them was a woman, a regular to the show, who spoke with urgency in her voice. Funnily enough I can't remember her question. After the formal phone-in she rang again, and this time asked if she could purchase several copies for schools in Africa. I agreed, and on meeting her later in the week, she told me of a project she was involved in helping schools in rural Africa. Things moved fast. I found myself, inexplicably, putting together education packs for these rural schools. Within a few weeks, out of the blue, other representatives from other parts of African schools approached us for materials and possibly training for their schools. A few weeks later we had donated over one hundred educational packs and agreed to set up a teacher-training centre in Ghana. It took this woman's insistent phone call to give me the vision, to make me see beyond my little corner of London and further, and realise that the expertise, the research and development that goes on in supplementary schools is of value to children everywhere.

It is the summer month of August. A new term will start in the optimism of September, and new faces of children all over the country will appear at supplementary schools; inquisitive faces, all, in their various ways wanting to learn, wanting to be somebody in the world, and it will be the noble job of these unsung educational projects to help them. Many years have passed since the *SS Empire Windrush* docked, and the ship of revolutionaries that was also guided to these shores and was/is the inspiration behind many of these Saturday schools. But there is more work to be done. The challenge gets greater, as the Black child's mis-education in the media becomes more awesome and catastrophic. It is time for the black community to support these seed-schools, to value the tremendous work they do, and for these schools to work together. In our work, let us remember the Ethiopian proverb: *If you can't hold children in your arms then please hold them in your heart.*

Notes on Building Family

It is important that we challenge all beliefs we have on family and the relationships that stem from family. If we look at these beliefs carefully we find that they are in fact limiting beliefs. Clearly we can see that this is what is happening in the case of Yvonne and Sebastian. The beliefs that they have about themselves as a married couple; beliefs on courtship, on marriage, on family life are now challenged due to the break-up of their relationship. Central to all of these beliefs is their 'me', their 'I', which they believe has to be important; has to have status. There can be no reconciliation to their relationship unless they tackle this belief system which of course makes them vulnerable and this vulnerability stems from fear.

All of us need to replace these limiting beliefs we have on family with positive beliefs, such as: family as a care system, family as your capital, family as your network, family as inheritance, family as wealth and so on. We need to build a kind of family altar that allows for all these dynamics around family to coexist and even be celebrated. The complexity around family means that at any one time people will want to give thanks for family, remember family, pour libation to family members that have passed and seek divine guidance on family matters.

Yvonne and Sebastian have made the mistake of thinking of family as solely about their relationship, even ignoring Theo at times. They believe that central to the existence of their family is their relationship. If we back track a little we find that the stages that have led to their family, that is, courtship, engagement, marriage, birth of first child, etc, have had community involvement. Now that the break-up is taking place there will not be much community involvement to rescue the emotional breakdown of Yvonne, Sebastian and Theo. Family is dynamic and involves many people, who, if a family altar had been made, would demonstrate just how extensive family is.

How will this family sit in front of the family altar? And let's not forget Grace. How will she, who for so long believed in her professionalism and in individualism that she learnt about at university, cope in this moment of crisis? To understand family, to re-engage with family requires that she also take off her mask, observe the masquerade of her fear and re-build her family simply through this honest self-observation and positive belief-system.

Family Wisdom
On Teaching

- The parent is the child's first teacher so let's all be patient on the growth of both.
- Do not abdicate your responsibility to be your child's first teacher.
- Each one teach one and then each one teach ten.
- To be a great teacher you need to reflect; to reflect without condemnation you need self-love, to have self-love you need forgiveness.
- Doing is learning, thinking is learning, laughing is learning, playing is learning so make life your classroom.
- When thought comes to an end, wisdom speaks and when wisdom speaks, real education begins.
- Family learning is about family learning about family.

Stage 4

Family, Sex, Love and Relationships

Duafe – symbol of beauty

This symbol reminds us of beauty, particularly in women and it might also imply the reverence and respect that a society should have for its women.

For our inquiry this symbol hints at a deeper understanding of beauty that is associated with the journey from girlhood to womanhood.

Theo's Diary

Every time I dream I see Amma from afar, and she points me to the forest. It's not like an ordinary forest. It's like people live there but you can't see them. I walk, following some music until I come to an old old tree and there, I see a kora player. This man is like he's older than the tree and he don't even stop when I come. It's only when I sit down that he almost stops playing, but every now and then his fingers will pluck one or two strings, and birds will sing, and flowers just open with magic, and their fragrance turns into butterflies, and he starts to talk. Each time he would start by saying: ' You must understand why we had to run into the bush and bring our great teaching here and hide it, but it's now time for this science to reach back to the people. Tell everyone about what you learn here in the bush, Theo..' When I wake up I feel disturbed. I know I was so close to some kind of old wisdom.

Stage Four

More boys have joined my gang. Like Biko and Tupac, they all have to take on a name. We now have Shaka, Menelik and Equiano, but I told them that in order to join they have to drink some rum. We had our first meeting after school in the park as we were waiting for the girls to walk by. Like me, Shaka had the idea that we should spread our revolution through rap. Everyone get excited, then Shaka asked, what revolution. I got so mad. One of the principles of our revolution was to start socialising with girls. It's then that I realise that I had to tell them. Pure Rubbish! Boys like Lumumba, and Toussaint made out that they knew everything, but when I asked them some real big questions about sex, they start telling me about what their big brothers told them. Anyway, my talk lasted almost twenty minutes. I told them about what herbs for sex; told them how to sing to a girl and to get her aroused. For the rest of that week we met in the park after school to do some press-ups, eat some raw nuts and start smile at the girls as they walk past carrying their school bags. And as them giggle at us with our shirts off, I just start lick out some Bush lyrics.

Yes, I want my gang to be the baddest in the whole of London. I want some respect!

In the science lesson I couldn't stop thinking about the girls. I Just kept looking out of the window, at the grass and thinking about the pretty one. Ms Arnold told me to pay attention and then asked me what I was thinking about. I told her I was thinking about the girls in the park and the lyrics of my new love rap. She became puzzled, then cross and then went red.

Headteacher told me that I have to see Dr Seamus again.

The Science of Learning

Emotions are essential for learning. The part of the brain which controls your emotions is called the limbic brain, which is situated between the reptilian brain and the cerebral cortex. The limbic brain consists of: amygdale, basal ganglia, hippocampus, hypothalamus and thalamus. This part of the brain also controls the release of neurotransmitters in the pleasure centres of the brain. In *Smart Moves'* by Carla Hannaford she writes:

> *The intricate wiring of the limbic system shows that in order to learn and remember something, there must be sensory input, a personal emotional connection and movement...*
> *In order to learn, think or create, learners must have an emotional commitment...*

This means that:

- children need to be emotionally engaged in their learning; to be challenged, excited especially in the first five years of life when 90% of learning takes place.
- children be in a learning environment where they are culturally comfortable.
- children need to be able to dream which aids the processing of emotional experiences.

In order to learn in accordance with the limbic system we should encourage our children to:

- Use movement exercises to aid learning. Remember, there must be motion to have emotion
- Use creative and imaginative play
- Use story writing, storytelling and joy
- Use emotional expression through drama and role play
- Engage in the caring of others
- Engage in group learning

The system of the brain and the whole nervous system is electrical, that is, the transmissions within the brain is of electrical currents which are dependent on water and nutrients. Two key nutrients are sodium and potassium, and their action is sometimes known as the sodium-potassium pump which gives the neurons their energy.

The Natural Learning Style of the Black Family

To understand the natural learning style of the Black family we should first look at traditional gatherings, gatherings of liberation in fighting oppressive situations, and gatherings of African people when celebrating their spirituality. A brief look at these organisations leads us to a number of components, the first of which is the brain.

The Human Brain:

1. Has 100 billion active nerve (neuron) cells and these nerve cells have 20,000 extensions.
2. Has an additional 900 billion cells that support the active cells.
3. Has 4 wavelengths with alpha wavelength being the one to be achieved for optimum learning.
4. Has two hemispheres which are joined together by the corpus callosum.
5. Is thought to have evolved in three stages: reptilian, mammalian and cortex
6. Is able to learn throughout a person's entire life.

In order for the brain to function at its optimum it must have oxygen, water, nutrients and movement, and have a learning environment that understands the conditions for peak mental performance and the science behind good brain chemistry. By looking at these components we can, scientifically, plan family learning events whether it be parenting classes, family learning, after school club, homework clubs, Saturday Schools, full time schools or family fun days. Africentric education, which is simply an organised learning experience where the African family in central, is based on a holistic scientific curriculum.

In the case of Theo, any issues around his learning should also focus on his brain function rather than simply the behavioural issues and how stress and anxiety might impact on his learning.

The Learning Space

The circle is sacred in many traditional African societies as with the Zulu nation, partly because it represents the egg of creation and partly because it determines equality at gatherings: there is no individualism, although someone might step out of the circle, but they are only representative of the group. The learning space is adorned with symbols of nature to group-teach principles or themes that require relational thinking (thinking about relationships). This type of thinking is superior to associative thinking, and so to accommodate this type of relational thinking glyphs were and are used in traditional African learning systems that incorporate models of intelligence within nature (Neter). This is the learning space where family learning should take place as the circle can be a place for the family to talk, to listen, to share, to forgive and to be silent.

How to Unlock Your Family's Genius

We can already see that Theo does not have this family learning space, so his learning takes place in the secrecy of his diary where he questions the world and it is only Amma that gives him hints of possible answers.

Breathing

Correct breathing is essential for us to realise our full potential. Correct breathing will give us much greater vitality, (as will good diet), improve health and prolong life. A system of breathing developed in Black India is called *Pranayama*, which is about the science of breath.

The first step in correct breathing is becoming aware of the body and posture. Become aware of both feet grounded on the floor. Then imagine a string at the top of the head gently pulling upwards and the body lengthening. Working from the head down imagine the facial muscles relaxing, the neck, shoulders (trapezium muscles), chest (pectorals), biceps and triceps, stomach (abdominal), pelvic area, buttocks, thighs, quads, calves, feet and toes.

Now that you are relaxed imagine the pathway for the air: first entering the pharynx, the larynx, the trachea (windpipe), the bronchi and then into the air sacs of the lungs. Imagine the lungs filling up with air and then emptying.

Breathing should be continuous, rhythmical and smooth even though there are four sections to it:

1. Inhalation (4 seconds)
2. Retention (2 seconds)
3. Exhalation (4 seconds)
4. Relaxation (2 seconds)

Simple breathing exercises should be part of any learning experience and definitely part of family learning. It can bring much needed calmness to a home or even an institution and its benefits to health must not be underestimated.

On many occasions when Sebastian came home late he would be stressed and his breathing throughout the day would have been shallow; so his thoughts would be racing, wild, condemning and when he finally turned the key and entered his home he would bring anger and tension. He and Yvonne might have argued about money or something else but part of the root cause of their disagreement would really be the lack of correct breathing.

Meditation

Breathing leads to meditation and the purpose of meditation is to take in more oxygen than normal, repeat a mantra (words of power) to help stop verbalisation/thoughts (at least slow thoughts down as you slow down your breathing), to visualise your objective, to remain conscious, allowing thought to come to an end and therefore allowing insight which is not limited by the apparatus of thought. When you breathe you should imagine your lungs filling up even in the abdomen area and then emptying completely. Make sure that your face, shoulders, chest, arms, stomach, legs and feet are all relaxed. Maintain a slow, even and smooth breathing rhythm, using a four count for inhalation, retention, exhalation and relaxation.

There are many different techniques for meditation; however, the basic approach is to meditate for thirty minutes each day, morning and evening, at least two hours after a meal. You should sit in a dark room but not in total darkness; be relaxed, palms on your lap and breathe slowly allowing your thoughts to settle down. Never end your meditation abruptly and try and write down insights gained during and after the meditation experience.

Movement and Joy

One of the main emotions leading to the alpha state is joy (ecstasy). To have the emotion of joy you must have motion. Therefore movement, even if imagined, are key to achieving optimum learning. Relaxation, happiness, joy cause the pleasure centres in the brain to trigger the release of neurotransmitters of serotonin, dopamine and endorphins. This is the brain chemistry of joy, and this state can be achieved through dance, percussion and music (healing music).

The first part of the brain to develop is the vestibular system which is stimulated by movement. For the vestibular system to develop it must have movement and sufficient sensory experience. So learning does not solely take place in the head; the body has intelligence too. The various movements we perform develop nerve cell networks. Movement is essential to cognition as it uses some of the same localities in the brain.

In the various Black civilisations like ancient Egypt, Indus Kush (ancient Black India) you have developed systems of movement to promote good health such as Hatha yoga and Kamitic/African yoga. Dance, percussion, call and response, multiple rhythms, words of power, ecstasy and trance (alpha state) are learning styles that Black civilisations have used which has seen them achieve rapid development in all areas of life. The slowest learning experience that Black people have experienced is the Western model, yet so many Black communities are unaware of their true learning style and the economic, social, psychological and spiritual benefits it offers. Certainly African leaders have not made education central to development. Africentric education based around the family is where true liberation will be achieved. What keeps so many families seeking the Western education is simply lack of choice, western propaganda and ruling class education monopoly.

Very often, especially in secondary/higher schools, students like Theo would get told off for moving in such a way, for walking with a 'bounce', for shrugging their shoulders, for talking 'loud', but sometimes, at the heart of this is a rhythmical expression that the intelligence system of the student needs for its 'awakening', for learning to be achieved, for brain development.

Sex Education for the Family

Sex education for most children starts around the age of 10 years of age (Year 6/grade 5) and this education mainly focuses on the biology rather than the emotional relationships around sex. School sex education mainly focuses on:

- The human body and sex organs
- The human life cycle
- Stages in puberty
- Sexual reproduction and genetics
- Sexual health

How to Unlock Your Family's Genius

However, within the family sex education might be referred to as sex intelligence for there are a number of factors that can impact on the various relationships within the home. There are a number of key conversations that need to take place in the home depending on the composition of the family. In the Taoist tradition sex (Sexual Kung Fu) is tied to spirituality and in this sex education the great focus is on harnessing, nurturing and circulating the sexual energy for healing, enhancing vitality and ultimately to assist in spiritual enlightenment. In the traditions of ancient Black India, the Karma Sutra is often cited, which again is the use of sexual energy for healing and spiritual upliftment. This sexual practice originated from the Black civilisations of India (who migrated from Africa some 60000 years ago), the Indus Kush and is a system of knowledge that taught courtship, positions for sexual intercourse, and about marriage. In the African tradition, rituals support this approach and apply strict protocols to puberty, courtship, marriage, sex and sexual health. At the heart of these systems of sexual-spiritual practices are:

1. Non-ejaculatory techniques for men, that is, withdrawing sexual energy away from the genital area through visualisation, thereby allowing the body to also conserve more energy and prevent ejaculation.
2. Techniques on preventing ejaculation, e.g., holding penis at the base.
3. Stimulating the sex organ through rubbing, massage, tapping etc to maintain good health of the sex organ.
4. Knowledge of breathing techniques to stop ejaculation and maintain good health
5. Knowledge on how to circulate the sexual energy (kundalini, Chi, Ra) throughout the body which promotes healing
6. Knowledge of sex cycles and key muscles, e.g., the pubococcygeus or pc muscle (the muscle that you use to stop you urinating)
7. Knowledge of sexual positions to aid healing and meditation; knowledge of the stages of erection and the time and consequence of ejaculation on men's health (loss of zinc and selenium).

For women the sexual-spiritual practices have always been followed in African cultures and the implementation of these sexual practices has been the responsibility of women of all ages:

1. Preparation for puberty through counselling from elder women
2. The knowledge of women's cycle, e.g., the natural mating seasons and the understanding of these cycles which ensure good health.
3. Courtship protocols to regulate sexual activity and keep the natural cycles of the body; e.g., the 28 day cycle, the cycle of pregnancy, cycle of breast feeding.
4. Knowledge of multi-orgasmic experiences and the endocrine glands that strengthen the immune system.
5. Knowledge of sexual union and how to circulate the sexual healing energy.
6. Knowledge of the bioelectric systems within the body (in the cell), and the use of water, herbs and asanas to strengthen sexual organs, and increase oxygen to the body.
7. Rituals for enhancing the man woman relationship; the use of music, crystals, dowries and dance.
8. Herbs that act as aphrodisiacs and the seasons when they should be picked, and used.

The above information points to the fact that sex experience is also related to brain activities. Though, there are various areas of the brain responsible for different aspects of the sexual experience, it is the hypothalamus which is involved in the emotional and sexual experience. We must remember that for couples to enjoy a healthy sex life then they have to train for sex, which is one aspect of yoga. During sexual arousal the pulse rate increases from 70 beats per minute to 150 beats and burns up 200 calories which is equivalent to jogging for 15 minutes. So we can see that health and fitness are also key aspects to a good sex life. What you should have gained by now is that to teach sex education

simply from the point of view of biology was never the African way. It is also important to teach both children and adults about sexually transmitted infections such as Chlamydia, genital warts, gonorrhoea, syphilis, pubic lice and herpes, and this can be done by an informed family member, or member of your church, or mosque or faith group as well as the school.

Perhaps, if Theo had been taught about this tradition of sex and the liberation of sexual energy he might have understood what was going on in his life and that of his father, and realised that the growing sexual energy and awareness taking place in his life needed to be cultivated and nurtured.

Sex on the Brain

The Amygdala	• Found in the lower region of the skull • Responsible for basic behaviour, memor and emotional reactions
The Hypothalamus	• Regulates sexual behaviour
The Pituitary Gland	• Manages the body's hormonal balance (testosterone)
The Septum	• Responsible for sexual pleasure
The Thalamus	• Also concerned with the instinctive sexual behaviour and arousal
The Cerebral Cortex	• Responsible for sexual fantasies

You can see from the above that the brain is key to the sex experience and this is why some sex researchers have said that orgasm takes place in the brain. But we must move on to the emotional side of sex, relationships and marriage, as this is key to teaching families about sex education.

In traditional African societies, when a young girl or boy reaches puberty, they are taken away from the home for a short while by elders of the same sex to be taught about sex education amongst other things. Fertility dolls are used to teach, but these fertility dolls provide a wider understanding of sex/ procreation in that they give a deeper understanding of propagation in the world, e.g., harvests of crops and the seeding of thoughts and its harvests/ gifts from Nature/Neter. It was this science, that the kora player was trying to tell Theo to tell his gang about; this science from Theo's family tree.

On Relationships

I remember a friend of mine telling me that he went to consult a psychic in Brixton one Saturday morning to find out when he was going to meet the woman of his dreams. Apparently, when he got to the place it was packed with Black people all wanting to ask the psychic, an Asian man who wore a lot of silk, the same question. Further investigations by my friend revealed that there were a lot of jilted lovers, all wanting the psychic to put bad spells on their ex lovers. According to him, the atmosphere was vex. Beautiful women, still with old tears in their eyes, came with pictures of men that they wanted to get back, or who they wanted to bring misfortune to. Then there were the men, many of whom were in complicated relationships, and therefore, some at least, came to consult the psychic on choice: that is, which woman to pick out of three or four. Over the years, I heard other stories like this. The sorrowful state of some black relationships are mirrored in other communities because of the attack on family, on culture. Many of us that live in the West are brought up on a cocktail of Hollywood love stories. How did these relationships start? At a dance, a party, a night club. Here, people would be drinking; there would be music, socialising: man watching woman, woman watching man. Body language is key. 'Did she smile at me?' Wine would flow. As the late hours approached couples would dance close; cheek to cheek. Phone numbers would be exchanged, and dates made. In a few weeks there would be intimacy, the first love making, the first promises to love one another truly. Things might work out, but the chances are that they will not. The context of the marriage is debt, unemployment, drugs, lack of family and societal support. There is no framework for the relationship; no understanding that marriage is really the marriage of two families, that it is also an economic relationship; an institution that ensures the stability of community and that private choice of partners is nonsensical, when family is the building block of community. Clearly what needs to be reintroduced into the Black community is a framework for not only the establishment of strong relationships, but the protection of women and family rights. Earlier I mentioned the use of dolls to signify stages in fertility, but if we look at their use to relationships generally we gain a sense of this sophisticated framework where equality is clearly embedded; where there are clearly understood codes, conventions and responsibilities.

African Dolls/Relationship in the Ndebele Dolls of South Africa

Type of Doll	Purpose
Initiation dolls	To signify that a woman has undergone initiation and has a certain status as a married woman and parent.
Ceremonial dolls	Dolls placed outside the home of a young woman by a young man who intends to propose marriage.
Maiden dolls	To signify that a young girl has gone through her rites of puberty and is now eligible for marriage.
Fertility dolls	Dolls made in secret that are presented in a ritual to the bride as she enters her new home after her wedding.

Such use of dolls and their accompanying protocols clearly demonstrate a framework for relationships to be initiated, consummated, celebrated, supported and even annulled, but at all stages there is community involvement and community responsibility. Many of the families that I work with are in turmoil, partly because of the break down of their relationship and the almost casual way the parents entered into the relationship. For many, there was no framework when they dated; there was no ceremony when they started to live together; there was no naming ceremony when they had their first child; there was no counselling when they began to argue, and there was no formal declaration to the community when they split up.

At each stage there is a silent impact on the community. The child that comes from a home where there has been a separation is more likely to separate in their adult relationship. The effects on children in a separation are, in my opinion, far greater than the parents are aware. I remember one single parent mother telling me: 'It's so hard and lonely being a single parent.' I wonder how many really understand her words. It is the collective responsibility of all the community to make this casual behaviour of abandoning children and not facing up to the financial and emotional responsibilities, unacceptable.

Love and Marriage

Building a marriage is really about building a community but in adopting a Western outlook on marriage many Black people look upon marriage as a solely individual and romantic affair. We grow up on a strict diet of Hollywood love stories. We believe in love at first sight, in big weddings and lavish honeymoons, or just living together for a few years then having a change. This approach to marriage soon brings its problems. During the last few years I find myself receiving phone calls from old friends. We talk about the good old days; when we raved, partied and clubbed. I ask them about their children and they ask me about mine. We talk the 'what happened to' talk, then they, almost in a matter of fact tone would say, 'you know me and xxxx split up. Twenty years of marriage just ended like that. Few ever really recover unless they actively seek help. The consequences of the separation or divorce is enormous to both the man and the woman, and perhaps even worse for the children. The sheer stress of it all often leaves both parties lacking confidence, low self-esteem; brings on panic attacks, illness and in a few case I have known, suicide. Anger, blame and even shame haunts these couples, as they then set about looking for a new partner, and in looking they are bitter, condemning. The new partner, who might have this same baggage, has to deal with all these emotions, and their own.

So is there another way to look at marriage. To make our marriages successful we have to look at good practice within our tradition and any tradition for that matter. In the African tradition marriage is looked upon in terms of spirit, and this spiritual union between two people, or more, needs experts at strategic times to guide and advise on this union. Fundamental to the support and therefore the success of the marriage is the understanding of what it is to be human. The African Tree of Knowledge says that humans are spirit, in physical body. Additionally, there is an understanding of what in the Igbo tradition is known as the chi, that is, the pact that your spirit makes with itself to learn certain things during its incarnation. Therefore, marriage is a spiritual classroom; the ups and downs of marriage is calling out this spiritual strength, so there needs to be constant revisions to pass the exams of marriage and these revisions and end of term tests are called rituals that sweeten marriage, that remind those involved of the centrality of spirit in the marriage. On marriage, Ra Un Nefer Amen writes in, *Black Woman's Black Man's Guide to A spiritual Union* (1981):

> *So that from an African perspective, it is not 'a man' dealing with*
> *'a woman', but the One Self dealing with itself. (p71)*

We can therefore see that those who can provide marriage/relationship counselling to families must also have knowledge of spiritual science, which is central to nurturing and the building of family. The issues in the marriage of Yvonne and Sebastian may well have been resolved very easily if they had the support and expertise that once clearly existed in their family tree and tradition. This insight gives us clues, as to the journey that Yvonne and Sebastian must and will take to understand what is going on in their marriage, and to what is going on in their spirit.

How to Unlock Your Family's Genius

Family Celebrations: Kwanzaa

Family celebrations are important to any family for they acknowledge achievement, invite others into the home to share in the celebration, allow people to pay respects to the creator, encourages appreciation to others who have gone before and it is a time to remind everyone of the family's and community's goals and ideals. At Ebony, In late December just before we break-up for the festive holiday, we have a pre-Kwanzaa event (a non-religious event) where we give gifts to the children and young people and thank the parents, staff and volunteers. Kwanzaa was started in 1966 by Dr. Maulana Karenga at the time of the Black Liberation Movement, and has as one of its main goals to restore cultural pride in being African and reaffirm the bonds between African people. Kwanzaa officially takes place between 26th December to 1st January.

On the official Kwanzaa website it states:

> *Kwanzaa is an African American and Pan-African holidaywhich celebrates family, community and culture. Celebrated from 26th December through to 1st January, its origins arein the first harvest celebrations of Africa from which it takes its name. The name kwanzaa is derived from the phrase "matunda ya kwanza" which means "first fruits" in Swahili, a Pan-African language which is the most widely spoken frican language.*

The seven principles (Nguzo Saba) of Kwanzaa are:

Umoja (Unity)	To work for unity and maintain this unity in the community. This takes place on the 26th December.
Practical Application:	Family meals, family conversations & family reunions.
Kujichaguilia (Self-determination)	Which means to define ourselves, name ourselves and speak to ourselves. This takes place on 27th December.
Practical Application:	Naming ceremonies, think tanks, Remembrance Day, African Liberation Day & Black Studies.
Ujima (Collective work and responsibility)	To collectively build and maintain our community. This takes place on 28th December.
Practical Application:	Build Saturday schools, full-time schools; stage Black History Month events, start or join susu/pardner schemes, or time banks and credit unions.
Ujamaa (Co-operative economics)	To build and maintain our own businesses and to profit collectively. This takes place on the 29th December.
Practical Application:	Join susu/pardner schemes, credit unions, or start family businesses.
Nia (Purpose)	To dedicate ourselves to the purpose of restoring our people to their former greatness. This takes place on 30th December.
Practical Application	Things to do lists; daily meditation on life's purpose; positive affirmation of our greatness especially when faced with negative media representation of African people; monthly goal setting.

Stage Four

UKuumba (Creativity)	To create beautiful and relevant cultural legacies. This takes place on 30th December.
Practical Application:	Patronise Black artists and art, and develop creativity in the whole community. Celebrate Black art in our homes, churches, mosques and community centres. Use our creativity to develop new models of education, healthcare and economics.
Imani (Faith)	Which means to define ourselves, name ourselves and speak to ourselves. This takes place on 27th December.
Practical Applications	Naming ceremonies, think tanks, Remembrance Day, African Liberation Day & Black Studies.

Greetings

The greeting of the kwanza celebration is in Swahili and is: Habari gani, to which the response is, Umoja or whatever day it is during the Kwanzaa period.

Gifts

Traditionally gifts are given to the children and are usually a book. At Ebony, as this event is usually a big occasion for all the families that attend we give gifts to both the children and staff, and offer gifts to the parents in the form of pupil performances that include poetry, song, dance and drumming. To bring this aspect of the celebrations alive even more, we normally hire an actress to play the character of Kwanzaa Queen and to hand out the gifts to the children. In keeping with the tradition of Kwanzaa, the Kwanzaa Queen is dressed in traditional African dress (ideally black, read and green) and offers some words of wisdom to the gathered families. Around her throne, we place African artefacts; kente cloth, harvest symbols and African musical instruments.

Whilst this takes place in our education centres, the ideals of Kwanzaa should be kept in the home by the presence of symbols on a mat (mekeka). The symbols should include the mishumaa saba (seven candles of black, red and green). The black candle should be in the middle and with three red and three green on either side of the black one. The black one (representing the people) should be lit first. The red candles, that represent self-determination (Kujichaguilia), co-operati ve economics (Ujamaa) and creativity (Kuumba) are placed on the left of the black candle and the other three green candles (future and hope) are placed on the right. These candles represent Ujima (collective work and responsibility), Nia (purpose) and Imani (faith).

When we stage our pre-Kwanzaa events that have proved to be extremely popular, what has become apparent is that the Black community are starved of their own culture and there is a real thirst for such occasions.

Last we must not forget the Kwanzaa Unity cup (kikombe cha umoja) which should remind us that Kwanzaa is one of the few events that brings community and family together. Its function is to pour libation to the an cestors that have gone before and who even gave their life in the struggle for Black liberation.

These family gatherings are important in building family and community, and it was the increasing absence of such experiences that saw Yvonne and Sebastian drift away from each other and their culture. They therefore made no community pledge; they didn't share in the community ideals and therefore could reap no love from other families as they lived a more and more isolated and unfulfilling life.

Writings of an Educationalist

The Local Housing Estate

I went to live on a council estate in1980; a typical housing estate with its lifts and puddles of urine, its graffiti, its loud parties, its dogs mess and irresponsible owners. There was an array of characters: a weed seller called Tony who wore a bright beaver coloured hat; a grumpy caretaker who spied on various tenants (including me) to see if we were guilty of dumping furniture in the walkways; an old mad woman who sang hymns with great joy as she walked about the estate in her rainbow coloured clothes and would later be found crying by herself in the stairwell. There was also Jamie, the drunk, who, in truth was the loneliest man in the world, for he would sit with his bottle on the bench in the courtyard and wait for someone to come along and then pester them, not for money, but a pleasant conversation. The inner cities then, were a time of sound systems, police stop and search, of Bob Marley, of cold figures of unemployment, of punk, of the emergence of the anger of the second generation of immigrants, of dub poets, of riots. It was the time of the Black and International Bookfair that brought literary radicalism to London. When I was in my flat studying for my degree, someone would be setting fire to the garbage shute, or jamming the lift, or breaking into a car. I would read George Orwell, George Bernard Shaw; I read book like *Love on the Dole* by Walter Greenwood and Upton Sinclair's *The Jungle*, but it was my alternative reading; books that were not part of my Humanities degree reading that really inspired me. I joyfully ploughed through the pages of Toni Morrison, Claude McKay, Derek Walcott, Mari Evans, C.L.R.James and other Black writers. I paid little attention to the estate as a living space. I knew one day I would be gone. I had my flat. It was a cosy bachelor flat where, a few student friends of mine, would organise parties.

Soon the partying stopped. The estate became more bleak. I was no longer an undergraduate but an unemployed graduate unable to find the work I wanted. My manuscripts kept getting rejected. My situation began to politicise me. I saw families struggling in all directions: caged into this concrete estate, trying their best to live. I began to see new immigrants arrive, and the problems of old immigrants would beset them; no one had learnt, or should I say no one cared. Their children would go to the worst schools, they would have the worst health care; get the worst jobs, experience the worst discrimination, and on top of all this, compete with others who also had little limited resources for these impoverished housing stocks.

I spent thirteen years on the estate, and saw the selling of soft drugs to hard drugs emerge. Not long after I left I heard of two murders. When I have gone back to the estate old residents tell me that Tony the weedsman had his flat repossessed and was now inside for selling crack. They tell me that Mad Matilda is in a psychiatric unit and not even her family visits her. They tell me that Jamie the drunk was found dead in his flat; apparently he had been dead for days. These people's lives all seemed to end in tragedy because they had no family. For some reason, whether choice, or misfortune, or through death, they had no families; no one to arrange their care, or burials. Every day I would see some one from social services with meals on wheels; a life line for lonely people, who, once, partied as I did.

In a few cases I have been asked to run education projects on local council estates and this experience of living on an estate is also what has informed me of the provision that is needed. The elderly are lonely and need befriending schemes. The mentally ill lonely and need befriending schemes, training and work; the alcoholics and druggies are lonely and sick and need programmes to address their addiction. People want to get out of their homes; they want to volunteer to help others though they can hardly help themselves. They want food cooperative schemes so that they can eat wholesome affordable food. They want debt support. They want health care. They want ecological projects on their estate so that they can green-up and big-up their environment. They want childcare support so that they can do something for themselves and their families and know that their children are safe. They want family education; Saturday schools, homework clubs, mobile toy and book libraries. They want someone to close down the crack houses. They want someone to stop arresting their children. They want some answers. They want family. Family must also be supported.

Notes on Building Family

Central to a good family life is the *celebration* of family. That is, the celebrating of a birthday, the arrival of a new baby into the family, the wedding anniversary and the family reunion. All must be marked and celebrated.

In addition, families have to do things *together*; they have to eat together, learn together, go on holidays together and practice their faith together if the family belongs to a religion.

All of the above promotes joy within the home and this joy achieves many things besides socialisation. Joy is part of the wellbeing as joy heals, promotes good physical and mental health and this joy, this celebration of family has to be worked on every day. Laughter, flowers, music, smiles, stories and dance are joy's tools. The colours of nature, the sweet smells are its celebration and the reminding to all creatures to celebrate and *propagate* life.

Drugs, drink, unemployment, debt are things that can undermine the joy within the home and when this happens early family support is crucial to the family member concerned.

It is important that a family have a vision of itself; to see itself being successful, growing, strengthening and changing for the better. Affirmations, prayer meditations are all useful in this regard.

If each and every member of the family is to be celebrated then we have to remove the cynicism around certain members like the mother-in-law whose ridicule is probably because she poses a threat to the bullish patriarchy of the home.

In the relationship of Yvonne and Sebastian we see a lack of joy as well as trust and friendship. Sebastian could have done with a smile, some new clothes, explored new music. Also, Yvonne could have acquired new friends, new interests new reading material and a smile. Of course both could have done with some new *love making* times, some more loving, and words of romance. This did not happen in the relationship between Yvonne and Sebastian. Instead, fearing that they were breaking up, they put on their masks and blamed each other.

Theo could see that things were breaking down so he accepted this change to an extent but sought to build a further home in his school so he *created* a new family. He used this *creativity* that excels in adolescence to bring about real change in his life. In this regard he was braver than his parents in that he accepted that things were changing and wanted this change to result in the building of a new and stronger family.

So we have to help this couple. We have to imagine them in romance, loving one another, talking and listening to one another and loving their son.

Family Wisdom
On Relationships

- When sad, brighten your home with colour, sweet smells, joyful music and real laughter then feel if you want to cry.

- Do not worry about the cobwebs when you spring clean; worry about those old thoughts that have kept you back for years, and get the broom and sweep them out.

- It is easy to forget about the importance of joy when you're sad, so be clever and be joyful just to be alive.

- Sometimes it is good to remind yourself and your partner that you are still lovers, and how do you remind each other of this: with love.

- The sex of flowers: its smell, its colour is the quiet conversation of Nature reminding us that to be in the arms of someone you love is the flowering of something eternal.

Stage 5

Family, Gangs and Youth Leadership

Gyawu Atiko: African Symbol of Valour

Gyawu Atiko is the symbol of valour and reminds us in our journey of inquiry to have self belief in our own courage even though others may doubt our abilities. So we have to be adventurous and courageous in our inquiry.

Theo's Diary

This time Dr Seamus was even more serious than normal. His glasses were at the end of his nose, and he was just peering over them at me as if I had committed murder.

With a slight tremor in his voice he asked me to recount what happened in the science lesson. Well, I cleared my throat and started to talk to him about some of the things I learnt in my dreams about how I must look after my t'ing and manhood. Each time I said t'ing he half jump, like he didn't have one or something like that. So I explained about how I was preparing to have sex. Well, who told me to open my mouth. He just started scribbling things down in his note pad; writing one set of big words. Suddenly he stopped, then wiped his brow. Asked me another question. 'Why have you started a gang in the school when you know that the Headteacher has forbidden it?' For awhile my head dropped, not in shame but in thought as I considered the words I should use. "Well," I said: 'We boys are becoming men, and school doesn't realise it so I've started my gang to teach them about sex, and politics, and racism, and lyrics: all the things the old griot told me.' I wanted to tell him what it means to start believing that we're going to be young men, but he didn't really understand. Before he could ask me more questions I just got up and walked out, and started to do my new lyrics even though he called me to come back.

Today, more boys came and said they wanted to join my gang. I understand why they get in trouble. I understand better than their parents or the teachers. They want to be men. I gave them names of real revolutionaries that my dad used to talk about. Like Garvey, Lamumba, Toussaint, Biko, Sobukwe, Bogle, Malcolm X and others. Did a bit of reading to find out what they did. The books had dust on them but I still read them. I am determined to create a revolution in school! .

Youth Work

Broke as usual, I got a job as a part-time youth worker whilst at university to help make ends meet. The process was quick in those days: you filled in an application form, got interviewed and started the following week. I started at St Giles Youth Club in Peckham, slightly hidden centre that served youngsters on the local estate; a mix of mostly Black teenagers who had little opportunities other than the club. When you entered you came straight to the heart of the centre. A snooker table, table tennis table and an old juke box that the youths thought too uncool too really bother with. I did not know at the time that Peckham had a real history of youth work that went back to the 1930s and beyond. Dr Harold Moody, a Black Jamaican doctor had arrived in London in 1904 to study medicine at Kings College, and then went on to set up The League for Coloured Peoples' which also raised money for destitute children and took them on trips to the seaside. A slightly run down club, Dr Moody's spirit was still strong and the need for his old society was needed for many of the teenagers who came from families that required help. So, I was now a part-time youth worker and soon got to know the young people quite well. There was one boy, a short stocky muscular boy who only smiled out of spite; that is, when he did something wicked he laughed raucously, and you couldn't but help laughing with him, yet there were other moments when he would become serious, and it was in those moments that you could see some kind of hurt he never wanted to expose. He was not only the roughest in the club but he also had credibility amongst the other boys for his cousin was a famous boxer. This boy, George I think his name was, also epitomised the lack of opportunities that so many of the youngsters had. He had incredible natural leadership, but there was no where for him to use this leadership other than in a gang. In an odd way he had charisma too, and humour and was incredibly intelligent in his observations of others, but this was Southwark, which at the time had a truancy level of over 50%. It was for boys like George, that the youth club had been set up, but it was surrounded by poverty, drugs, crime, yet the families that lived on nearby estates were strong; just as caring and as ambitious for their children as any other family. Young people like George were in a very precarious position; the streets were calling and there was little that these families could do about it.

I continued to work at the youth club during most of my final year at university; reading Dickens, Joyce and Lawrence by day, and, by night reading Toni Morrison and Claude Mckay. I was studying day and night; reading, and writing my first poems, and increasingly seeing the slightly younger me in these boys. I could relate with them to an extent as I too, as a youngster, had been stopped and searched and arrested. This was my awakening, helped by strong family support. Some of these boys had this, others did not.

A few years later I came home late from a party in Brockley that night to get news that there had been a fire in New Cross and many youngsters had been killed. There were accusations from the Black community that it was racially motivated but the police refused to take this line of inquiry and to this day the cause of the fire has never been discovered. Later, 20,000 people marched through the streets of London demanding justice. Soon afterwards 'Operation Swamp' was supposedly launched to combat crime. Stop and search became the everyday reality for Black youth and the Black community as a whole. In 1981 rioting broke out in Brixton; the Black community had had enough. At this youth club, I could see the same trauma in the boys that I had experienced, and they too wanted to riot.

If I had been arrested today, I would have had my DNA taken and put on the national DNA database. It is estimated that Black males in the UK are four times more likely to be on the DNA database. Currently 32% of Black males are on the database compared to 8% of white males. By 2010 over 50% of Black males will be on the DNA database. The Black male, the Black family is under attack. Any community under attack has to build defences, and this must start in the mind. Our youths must see their community organising, and this organising, for it to be lasting, must start in the home. At present what do they see. They see guns, drugs, porn, junk food and junk advertising all being freely brought into the Black community, and little organising to stop this. The mere act of organising and for this to be witnessed by the young people is part of their youth leadership training. It does not necessarily have to start in the youth club, it starts in the home. The empowerment of the home is what is key, but it is difficult for this to happen if the parent is unaware that actually the reverse is happening in the home. Besides the home being inactive, the Black youth, like Theo, watches television that portrays them as criminal, unambitious, underachievers. They see no heroes, no love stories, no fairy tales with them as Prince or Princess. Successive generations of some Black youth witness this same omission in the classroom and inactivity in the home. No species takes their survival for granted, or does not prepare them for the world, or puts in place defence mechanisms for the realising of their potential. Clearly there needs to be a youth leadership framework that operates in the community and the responsibility of this framework is with the community.

How to Set Up Youth Leadership Programmes

Aims and objectives:

1. To help raise self-esteem and self-confidence in young people and their families
2. To help raise the cultural pride in young people and their families

3. To help young people understand leadership in a holistic sense; that is, non-traditional leadership, community leadership and traditional leadership
4. To help and encourage young people to think critically and develop problem-solving skills on life issues
5. To help raise young people's awareness on community development issues
6. To help young people express themselves creatively, responsibly and realise the positive contribu   tion they can make to society

Designing the Leadership Programme

a) Set up steering and advisory group that **must** include young people
b) Explore ways that give young people immediate shared ownership of the programme design
c) Look at good practice of existing youth leadership programmes that fit in with your aims
d) Develop a framework for the programme but always trying not to make it too prescriptive as to undermine innovation and improvisation
e) The workshops should not be tutor dominated and skills dominated, but allow for young people to learn through their own inquiry at their own pace in their own or group learning style
f) Use mind mapping and nature models if appropriate to allow for creative thinking, planning, problem-solving and strategising
g) Youth leader should remember that they are a learner as well: this allows for creativity
h) Try using a warm-up exercise like Brain-Gym, or yoga, or African-Caribbean dance to start the steering group sessions
i) Be aware of current government guidelines on working with children like The Every Child Matters Agenda and health and safety guidelines/policy

Possible themes/workshops of the Youth Leadership Programme

- How to learn about sex and health
- How to be a positive young person
- How to think big, create wealth and be happy
- How to avoid the trap of gangs, crime and underachievement
- How to do well in school
- How to start your own business

The Leadership Environment and Resources

- Try to obtain an open plan space that allows for young people to move around and learn in groups as well as individually
- Allow quiet space for young people to dream and imagine
- Have positive images on the wall and positive and cultural music available
- CD player, dvd player, digital camera (to record journey, to reflect & celebrate) and computers
- Creative and tactile resources like flip chart paper, coloured pens, pictures, photographs, coloured paper for those with dyslexia
- Mind games (oware), puzzles and drawing paper
- Fresh air, water & plants
- First aid box

Staffing and Facilitator Training

- Ideally staff/facilitators should be multi-skilled and have a sense of fun and responsibility
- Staff /facilitators should have specific training in youth leadership for the programme and the

Stage Five

87

> training should involve the young people on the steering/advisory group
> - Ideally, but not a necessity, staff/facilitators should have themselves gone through a youth leadership programme
> - Staff should be aware of the community and youth issues that are current
> - All staff should have CRB checks and references

Family Viewing and Online Childhood

There are so many studies on the effects of television on childhood and the growing use of social sites that parents seem to be becoming more confused as to what strategy to adopt. 'Should my child have a television in their bedroom? How much television should I allow my child to watch? Will computer games make my child aggressive or give them behavioural problems?' These are some of the common questions that parents ask. The American Academy reports that children who watch too much television tend to be overweight; see thousands of acts of violence by the time they are in their teens and will see four thousand commercials per year. The key issue is, does this affect their synaptic development in early years? Are children simply passive consumers of television; defenceless to the sneaky advertisers who know that they are both gullible, or are we not crediting children with far more critical thinking than is often quoted. Advertisers are fully aware that 50% of the time children are able to successfully influence consumer choices. Once a cartoon series has proved successful its characters are licensed to sweet and toy manufacturers who then also target children. However, limited good quality television where the parents watch television with their child or children can develop language skills and widen the learning opportunities.

Here are some tips that families might use:

- Set time limits of the amount of television your child watches or indeed the family watches.
- Plan and negotiate (depending on the age of the child) programmes to be watched.
- If your child is very young watch television with them; discuss what is viewed and encourage critical thinking.
- Monitor your child's exposure to commercials and do not succumb to their requests to purchase every consumer item they see advertised.
- Often habitual watching of television starts with boredom so encourage your child to develop other interests. It is worth noting that by the age of six children have spent one year of their lives watching television, which, according to Dr Aric Sigman, can lead to obesity and hormonal changes.

In regard to children and the internet, especially on online social websites, we find that British children are spending 20 hours per week online. Coupled with this is that parents are not aware what their children are dong on the net. The Institute for Public Policy Research report (Behind the Screen: The Hidden Life of Youth, 2008) found that 57% of young people have browsed on pornography sites. One of the recommendations of the report is that computers are placed in communal areas rather than in children's bedrooms where monitoring is more difficult, and to improve media literacy for young people so that they can of course monitor themselves. However there can be no denying that the internet has opened up wonderful learning opportunities for young people but they also need to be taught about its possible uses and abuses.

Writings of an Educationalist

Boys' Football: from boyhood to manhood

Since Theo had joined Ladywell Boys Junior Football Club he had felt he had been living in a dream, especially the morning when he played his first mat ch, and kept smelling the brand new boots; kept trying on his new kit and staring at himself in the mirror. All this took place in his bedroom, the attic room, where he could cut himself off from everyone; be lost in his little world, especially his world of football where he played amongst his heroes and scored the winning

goal in his imaginary cup final of dirty fouls and last minute penalties. Here, he lay late at night looking up through the skylight, surrounded by pictures of his football heroes and letters from his grandmother in the Caribbean. Here, his mother, Yvonne, knew he was safe; safe from the headlines of guns, crime, stabbings and all things bad. This was why she had brought him to the club, to toughen him up; to give him some kind of initiation into a changing world that waited for him. And somewhere mixed with this feeling was the usual mother's guilt at giving him away. She was losing him, like she was loosing Sebastian, her husband: one to football, the other to local politics.

'Why can't you spend more time at home, with Theo," She'd blurt out; perhaps at the wrong time, but she just had to speak her mind.' Sebastian would sigh; he'd look at her then out the window, then back at her.

'Understand Yvonne; this is my chance; my chance to be someone, to do something. I want Theo to respect me, not just be with me!' Soon she saw him stretching into his coat as he made off to another meeting of rowdy local politicians. There was more she had wanted to say as he left. She wanted to say that she didn't like his new politics. It was different. Since he cut off his locks he talked about Garvey less; talked about Malcolm and Martin, and Biko and Nkrumah less. Now, he seemed to read books by people with Russian or German names. She never cried outwardly. Her mother would not have it. So, since she was a child with ribbons in her hair, she had learnt to cry inside; a place she thought no one could see her, only God and her God never betrayed her pain.

It was the day of the big match. The previous night, animated by a wind that was intent on breaking down the little old shed by the apple tree, Theo had prayed to his Grandma in Jamaica. He had promised her he would do his best. It was a response to the letters that she'd sent to him. In the background of his thoughts, as he stared at the kit bag, he heard Yvonne shout:

'Theo, come on; it's time to leave.' He heard the front door open, as Yvonne went to start up the car, and he knew his big day was truly here. He picked up the kit bag that had his initials on it and made his way down the newly carpeted stairs, now with his heart beginning to beat hard.

They arrived at the football ground which had a new sign towering over it reading: Ladywell JFC Sports Ground. As they drove in they could see the tall alien-like floodlights towering over the astro turf; now, a far cry from the once under used and untidy park wasteland that it had been before, which was only frequented by old men and their restless dogs, together with drunks, addicts and the sad wanderings of the homeless. In the car parks were dozens of white cans belonging to builders, roofers, plumbers, carpenters, and all those who worked in the construction trades; all there with their sons, wanting them to be top footballers. All week, these boys and those in Theo's team had been training for the finals; they'd been on the cold floodlit mini pitches going through the gruelling training schedule: passing, shooting practice, fitness work, heading, positional play. Yvonne had already become concerned how serious the parents took the football; shouting and sometimes bullying their poor little child, and even secretly having a word in the manager's ear as they tried to persuade the coach that their boy should play up front so that they could score the wining goal.

Theo, with a grin that threatened to split his face, raced ahead to join his team mates on the training pitch. Yvonne, collar hitched, walked over to the other parents; many with smoking cups of coffee and tea. She looked over to the boys again. The coach, a balding cockney man who wore a black track suit and woolly hat, had them huddled together for the team talk. With red cheeks, he gave instructions; explained tactics, pointed at the boys individually as he reminded them of their job. These young footballers, carried on warming up before the kick off. Yvonne tried to make conversation with the other parents; joking, smiling; a little chit-chat, but every parent was just there for their own child; this wasn't really about the team. There were parents who had grown up on local LCC estates; working class people who now thought of themselves as middle class; now able to afford holidays in Spain; buy homes in the suburbs, yet still liked their fish and chips, their pint of beer, their local pub. Their parents, in turn, had lived with the promise of a better world after the war when the NHS was established. They had seen their local community change; they had seen immigrants come and in some cases do better than them, and they had seen local politicians come and go who had promised so much. There was a sense of betrayal, confusion and anger all mixed in with their layers of colourful woollen hats, scarves and coats.

It was time for the match to start. Yvonne glanced over her shoulder hoping that Sebastian, who had promised to come. As she turned back she saw Theo standing on the touchline. He had been made substitute once again, despite him scoring so many goals; despite him being the most athletic boy in the team he had been made sub, and the manager's son, Johnny, was playing up front where Yvonne had always argued was Theo's best position.

The two teams played hard. The boys tackled, and ran, and headed, and argued with the referee, and cried, and shouted back at their parents who screamed at them to pass, or tackle, or shoot at goal. On the touchline, the manager of the other team, a tall Asian man, would keep encouraging his boys to try; remind them that they had to enjoy themselves, and he would clap loudly when they tried something different but it did not quite work, much to the annoyance of some of the parents who simply wanted to win the game. This was in contrast to Arthur, Theo's manager, who shouted at the boys for every mistake, even his own son. Finally, Johnny, his frail son, received a pass from the right-wing in front of the goal. Johnny trapped the ball. He could hear the parents shouting at him to shoot. Johnny's heart was beating hard. He knew he had to kick the ball at the goal quickly otherwise the other boys would tackle him. But amidst all the shouting there was one voice he could hear the most; it was his father's, Arthur, screaming at him to f'ing kick the ball. Johnny almost closed his eyes, kicked the ball the best he could and hoped for the best.. It turned out to be a feeble shot.

'Johnny,' screamed Arthur, 'why didn't shoot properly. Before Arthur could finish his cursing, the goalie had thrown the ball out and the other side scored with a slick passing move. The poor boy, Johnny could hardly make his way back for the kick off. Arthur was still cursing. The parents, some of who had no qualms about shouting abuse at the boys of the other team, were beginning to turn against him and his bullish tactics. The referees whistle blew to end the first half. Theo's team came off crying, perhaps afraid more from what Arthur would say to them than defeat.

It was now the second half. Arthur, who had apparently calmed down, had put Theo on to play, but much to Yvonne's annoyance, Theo was to play at the back, in defence.

'Why can't he play up front?' she queried. Arthur turned away from her and once again began to shout at the boys. The second half started and for a while Theo's team played hard, just as Arthur had demanded, they competed; they 'played the long ball game' but the other team had a good defence. Theo had played well in defence, but his dribbling skills couldn't be used there. It was now only a few minutes to go and the other team were holding on, occasionally threatening to score again through their star player a mixed race boy who moved with dance-like grace. Then suddenly the ball came to Theo. He ran with the ball picking up speed as he beat one boy then another until he found himself in front of the goal. He had options. Arthur was screaming at him to pass to Johnny, his son, even though Johnny still had tears in his eyes. But Theo also had dreams; dreams to score the winning goal in a cup final, dreams to play up front. For a moment he did think about passing to Johnny, but the look in his eyes said that he was scared, scared of what Arthur would do if he missed again. Theo saw the goal in front of him and he kicked the ball hard. The goalie, a chubby boy dived but it whizzed past him, and crashed against the cross bar, disappearing into the grey sky. Theo had missed. Arthur screamed at him.

'Why didn't you pass to Johnny?' What confused Theo more was that Johnny was now shouting at Theo, saying the same thing, which made Theo sense some kind of betrayal. At that moment Theo could see that he had never really been part of the team.

The two sides continued to play for a couple of minutes. The parents were either wild with excitement, or cursing the poor gangling referee. Finally, having endured so much abuse, he mustered enough energy and blew for the match to end. Parents of the winning team went crazy with joy. They ran onto the pitch and hugged their sons. They hugged the Asian coach who was modest in the congratulations. Theo's team came off crying. Arthur could hardly speak. Later, they collected their runners up medal. There was silent blame of Theo. The team needed a scapegoat. Johnny, Arthur's son began to whisper to the other boys that they lost because of Theo. For the first time Theo felt threatened. He felt physically threatened by the fathers who really only wanted their boy to score the winning goal. Funnily, Theo was calm. He knew that something had changed; a lesson was there for him to find and then dwell upon.

The story should have perhaps ended there, but it did not. Yvonne changed football clubs, bringing Theo to another club; this time to a club with many Black boys which Sebastian thought was wrong. They played 'Black football'; using skill, speed and intelligence, with Theo playing up front. The coach was a big Jamaican man and he seemed to communicate with the boys through a combination of good humoured cursing and grunts and Jamaican English.

Another year passed and the same cup competition came round again. It seemed that the same parents with their boys came, arriving in the same white vans; wearing the same woolly hats, coloured gloves and thick winter coats. It was all the same but Theo was different. His team played well: skill and speed made them walk over the other teams, with Theo scoring many of the goals. The story should have the expected happy ending. Theo's team should have met Arthur's team in the final, but Arthur seemed to have aged from all the pie and chips and shouting at the boys. His team lost again, this time in the semi final. There were some new boys in the team; many had left; bullied and harassed, and fed up with Arthur taking away their simple joy for the game they once loved. Yvonne's eyes met Arthur's. His smile, that once fooled her, this time revealed himself, and the more he smiled the more dishonesty she glimpsed. Later, she watched Theo play in the final. His team won. He did not score the winning goal, a young Nigerian boy, now being scouted by Arsenal, scored a fabulous goal. Theo played his part in the winning. They were young Black boys and they played with a realisation of their genius; realisation of how some people were to see them, and a realisation that they had to band together to protect themselves. In later matches they would even be stopped by the police as they made their way to the ground, believing them to be a gang. For now Theo was a winner, and when he went to collect his winners' medal he turned back to look at Yvonne. He kissed the medal, held it up as if to prove to the world that he was someone. Evening came. Sebastian was at a meeting, though Yvonne suspected otherwise, and Theo took one of Grandma's letters from his bag. To himself he said, 'Grandma, I did my best, just like you always told me to.' That day, in that house, a boy became a young man and a man became a boy. For a while the team were a little family to him, but he always had to go home; knock on the door that used to be his father's office, and look at his books, his posters.

On Leadership

I have learned over the years that when one's mind is made up, this diminishes fear.

ROSA PARKS (Mother of the civil rights movement)

Notes on Building Family

Leadership within the family has to be taught rather than assumed. The complexity of family, the various stages that each family member will go through such as birth, adolescence, courtship, marriage, adulthood, eldership, all demand preparation. The array of leadership skills needed in family might include *nurturing* when raising children, *patience* in the marriage or relationship, *discipline* in setting boundaries for behaviour and *courage* when having to end a relationship or in battling for a right cause for your family like a good education for the children.

The various stages in building a family can bring what might appear as disturbances, which are really stages of *growth* and *change*. For example, when a new baby is brought into the home and the disturbances this might bring to the partner or other children, or the disturbances that teenage years might cause, or the effects of a divorce. What is required here for these periods of transition is *planning, surveillance* of family, *self-observation* of those thoughts that say 'I can't' or 'I'm fearful.'

If we return to Yvonne we find that there are several disturbances going on in her life, none of which she has planned for. Her mother, residing in Jamaica is getting old and in need of more support, though she has friends and cousins around her. Yvonne worries about this,

Stage Five

and she worries about Theo's education and about him hanging around with 'bad boys', and of course she feels ashamed about the breakdown of her marriage. Yvonne needs support, guidance and courage from somewhere.

In the case of Sebastian we also find several disturbances in his life, some of which he is unaware of regarding his role as a father and husband. Unemployment, racism, low self-esteem, class discrimination are working against him in subtle ways, but he somehow blames Yvonne. Blame culture allows him to wear another mask which means that he does not have to watch these constant negative thoughts that make up his 'me'.

Fatherhood and being a husband/partner is very much dependent on accomplishing tasks, on building institutions, on grasping challenges and on the community acknowledging all of this. If these things do not happen then the vibrancy in fatherhood, in being a husband, diminishes. These disturbances and circumstances mean that neither Yvonne nor Sebastian can function at their optimum level in the family. As in many families, arguments in the home become common place and children all over the world hear these rows that centre on blame. Yvonne and Sebastian, to an extent, then begin to believe they can migrate to a world where the circumstances are different; migrate to a different work environment, to a different cultural group and so the result can be the abandonment of the home and a further abandonment of self.

When the home is abandoned it is unprotected, vulnerable and open to abuse from any internal or external source whether it is the education system, the criminal justice system or even junk advertisers. There is now no one to defend this family capital and institution. So, although they are both loving parents they have left Theo vulnerable. His family is not functioning as it should and he knows it, and he perceives these external threats to family are also targeting him, so he builds his family, his gang in order to protect himself.

All Amma wants both Yvonne and Sebastian to do is to be quiet and watch the negative thoughts of blame until these thoughts grow tired and don't have anymore to say, and become totally quiet, totally still, so that *peace* can return to the home.

Family Wisdom
On Teaching

- Be both courageous and quiet when confronting your fears.
- Being a parent is also about being a leader and all leaders should listen to those they 'command'.
- Leadership is lonely but rewarding, and for those who are called there is no choice but to lead.
- Great leaders know when to declare their greatness despite being ridiculed.
- Prepare for leadership; prepare for the opportunity and prepare for success: this is greatness.

Stage 6

Family, Adult Education and Manhood

Themes of inquiry: manhood and adult education	

Pagya: symbol of manhood and militancy

Pagya symbol represents ideas around manhood and the skills needed to be a man who brings positive change to the community. It is also the symbol of militancy.

In our inquiry we must have a strong state of mind in wanting to inquire and then take action in building family and community.

Theo's Diary

My gang is under threat of breaking up. Biko is living with his aunt now because his mum kicked him out. Toussaint's parents have found God and a new home in a white area and they're going to take him out of school and make him join a grammar school in Bromley. He doesn't want to go and has gone quiet, and a bit angry; that's why he shrugs his shoulders when the teachers speak to him. And Garvey's parents want him to go to university like his elder brother, and doesn't want him to have no African name even though his parents come from Nigeria. He says they both have two jobs so that they can pay for him and his sister to have tutors, and so he can only sometimes hang out with us sometimes. Parents always spoil things. But he doesn't want to be a doctor, he wants to draw on walls, and tell our story; tell the world what's really inside of us, especially when we leave school, or we get excluded, or we get left alone and we can just be ourselves. His parents mean well, but they don't understand; no parents understand what we go through. How we feel when we walk the streets, and police drive past; how we feel when the teachers stare at us in the playground when we meet up, or how we feel when we get our exam results. Parents and teachers don't really understand.

Met after school. Hung round the park, but police the came and we just went home.

Kept hearing the music of the griot in class and when I looked round there is nothing. I know what he's trying to tell me. My gang need initiation. They've joined but they have to prove themselves. I don't care if we're in school or not, I'm still going to do it.

Had to go to Headteacher's office again. We got blamed for trying to burn down the gym during the night. I said we didn't. Police came and questioned us in front of our parents, even though mummy cursed them, and argued. More police are in the school now. But drug dealers are still outside the gates. They never seem to get arrested.

Garvey said that his father said this was the final straw and that he shouldn't belong to no gang. Today was his last day. On Monday he's going to start his white school where you can go rowing, play chess and boys get picked up in a Mercedes. My gang is almost finished. Although some more boys come and join my gang, they don't know what it takes to be a revolutionary: the commitment, the thinking, the reading. One of the boys even asked me if I had a gun. I got so angry. 'My gang don't deal in no gangs,' I shouted. 'We deal in mental revolution!'

Later on Malcolm X came to see me to say he don't want to be no revolution anymore; that he wants to be a rap artist. I got real mad. Everyone is deserting the revolution for rap music, drugs, guns, junk tv. It's as if these things have been put into our community deliberately and we just don't seem able to see it.

Protecting the Home: Electrostress

We have already talked about protecting the family's health, protecting the family from junk tv, junk food, and today's home is also filled with electrical appliances that are harmful to the home. When electricity flows through a wire it produces a electromagnetic field. It is estimated that electromagnetic fields pass through us 200 more times than our ancestors. Electromagnetic radiation (natural or artificial) can alter our cellular processes. In addition, there are frequent reports of how low level radiation (from power lines) are linked to illnesses in children. When we looked in our homes we find non-ionising radiation being emitted from common household appliances, the television, computer monitors, lap-tops, cell/mobile phones, vacuum cleaners and microwave ovens. Scientists say that the earth's electromagnetic field is between 1 and 30 hertz (hz); human brainwaves between 5 – 30hz, while household electrical appliances are in excess of these, that is between 35 to 100hz. Microwaves ovens are potentially the most dangerous of all the household appliances as they have been shown to emit low frequency radiation in amounts over what is believed to cause lymphatic cancer in children. One of the best ways to therefore protect the home is gaining some knowledge of crystal science (and feng shui) which has been a great part of the curriculum of Black people for thousands of years.

Before we look at how we can use crystals to protect and indeed heal the home let us first remember that where your home is situated might be where there is unstable electromagnetic fields which can in turn cause geopathic stress, might cause depression, suicide, multiple sclerosis, high blood pressure etc. So, in order to protect our homes from this electromagnetic stress we can use plants like Peace lilies, Peperomias and goosefoot plants. Amethyst crystal, which is part of the quartz family of crystals, is an excellent crystal in counteracting harmful electromagnetic emissions. Generally, in order to clear negativity, you should use a smoky quartz.

The Science of and About Crystals

The earth's crust was formed by extremely heated rocks (like basalt and granite) that surfaced through cracks, forming rocks. Super heated gases and liquids surfaced, crystalising into minerals of great beauty and harmony (diamond and amethyst). Crystals have been used throughout the ages for different purposes such as for personal protection (ancient Egypt), to enhance good fortune, and for health and wealth. Crystals have a wide use, ranging from modern industry to Native Americans healers who use them as a diagnostic tool and even to Feng Shui (traditional Chinese art of arranging objects) who use them to create positive environments.

Below are some key crystals for healing and protecting the home and family.

Important Crystals for the Home

Name	Associated words/phrases	Chakra
Botswana Agate	Balances; raises self-esteem; relaxes body promotes calm; quietens emotions.	All Chakras

Name	Associated words/phrases	Chakra
Aquamarine	'stone of courage'; helps stops nervousness; promotes creativity	Throat

How to Unlock Your Family's Genius

Name	Associated words/phrases	Chakra
Blookstone	Detoxifies; purifies; promotes talents; gives insight.	Base

Name	Associated words/phrases	Chakra
Jade	(The symbol of the heart in Ancient Egypt). Increases vitality; harmony; wisdom; protection; helps dreams	All Chakras

Name	Associated words/phrases	Chakra
Moonstone (Potassium aluminium solicate)	Calms; balances; increases intuition; aids meditation; supports properties of other crystals.	All chakras, especially the crown

Name	Associated words/phrases	Chakra
Rock Crystal/ Clear Quartz	('The master crystal') Balances; aids meditation, supports energies of other crystals.	All chakras, especially the crown

Name	Associated words/phrases	Chakra
Tiger's Eye	Helps concentration; gives inner strength; optimism; balances ying and yang energies and promotes creativity.	Solar plexus & heart Solar

gangsta rap, single-parent families and so on. They hadn't taken the journey that we now take, for the real researcher enters this task armed with understanding, forgiveness and a genuine quest for truth irrespective if it means they abandon their theories. Pathetic careers are made with research that portrays the black child as delinquent, social outcast. And these researchers will go away. Once, I was teaching a small group of students on a 16-19 year old course which focused on life skills and there was one student who was particularly disruptive. Eventually I called him into my office and began to speak to him. It did The use of crystals in the home hints at a much greater science which was used in traditional communities to promote harmony in the home. For the traditional African, the world, as with the living space, is animated with energy. The living space was also understood in terms of proportion, geometry and ratio etc. What we begin to see is that the home was not just a place for shelter, but a place for growth, a place to create wealth, a place of education and a place to learn about citizenship. This all means that the home has to be programmed for health and wealth and this was achieved by Africans through the actual design of the home or building, the village and its compounds. For example, R. A. Schwaller de Lubicz who studied the Shamayit-Ipet (Luxor Temple) from 1937 – 1952, found that it was based on the human body and that this science of architecture allowed people to live by the natural laws of the universe.

In our inquiry into family and the marriage of Yvonne and Sebastian, we can see that this science of making the home harmonious, this science of programming the home for health and wealth was absent, which partly resulted in their problems. Ideally, to have made their home this powerful institution, they needed to have first blessed it with prayer, or affirmations or chants, and they needed to have burnt frankincense and myrrh, and to have poured libation to their ancestors and those of their family tree, and to have put up some kind of family altar; to have played harmonious music, and to have learnt the science of furniture placement, and to have routines in the home that showed Theo what he has genius within him and what he was capable of achieving with this genius on this wonderful earth.

Diagnostic Assessment: Prison, Race and Education

Theo is now a teenager and already he has friends who have gone to prison, written poetry, held a gun, sung in a church choir, robbed on the street, scored brilliantly in mathematics, been initiated into a gang, or secretly wished at night that they could go to university. This is more dangerous than people realise, for these children that once ran to the school gates sensing adventure were now completely disengaged with learning; some, confused as to what it was all about, whilst others were in open rebellion. Theorists, both black and white speculated in pseudo research papers; claiming it was peer pressure, not take long for him to open up. His mask was gone.

"Sir," he began fidgeting with his sleeves, "I've just come out of prison. I don't know why but I just feel I want to cry." I knew he wanted to tell me more but he said little after that. I talked to him about what we expected of him and asked about support he was getting. What he said made me think for some time, about these masks the black child and teenager are forced to wear. I realised that these are masks of tragedy, and yet they can become permanent masks which can lead to psychotic behaviour; schizophrenia, self-hate, suicide and violence, what 'popular' press sometimes call Black-on-Black violence. Here, I have to introduce you to Mad Martha. She was tragic and comic; colourful and drab, entertaining and annoying. I used to see her around the early 1980s when I was studying for my degree, and she would be around the bustop wearing bright coloured stockings, worn stiletto shoes, white gloves, layers of shocking skirt material, vulgar lipstick and make-up, and an unmistakable Caribbean church hat, and a look of total surprise. Each time I saw here she would look at someone in the bus queue, stare at them good, then, as if seeing their entire history curse them in a ritual of public humiliation. One day, as I stood at the bustop anxiously waiting to get to college for a lecture, Mad Martha looked in my direction. I felt an emptiness in my stomach. She walked over to me and began to sniff. I thought to myself, 'Oh no, I've put on my cheap bottle of Old Spice after shave." She pursed her lips. "You t'ink you is ah sweet boy. You t'ink I fancy you!" Nearby school girls giggled. People were staring. I tried to look in another direction, but she came up right in front of my face and smiled. "Where have all de children gone. Dem gone y'know!" With those prophetic words she herself went onto the bus where she started to curse the bus conductor. Each time I saw her she would be walking up and down the high road asking this same question. Now I know that Mad Martha was right. She talked more sense than the few local Black politicians. Many in the Black community didn't want to hear. The truth was that black children were going to prison. In Britain and the US there are more Black people in prison than in university, though these statistics can be a little misleading in that the university age tends to be 18 – 25 tears whereas the prison age population is much wider, but it doesn't hide the crisis. The children are going to prison to be bullied, molested, and kept miseducated. Prison is mainly for the poor, the mad, the uneducated. Behind these prison walls some will take their own lives; some will self-harm, some and some will secretly pray.

A detailed picture of the tragic situation that exists in British prisons can be gleaned from the Howard League for Penal Reform briefing paper which states:

1. Suicide in prison: key points

- Two people per week take their own lives in our prisons
- Over half of those who take their own lives are on remand

- Overcrowded local jails suffer from the greatest number of suicides
- Hanging is the most common form of suicide
- The average age at which people take their own lives is 32 years
- Between 1995 to 2004, 804 men, women and children committed suicide
- Prisoners are five times more likely to take their own lives in prison than in the community
- Young people are eighteen times more likely to commit suicide in prison than in the community

Prison Education

The prison experience is traumatic and for the black prisoner with little education prison offers little hope of any educational achievement which can support their life of not offending again. Eighty per cent of young people in prison have been excluded or played truant whilst at school. It is said that two thirds of prisoners have no education or work. This world is not too far away from Theo. He is in school, but underachievement, poverty and race make him a prime candidate for prison and the statistics that surrounds the penal world. His friends who are already inside lie on their beds wondering what life will bring next. Some still dream of being *someone in the world*, or dream of a good life, surrounded by people they can trust. Trust is key, because they have been let down so many times that they distrust the world, and sometimes hate the world.

How to provide prison education initiatives that stop re-offending

- Basic skills provision in literacy, mathematics and ICT
- Race and education workshops
- Formal accreditation courses
- Higher education opportunities
- Parenting training courses
- Boyhood to Fatherhood & Girl to Womanhood programmes
- Online jobsearch opportunities
- Employment and volunteering opportunities
- Post-sentence placement in education or work experience
- Counselling and critical thinking opportunities

Will such a programme reach Theo's friends, or will they become one of the suicide statistics? The black community cannot forget these children, or give up on them no matter how horrible their crimes.

The Story of a Black Prisoner: Killerman's Letter

In my novel *Garvey's last Soldier*, I featured a character called Killerman; a black Jamaican man living in England who is now imprisoned and, as a result of coming into contact with Professor Rollins who teaches him about African spirituality, he begins to discover the truth about himself and question actions that he took in his life of crime. His thoughts are revealed firstly in an open confession to other prisoners at a black inmates meeting, and then in a moving letter that he writes to his woman, Marcia. I present them now in the hope that they can move us as a community in an attempt to do as Professor Rollins has done and reach out to these men (and women), not with sentimentality, but with education, empowerment and employment opportunities. So let us read what Killerman has to say.

Killerman's Story

Man them call me Killerman, 'cause me kill plenty man dem that no one know 'bout. Me is a man that don't like speak; me and words not really friend. Me live me life de way me does because de world wicked, and me must stay more wicked than she. Me can hardly read nor write. Me have two children that me can barely recognise cause me been here so long, and me have a good woman who me don't deserve and who don't give up on me yet. Me still have five years to serve, and when me get out me was gone take a chance and rob another bank, but now de Professor come me start see t'ings differently. When him reach in me cell me did want to kill him, because of de African shrine him keep which frighten me raas! I did want to t'ump him. But hold me hand, what stop me from just boxing him in him head was how him did stay; how him carry himself; like how him not afraid of anything or anyone. It puzzle and vex me. And when him look at me, he not seeing Killerman who everyone afraid of, but someone who him respect; as if he seeing heaven seed plant inside of me.

When me born me daddy name me Joseph before him take off to find work in England. So me grow wid me sweet mummy in Jamaica. Eventually me daddy, whose lung was already sick wid factory work, send for me, me mummy, me brother and me sister. Daddy was a man me never understand, but now me is a man me understand de pressure him was under. Me regret me never see him cry, den me would have began to realise how hard life is for our people. It wasn't until him was 'pon him back in him death-bed dying of somet'ing me can hardly pronounce, that me and him talk like man to man. Me never know it but him guess that me had started keep bad company. Last time me see him alive him look me in de eye and say: 'Bwoy, be a soldier for me, not a t'ief!' But me heart wasn't fill with grief; instead, it was filled with blame; blame because it was Daddy that bring me to England and promise

Stage Six

The narrative continues and Killerman begins to cry. But he is rescued by Professor Rollins, as we must rescue those Black men and women who are in prison, 80% of who can hardly read or write. Killerman is finally given a task to write a love letter to his woman, Marcia. This is fiction, but I want you to write a love letter to your community to say what you will do….

Killerman's Love letter

Dear Marcia

Don't be surprised when dis letter reach you. Me is a man that never write; a man that never talk much, but since de professor reach in de prison, him show me so many t'ings that me want make you understand. Understand why me couldn't function as a man before. Marcia, strange t'ings happening to me. T'ings happening in me sleep, and when me awake too. People me know who dead just start talking to me.

Recently, when de night creep up on me and sleep stay stubborn, I been t'inking back to de time when me was a bwoy, and how me did always want to be someone; but who was dis someone? White man on tv with flash car? White man with big house and money? I did never want to be like a man de professor tell me about who dem call Marcus Garvey. You see, me never really have anybody to tell me what me should be, or what man is truly about. I just want to copy, and begin to want t'ings, and when dem t'ings deny me, me just get vex and just t'ief dem. Marcia, you did never know how me did feel when me couldn't get a job, or when them cut off de electric. Me feel like little bwoy! Crime give me opportunity and dream. Fool me to t'ink that me can walk de street like big man. When me did beat up de security guard, me remember that me keep beat him as if him was de same man that keep me down; de same man that stop me from having de t'ings me did want: job and clothes. De professor say that me must repent; that this isn't de way to beat the system. He say some people want us to get on like this so that dem can lock us up some more. And now, when me tink about de criminal t'ings me do, I does cry, yet, somet'ing deep inside of me does grow. I just want to give you de t'ings a man is supposed to give him woman.

Marcia, me just want to say dat me love you; dat me want to be a man that you can love back, and me want to be a good father. Me have a few years leave of me sentence and when he get out me was going to go evening class, try a little self-employ business and try sell me art work. Suddenly life exciting. Life is like it was when me first met you. Like it was when me eat fresh mango back home, or drink coconut water and it dribble down me mouth.

Once de Professor tell us about de African goddess of beauty and love call Het-Heru. He say we should close our eye and imagine a beautiful black woman smelling lily. Well, me imagine you, and dat night me dream about you. Dream of you naked; of you in bath scented with honeysuckle wid yellow petals floating on top of de water. And then me dream of de two of us making love.

Marcia, me is man now. Kiss de children for me. Tell dem that me will be home one day and dem will be proud of me.

Love Leroy.

Stage Six

Killerman (Leroy) is lucky that he has his partner, Marcia there to support him. The situation for many Black men in prison is that they do not have anyone, and so they are faced with the same problems of unemployment, mental health issues, housing, health and companionship. What is important is that we address their training and education issues, by providing support in basic education both in and outside of prison. So now let's look atbasic education and how best it can be tailored to meet the needs of the Black community.

How to develop an adult education project to help the community

The term basic education is often used when talking about the literacy and numeracy of children or adults and, depending on the context, can also mean supporting learners when English is not their first language. This area of education is also very political. When we begin to consider, who, traditionally, has been uneducated; in need of basic literacy and numeracy, we begin to once again see the politics around the education of the poor, the dispossessed and the discriminated against. Here in England, the government has had to respond to the 7 million adults who have difficulties with their literacy; basic difficulties that includes writing a letter or even reading a piece of text. The government's response has been to initiate the introduction of a core curriculum; the introduction of a new set of teacher qualifications and the increased professionalising of the teacher workforce. However, despite these initiatives we should not loose sight of the politics surrounding basic education. One educationalist that has addressed this is Paulo Friere, the Brazillian educationalist who dedicated his life to the study of education of the oppressed people of the world and who wrote the classic, *Pedagogy of the Oppressed*. For Freire, literacy was a tool to help liberate oppressed people, by helping them to understand their oppression and raise their consciousness. Freire hoped that from this point of reflection, the oppressed people would engage directly in the everyday struggle for their own liberation. So, from his point of view, the teaching of literacy (basic skills) is a political act, which, therefore can act as further oppression if it simply imitates the education provision that the oppressors, in their 'benevolence' have provided the oppressed communities with. So we see that Freire wants a system of teaching and learning that is not distant from the people; where the consciousness of the people is central to the whole learning exercise and experience; where the narrative of instruction from the oppressors (teaching) is broken and where education is not simply a 'banking' system where 'chunks' of education are deposited. He writes:

> *Education must begin with the solution of the teacher-studentcontradiction.*

I once worked in basic education in a large further education college that was perhaps living on its reputation. I was part of a small team that had to deliver additional learning support to students undertaking vocational courses. It was a fascinating job as the area was a growing one at the time, and as I was one of the first to set up this department I had the opportunity to go on a whole variety of training courses in this area. This, coupled with the fact that I was running Ebony Education in my spare time meant that I was rapidly delving deeper and deeper into this how children and adults learn, and the politics around learning of Blacks, women and children and adults with so-called learning difficulties. For months, in a modern study centre I taught literacy to these students; young men and women from Africa, Asia, South America, Europe and in some cases from the poorer communities of London. We had a wealth of resources: computers, the latest computer packages, slick teaching materials, but there was no soul to the teaching or learning despite good inspection feedback when the College was inspected. Slowly I began to understand that what was central to my teaching was allowing the learners to think about their lives; to think critically as to how some of them couldn't read, why some of them had just come out of prison, or even how some of them came from countries where there was dire poverty. I didn't see myself as being political, just an effective teacher. In particular, when I questioned Black students who were studying media courses about Oscar Micheaux, or Ousmane Sembene, or Spike Lee they simply didn't know who these people were. Again, when I questioned Black students studying performing arts about Paul Robeson, Harry Belafonte, or

How to Unlock Your Family's Genius

Dorothy Dandridge or Sidney Poitier they simply didn't know. When I questioned Black students studying fine art about the Harlem Reniassance, or about the Benin Heads, or the Ndbele decorative art; or those studying literature about Toni Morrison, or Chinua Achebe, or Wole Soyinka, or questioned those studying engineering about the great accomplishments of Black Egypt they simply had no idea. They had arrived in the College and in this class in additional support, having gone through their education with no opportunity to think about their lives, think about their communities, think about the issues affecting them or even celebrate themselves. Now, in my class they sat there waiting for me to 'bank' chunks of education into them. From an early age they had had intervention with its benevolence and irrelevancy thrust upon them, but it hadn't worked. This is what senior management, inspectors and the whole education establishment wants. Anyway, I started to depart from just teaching grammar, and started group discussions around films, books, photographs, music and poetry that I would sometimes read, or have them listen to. From these discussions our loves, ignorances, interests and prejudices came out. Sometimes, the lesson plan that I had prepared was virtually torn up by the students leading the discussion in a completely different area. Attendance and retention was high simply because of the joy, the fun, the discovery and the variety of 'intuitive' learning that went on. But I was under pressure. These students had to get through an exam, and so I would have to return to the exam preparation. Many years later I met one of these students. Now a young man in his mid twenties, he shouted over: 'Hi Sir, it's me!' When I looked it was Jerome. Before I could speak he boastfully told me that he was in his second year at university. 'You still teaching Black Studies Sir,' he enquired. When I explained that I never actually taught Black Studies, that I simply embedded it in the cause he laughed. 'Loved it Sir; made us think.' It was a kind of triumph for me. We talked, and he kept recalling what he learnt in the classes. For him and the other students in the class, basic education was about critically thinking, cultural identity, power; about their lives and environment.

How to Provide Basic Education in Your Community

Utilising Useful Research in the Design of Your Basic Education Provision

Whilst there is much research out on basic skills and the teaching of reading and writing, the recent publication of research by the National Research Development Centre (Brooks, et al. 2007) is useful in informing the design of your basic education provision, and one must remember the cultural implication of a provision that does not address culture and power. The summary findings of the research are as follows:

Reading

- Pair and group work encourage progress
- Women tended to make slightly better progress than men.
- Learners who spent more time in self-study made better progress.
- Employed people made better progress than unemployed people.
- There was evidence of significant increase in confidence amongst learners who read regularly.

Writing

- Improvements in writing cannot be measured quickly
- Younger learners, learners in employment and full-time education made the most progress
- Learners' confidence in writing and uses of writing outside of class increased
- Learners' confidence in writing tended to be higher at home than in the classroom

Venues for basic education

Basic Education can take many forms and doesn't always have to be in the traditional classroom. It is important that the Black community looks creatively at basic education and sees the effective delivery of creative and empowering support in all age groups. Here are some ideas for staging basic skills.

1.   In your church, mosque or temple. Here Saturday schools, reading, maths and computer clubs might be useful. As these groupings have members of all age groups it's important that the whole group is mobilised and the variety of skills of the group is targeted at the delivery of basic education whether in the form of family learning (parents and children learning together), parenting skills, reading clubs or adult literacy and numeracy.

2.   In your place of work. Whilst some employers make provision for work based learning (WBL), many do not and it is therefore the workers to prompt their employers to undertake the raising of the literacy and numeracy levels of the workers. Unions are now quite active in these areas and workers should consider union involvement in order to prompt management to provide basic education/basic skills support and qualifications.

3.   In the prison. Prison education is more problematic but the black community needs to become more active in this area. Security, poor funding and resources, and the movement of prisoners from one prison to the next makes education in prison difficult. In some prisons prisoners are kept locked up in their cells for the majority of the day. If the circumstances are that there is little or no education provision at the prison, then family members outside of the prison might, on the agreement of the prisoner, enrol them onto a vocational or basic education course at a further education (or technical) college. However, as I mentioned earlier, key to basic education is the opportunity to think about the real issues affecting one's life and even the act of thinking about thinking, and to engage in real cultural empowerment.

For those of us in the African Diaspora the support of basic education initiatives is of vital importance and can be addressed if we are creative, resourceful and dedicated. In Africa, 24 million girls aged 11 are out of school. In terms of basic education and gender, two thirds of the worlds 781 million illiterate adults are women. Yet the education of women is central to a community's prosperity as educated women utilise the resources of the home more effectively by devoting them to childcare and education.

Writings of an Educationalist

My Inheritance: Education on Manhood

My father, my uncles and cousins were of a type that only the Caribbean could produce, for their history was unique; tragic and heroic at the same time; history scarred by slavery that school books have forgotten, and fading as memories of these old folk die out. These men taught me about manhood. These men, in the heat of the Caribbean, built each others homes from local wood and stone on designs fashioned in Aruba, Trinidad, Scotland and Africa. These men by day worked hard, drank rum, cursed their low wages and by night danced to Shango, and beat Big Drum, and sang in Igbo, and lit candles for ancestors on All Souls Night, and boiled Secret Bush, and made story at Stone Feast. These men, my father, my uncles, my cousins, grew up together and shared and carried water from distant wells; shared clothes, suitcases; shared their little savings, and bush medicines, and funeral expenses; shared their ground provision from the big pots of brown women who brought them into the world These were the men who gave me my education on manhood.

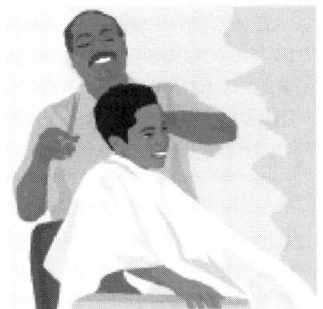

My education started when, my grandfather, under a hot colonial sun, took his own worn Bible that he had inherited, then uttered the words, 'Trust no man', before naming my father Samson. Many years later, draped in a heavy winter coat, Samson, who I now called Daddy, took the same Bible, uttered the same words, and named me David; perhaps so that I would stand up for myself, even if it meant defeating giants. This was the story that Daddy repeatedly told me in his more sombre moods; it wasn't true, but it was his way of trying to tell me that the world was more cruel than any little child, as I was then, could possibly imagine.

Daddy and his generation was a man that I feared and loved; a man of immeasurable charm and sternness; a man that I adored when he played his sweet parang on his Spanish guitar; a man that I wanted to strike down with my legendary sling when I saw him bullishly argue with Mum about another business venture that would leave him broke. Yes, a man made from, the rainbow of races inhabiting the West Indies, who once fraternised with beautiful women and low level politicians from the islands. In many ways he was a gentleman, but he had also been brought up to believe that life was a dog-fight: you took some blows, you gave some too; and if your mouth got bloodied, you didn't cry; you dusted your pants and cursed the next man that got in your way. He was my teacher of life but it would take me over thirty years to understand the inheritance that he left me.

Perhaps I had too many contradictory feelings towards him: feelings that I would later question as I realised that I judged him and not the times he lived in; that I didn't understand the lessons in manhood that he gave me. And I remember him telling me how, when he was a boy, how he had to walk to a well miles from his house to fetch water and how that toughened him; prepared him to take blows in life; and I remember him telling me how he used to do 'stick fighting' and what a dangerous sport it was but it toughened him up, and so when he saw me weak he wouldn't baby me because he knew that I had to 'walk to the well, that I had to compete in stick fights', and I didn't know it at the time but he was schooling me to take those silent blows that he faced each day as he walked the streets of London back in the early sixties.

I was the youngest boy, then, unaware of those 'swinging' sixties; his little *bwoy* who he tickled with Anancy stories one moment then became oblivious for my need for love as he embarked on another business venture. It wasn't until the '83 the sun was fading from his smile, and his fingers rarely held his sweet guitar, that our relationship seemed to become more important to him as well as me. In the summer of that year, now both men – I, the age he was when he first stepped from the boat-train, and he, an ageing man – we became angry and almost unforgiving towards each other.

My first memory of Dad and the men of his generation was of him in '63 drinking rum; rum because he was a man from 'Back-Home', 'Back-Home' that made strong rum they called *Jack Iron* and made strong men. These were the men that could drink one whole glass straight; men that slapped one another on the back, laughed loudly so that God could hear and men that bore the scars of travel and hard labour in various parts of the world. But amidst the raucous symphony, there was a silent brotherhood amongst men of colour who simply got on in life but one day I would see the toll this would take. Why couldn't these men speak to me more? Why couldn't they, like their wives share each other's hurt and pain; why couldn't they talk openly about the wounds that were still bleeding, and why couldn't Dad tell me of the herbs and bush and curse he used to heal these men and himself when they came to our house to pay their susu 'hand'. And then he would change; he would bounce me on his knee, measure me with his fatherly eye, whose look somehow contained the belief that I would someday inherit something he was building. I wanted to be like him, to have his smile and broad shoulders and muscular arms that built houses in Trinidad, lifted oil barrels in Aruba and punched down men bigger than him who came to make trouble.

By the mid seventies Dad's dream and those of his generation's dreams were fading. He, and they, had tried several business ventures but failed. I had no idea at the time but Daddy was clinging to those things he had learnt from his uncle, who had learnt them from his grandfather and so on. And theirs was a tradition that I didn't understand, of men supporting men, of men not speaking about this; only when they dressed in white under a full moon and danced Big Drum, or were possessed by Shango and then their spirit was free. I began to glimpse in Daddy a spirit of resistance that made him rise each morning with the sunrise. And it was in the late evenings that he would tell us, his eight children, stories of back home; stories that as we grew we thought were just stories, but his mix of folklore, magic a tall-tale was both strategic and scientific, for he wanted to educate us about manhood as he saw it; from the times when Shango was Heru on the Nile to then. And his education might have been on diet, so we ate unsalted food for a day or two; or it might have been about our history so he told us about how Fedon fought the British, or his education might have been on doing well in school so he scolded us if we brought home a bad school report. I never understood his anger at our failure stemmed from him being, an educated and talented man, having to perform mundane unskilled work. There was a great education in this daily sacrifice that I missed, and that he never had the time, or the will to talk to me about.

I graduated in '83, and in that same summer I left England and made my pilgrimage to Carriacou, knowing that I was going to trespass on Daddy's history, and perhaps in someway understand his past that could somehow bring us closer. So I found myself sailing in a fisherman's boat to this tiny and beautiful island, I having just left Maurice Bishop's revolutionary mainland Grenada, hearing Dad putting down the young prime minister, not because of politics, but because he had played cricket with the opposition leader in his youth. And I came to find the house Dad grew up in; I came to speak with people he had gone to school with; I came to pour rum and water on his parents, my grandparents grave, and to sense and understand the fight they gave to my father, and perhaps to me.

The next day, slouched on my aunt's verandah, I could hear the parang music of my father. People that came to the house just to visit would look me up and down with a sun squint and say, 'Yeah man, you 'ave your Daddy nose; it stay big just like ya fathers.' After this they'd talk about Daddy and Mummy; about how they were when they were courting. It made me proud and sentimental, but then their expression would change; become sad as they looked out to the sea slapping the sand for they knew that many of the men who travelled to England things hadn't quite worked out; that England had somehow broken their spirit. Was Daddy one of them? But I would quickly tell myself that Daddy was Samson, the strongest man in the world, hoping that this would console me.

The very next day, my aunt, perhaps knowing that this was a pilgrimage, gave me two bottles of rum; one containing rum, the other water. She told me where my grandfather's grave was and then sent me on my way to pay my respects as old customs demanded. It was the rainy season; it had just poured, so there was an unreal freshness all about. As I continued I came to an old church that I assumed was now derelict. Walking by I began hearing the reciting of school children, so I came off the dirt track road, walking along a small path flanked by tangled shrubs, and looked through the broken window of the church. To my surprise there were dozens of small children crammed into this one little classroom sitting on the floor with slates and chalk. Their eyes and mouth were open, taking in everything they could. In front of them was a young school teacher writing on a small blackboard. There was no doubt in my mind that this school was old enough to have been the one that Daddy had studied in; that he left when he was thirteen; the same school that he used to tell me that he wished he could have stayed on longer in.

I continued to walk, half worried that there would be another downpour, while at the same time observing the beautiful wild flowers that Daddy had once picked and brought to my mother waiting on her veranda. It was when I came to a tiny house with its old Scottish stonework, that I realised that I was lost. A few noisy fowl in the yard announced my arrival. A voice called to me. An old woman with wet hands and a chuckle in her throat, parted her tatty washing that hung in the yard.

'You is foreigner?' I told her I was Samson's son. A smile came to her face; she began to sing one of the songs Daddy had composed for Mum.

'An' is where your guitar?' She asked. I smiled. She insisted that I come into her modest home, that had two rickety chairs, a table with table-mats that had been sent from abroad. I sensed the presence of absent children. I knew that this house was where Daddy had lived as a boy; that he had sat on the veranda, looking out into the glory of the sunset, dreaming of work and dollars, and life in the big city. At that moment I felt to write Dad, to tell him I forgave him, that I understood both his anger and love, and perhaps why he kept his feelings so private…She offered me food, but I refused it; my thoughts were thousands of miles away, wanting to care for an ageing man with arthritis.

I left her house and continued walking in the direction that her crooked finger had pointed. At long last I came to my grandfather's grave, where an old stone stood; placed there by my father and aunts. Tears threaten to spill down my cheeks. I quickly opened the two bottles of rum and water, but as I was about to pour a little from each one on the grave as part of my libation, an old man held up his loyal walking stick and shouted. His smile gave his face youth.

'Bwoy, me mout' dry; pour some rum in it na!' He pointed to his mouth. I was angry because he had interrupted my special moment. Then he walked shakily over to me; took one of the bottles from me; threw

How to Unlock Your Family's Genius

his head back as he drank as much as he could, before smacking his lips together as Daddy always did.

'Bwoy, next time your foot reach 'pon dis spot, bring some good rum for your grandfather!' I immediately wanted to know how he knew I was the grandson. As I was about to ask him he looked bitterly down at the grave and spoke again: 'Tell him from me that a man can only inherit love. Everyt'ing else is not real.' With that he walked away, ignoring my jumbled questions.

When I returned to England I told Daddy the story of the old man at the grave. I remember how he froze, asking me to describe the old man. I did, recalling every detail that I could remember. There was a long silence when I finished, except for quarrelsome garden foliage. Dad turned his face from me. I sensed it was to hide the emotion. He turned to me again: 'What else him say? Tell me!' I became scared. Daddy became strong again, and he looked around the room as if sensing some unseen spirit. 'What's wrong Dad?' He looked under his pillow for his bible, before trying to find a passage that would give him comfort but the bible dropped and Daddy followed as he fell back onto the settee.

'That old man you meet; it was your granddaddy; my father.' I stayed there with Dad, sharing his muse, pretending not to notice him wipe away the tears. I knew the old man wasn't my grandfather, but why should I tell him otherwise and spoil his moment. Many years later I would bury Daddy. In grief, I would review his life; realise that he, and his generation had given the best education they could have possibly given, and I would be almost broken by guilt, for I had never taken the time to tell Daddy thank-you for this education that allowed me to build a family, a career; stand up to my own fears, stand up to criticism. Dad belonged to that generation of African-Caribbean men who came to England in the late 1950s and these men were, in part, made of stone for nothing could knock them down, and yet they left so much which many of us did not thank them for: their love. So I say to Dad and my grandfather, and to all those men that educated us on manhood the best way they could; I say thank-you for everything. In February 2003 I climbed the pulpit, as my friends did, and their friends too, and read a poetic eulogy for not only my father but for those men of the Windrush generation, for those great black and brown men, who gave love as our inheritance.

Man of Stone and Work

We, who salvaged your resemblance,
Offer words to plant your memory.

Did you take the mason's ship to another small island,
That turned your hands to stone?

Did you sail to Aruba: you at the helm,
To discover oil; yes you, Captain Adventurer!

A living you chiselled, sculptor of our family tree,
Then married Mum, under Yemaya's moon and palms;

Honeymooning in London's romantic fog,
With guitar and trunk in a strange winter.

There, making your children study books by day,
African Big Drum and Stone Feast by night.

Now, time has made your portrait our reflection,
Your rainbow-life, our proud boasts.

Your memory is both muse and magic,
Like the parang of your quattro that sweetened our childhood.

To you all, we raise our glass of rum,
And toast your lives: men of stone and work.

106

Stage Six

Notes on Building Family

To build family we have to set goals and part of this journey in achieving these goals is *self-challenge*, that is, we have to further deal with our fears by having courage and be prepared to remove the fears and negative emotions that limits and destroys the family.

Again our reference point has to be our family tree which we now need to study in more detail to see the heroes and heroines of the tree who have demonstrated this courage in building family. Superimposed on this family tree is another tree consisting of principles of the African tree of Knowledge that we have seen is an organised understanding of nature. Representing these principles of nature we have images that remind us of our lower and super intelligences. At this stage of our building of family we have images, as our metaphors, of knives, swords and cutlasses. These symbols are also symbolic, and show us that in order to have the courage and to go onto the battlefield of our fears we must be able to cut the negative emotions away. We see Yvonne's grandmother, and her grandmother until we go back to the women of the Maroon communities and we find them with cutlasses that they used to cut cane and their own fears as they plotted to escape from slavery, and if we go much further back we find African women with knives and swords and hawk and falcon headed human sculptures, and drawings of people in our ancient tree, again indicating that they battled with their own fears to ensure they had the courage to be able to build sustainable family institutions like schools, health centres and homes. So the achievement of these goals requires a certain mindset and metabolism which will ensure success.

Theo might not be aware of this explicitly but he is aware that if he is to build his new family he has to associate it with those who have gone onto the battlefield of self and conquered their fears; those who have cut their anger, jealousies and hatred to pieces. Steve Biko, Robert Sobukwe, Toussaint L'Ouverture, Paul Bogle and Marcus Garvey were all family men who made a sacrifice. They, along with others, set themselves the goal to create revolutionary change so that their communities could prosper.

Sebastian, an ex-community activist, had once read the work of these men but was now trying to distance himself from them. In contrast, Theo, was fascinated with these men; began to keep a scrap book with their pictures, quotes etc. Why? Perhaps the answer lies in the 'heat' needed to achieve these goals. Youth, by their very stage of their evolution need 'hot' energy to begin to build home, family and community. This 'hot' energy is the hormonal changes that take place at adolescence and which changes the metabolism of the body and prepares the young person for adulthood. This new 'hot' energy and its possible effects on the young person has to be guided. Theo senses this and therefore senses that he can achieve anything in the world that he wants to but school, through its limited expectations and even those of the parents, say that his 'gang' can't achieve. Sebastian, now following mainstream politics and therefore subscribing to this 'limiting expectation' commits acts of betrayals by organising his politics in a way that does not even acknowledge the purpose, function and possible use of this 'hot energy', this fighting spirit. He now engages in meetings with tea and biscuits, training sessions with flipcharts, and every time there is a murder of a black youth and he is asked by the local media for a statement, he commits another act of betrayal by blaming the youth, the family and the community which he has himself abandoned. Yet his ancestry demands of him that he build,

build youth leadership schemes to guide the young.

The day Sebastian cut off his locks was a day of psychological betrayal, not simply to his family and community, but to his family tree, his ancestry. He cut off his locks after becoming increasingly disillusioned with his own community, not simply because they would not organise, but because they wouldn't accept him as a leader. And that night Yvonne cursed him for he betrayed something deep in their marriage. This incident made Yvonne more militant. Metaphorically she held the cutlass in her attitude to life wherever she went just like Nanny of the Maroons, for she was determined to defend her culture regardless.

In moments of quiet Amma is there to remind this couple that they can solve their problems by making reference to the family tree and the great indigenous knowledge that it holds; that they should pour libation, that they should cut kola nuts and say some prayers and reminds them that the great Yoruba god of war, Ogun, only fights fears and other negative emotions to bring about peace. Let them stop fighting one another and see the roots of the disharmony of their home lies in the *mismanagement* of their emotions.

Family Wisdom
On Thinking

- **When you have cut away all the arguments, anger, shouting and fighting you'll see the real beauty of your family.**

- **Love is the greatest protection you can give your family, but daily protection means daily love.**

- **Don't be over critical on yourself or your family but remember that we all make 'mistakes' in order to learn.**

- **Remember that critical thinking is a compassionate art.**

- **Teach your family critical thinking by thinking before you act.**

- **The success of any strategic action you take to improve the circumstances of your family will be based on the fire within you, which in turn is based on the passion and heat in your daily breathing.**

Stage 7

Family, Wealth and Culture

Themes of inquiry:

- Creation of wealth in your family and community
- Understanding how wealth is created
- The understanding of relationships in family, in society and in nature

Nkonsonkonson: symbol of unity and human relations

Nkonsonkonson is the symbol about relationships and the bond between people from the same lineage so this symbol represents community unity. This symbol also represents the honouring of the ancestors who are also part of the community.

Nkonsonkonson is useful to our inquiry on education and family in that encourages us to conceive of family in a way that includes our ancestors, and therefore we begin to understand our true interdependence with previous generations.

Theo's Diary

Toussaint's parents have been told they should send him to another school because of his autism. Dr Seamus wrote some kind of a report. They reckon that he'll get more help, but I know it's because they want him out of my gang. Toussaint doesn't want to leave. He wants to stay and start the revolution with me. Since we started our revolution, Black History Month is taken more seriously; some teachers that took liberties with us just shut them mouths, and our parents are beginning to be more active in school as if they're finally realising what we go through in school.

More trouble at school. Dr Seamus has had his laptop stolen. Police came into the school and questioned Toussaint, and then they questioned me. I felt betrayed when I heard that Toussaint began to cry. How can a great Black hero like Toussaint cry when the history books say that Toussaint L'Ouverture defeated Napoleon's armies. How?

Garvey, says he over heard the Headteacher talking with Dr Seamus saying how us Black boys need help. One of them said that there's going to be a man coming to come to talk to us in assembly. Some kind of Black role model. Then Dr Seamus began to talk about his laptop.

Worst day of my life. Role model? What kind of role model do they think we need. Looked up at the stage where the headteacher was and who do I see sitting there, lockless and clueless. My dad! Next thing I know he steps forward to speak, cleared his throat and began talking some rubbish about how he worked himself up from rags to riches. Lumumba yawned, then I yawned. Next, he talked about leadership. I wanted to stand up and shout him down. 'What leader walks out on their family!' When he finished everyone started to clap as if he was a real hero. I didn't clap. I knew my mum wouldn't want me to.

Toussaint and me got questioned again about Dr Seamus laptop. Mum was real mad when she found out.

Today is another sad day. Toussaint has been excluded from school. He admitted to stealing and destroying the laptop by throwing it in the recycling bank. He said that he didn't want to go to no special school, or keep having special lessons, and keep having people look at him like he's dumb. Thought that if he threw the laptop away then Dr Seamus wouldn't make no report on him. I saw when he and his parents walked out of the school. Toussaint had his head held down. His mother had a white handkerchief by her nose. His dad was mad. I wanted to shout out the window to him that Toussaint L'Ouverture never held his head down, even when Napoleon finally caught him and imprison him and starved him and make him die in the cold.

Since Toussaint has gone there's been more police in the school. Everyone is scared. This is why some of the boys are joining other gangs that have knives and things, but most keep themselves to themselves. Black and white. Everyone's scared on the streets; scared in school, and some are even scared in their homes.

Family Wealth

In this section we will look at the creation of wealth in the family and community and how the understanding of relationships is central in this, just as Theo has tried to understand the key relationships in his life. First we will look at some tools, innovations and schemes in the creation of wealth and further our understanding of wealth creation by looking at good practice in Black history. This financial literacy should have been Theo's education, and that of his friends, allowing them to direct this energy to build meaningful projects and even businesses in their community.

Time Banks

Modern Time Banks were started in the US by Edgar Cahn, a civil rights lawyer, with the aim of building and empowering communities, by using time as a currency of exchange. The emphasis of time banks are to develop social capital and encourage active citizenship through volunteering and social inclusion, thereby transforming their communities for the better. Time banks promotes regeneration in the fields of education, welfare and health and can therefore be said to be a key tool in community development where people are marginalised, historically disempowered and on low incomes. A key philosophy of time banking is to give families back valuable quality time.

Time Banking is Based on these Principles & Ideas:

- Valuing people and the recognising of their real worth
- Everyone has skills that can be shared and of value to the wider community
- The recognising of unpaid work in the community
- The developing of genuine reciprocity amongst all participants
- The active development and growth of social capital
- The sharing of skills and learning
- Developing grassroots community development

How do Time Banks Work

1. A group of people come together who belong to a community or organisation and list their skills, experience and offer these skills and experiences, whilst also indicating what skills, services and experiences they might need.
2. People are awarded time credits in the exchange of the giving and receiving of services.
3. One time credit is normally equal to one hour of service.
4. Volunteers can bank these time credits and withdraw them at a later date.
5. The banking of these time credits are handled by a time-broker.
6. The time bank philosophy encourages everyone to spend their time credits thereby making everyone involved and valued.

Susu/Partner Schemes: African Microfinance

On 22nd June 1948 the SS Empire Windrush sailed from Jamaica to Britain carrying 492 immigrants from the Caribbean. It was the start of the mass migration of West Indians to Britain. The West Indians responded to advertisements from Britain for labour to help rebuild the country after the Second World War and to have better educational and employment opportunities. Additionally, there had been a severe hurricane in Jamaica in 1944 which had destroyed much of the coconut,

111

coffee and banana crops, resulting in high unemployment. Though some West Indians were able to find accommodation through the Caribbeans (and West Africans) who had served in the war and had stayed on, many had to pool their resources to raise enough money to buy their own properties as the white landlords did not want to rent to 'coloured' people. It was common to see signs in front windows which read: 'No Irish, No Coloureds or Dogs'. Sam King who came over on the Windrush says: 'Because we couldn't get mortgages we pooled our money to help others. We called it a partner and it worked well.' May Cambridge who came in the later fifties also says: 'People had to share rooms and even cellars were used.' These pools of money were known as Susu or Partners. Many of the principles of time banking were in operation in these early immigrant communities.

In many countries like Jamaica, susu is said to be the most important savings scheme in operation as it provides cash and credit for people on low incomes. It is a system largely based on trust and established relationships. In Ghana, susu collectors traditionally operate in specific areas or with families they have established a long standing relationship with. So important is susu that many mainstream banks are now offering services to these micro-financers who constitute 70% of banking activity.

How Does Susu/Partner Work?

1. The scheme is organised by a susu/partner banker who is the person responsible for organising the project.
2. Once a group of people had been organised, 10 to 20, an amount is agreed to be paid periodically (usually weekly or monthly). This contribution is called 'a hand'.
3. The banker is the one who collects the money and gives it out to the member whose turn it is. This is called a 'draw'.
4. This process is repeated until each member of the partner receives their draw.

The Advantages of Susu/Partner

- Easily accessible and flexible as it can allow credit to members
- Informal as it does not involve taxes and the completion of complicated forms
- Allows for geographical convenience as it is often in the locality of all participants
- Operates amongst familiar group of people
- Few and low transaction costs

Yvonne and Sebastian, Theo's parents, had actually used this scheme to raise money not only for their wedding, but their first home. They would get their money regardless, go to a friend's house, hand it in and before they knew it it was their turn to draw out the money. Perhaps they had not realised that susu wasn't only about money, it was about socialising, about culture, so when they both began to establish careers and get money paid into their bank accounts they did not realise that they had let a little of their culture go. Then, when the arguments came about money, there was no little scheme to help them out, no network of friends to offer a few comforting words.

Black Wall Street: The Story of Little Africa

Black Wall Street (also known as little Africa) was the name given to Greenwood Avenue, North Tulsa, Oklahoma during the early 1900s. It was a time of racial segregation, where Blacks were restricted in what they could and could not do. Part of this restriction was in their economic activity with white businesses, and this meant they had to develop and run their own businesses. The Black community had been established in the area around 1908 as African-Americans moved in the area to gain employment, and those that had land discovered gold. The circulating of the Black dollar (36 to 100 times) meant that businesses flourished in this 35 block area, with dozens of Black millionaires emerging. By 1921 Blacks had their own churches, libraries, hotels, stores, theatres, hospitals and even high schools. In total, Blacks owned and operated 600 of their own businesses. This economic prosperity did not mean that racial violence was lessened. In 1919 two Black prisoners were lynched by a white mob.

In 1921, after an alleged accusation of rape by a white girl called Sarah Page, a young Black man, Dick Rowland, was arrested and charged with the rape. 2000 White men went to the jail to lynch Rowland. Meanwhile, 75 Black men, hearing what was happening went to the jail to give the sheriff support. However, the sheriff refused this help, and instead deputised the 2000 white men to keep the 75 Black men from having access to the prisoner. The 2000 mob then went and looted the Black businesses before burning it down, assisted with aeroplanes that dropped kerosene and dynamite on the homes of those living in Greenwood. On 21st June 1921, Greenwood, the Black Wall Street, was burnt to the ground. 1400 business and homes were destroyed, with some experts saying that 3000 people lost their lives. Many of the Blacks were buried in mass graves, whilst some were thrown into the river. Although Greenwood was rebuilt, it never recovered as the thriving centre of Black economic life. In 2003 a lawsuit was filed against the authorities for reparations.

Family and Finance

Many families are unaware that they have the skills and means to diversify their income and therefore be more financially secure. In a few years time 60% of people in the West will work for themselves and this is going to mean people having flexible skills. The home office, the family business is going to be quite normal and for Black people who traditionally have been multi-lingual, multi-talented, this should mean a return (aided with modern technology) to self-sufficiency. Families should consider network marketing, online businesses, investment schemes, susu/pardners and franchise businesses. This is also part of your home education provision. There is no better education for your children than to witness a business in the home.

Amma's Harvest for the World

Indigenous African crops lie at the heart of Africa's food security. These plants are tougher than the foreign exotic crops. Perhaps, through Theo, Amma is trying to tell us this. She knows the land of Africa better than anyone. As she walks over different terrain she sees families trying to grow cash crops, cutting down trees to use as fuel; she sees the planting of foreign crops that cannot take the African climate, that then perish in drought conditions and she screams at modern Africans: *'Grow your own food, eat your own food.'* But the modern African wants pizza, hamburgers, friend chicken and fizzy drinks. All she is trying to tell everyone is that if they grow indigenous African foods upon which the gut of modern Africans has been built then their immune system will be stronger, then we wont have failed harvests. People in rural areas, all over Africa see the shadow of an ageless woman working the land. She plants traditional seeds during the day, at night she picks medicinal herbs and leaves them outside the huts of rural families. When it's time for harvesting, these same people say the lost knowledge of working the land returned to them. Eighty per cent of Africa's population live in rural areas and here is the wealth. This is why Amma, who is always hidden but present, is here. Amma, will show Theo this in his dream and hope that he will value this knowledge and create a harvest for the world.

Amma calls out at night, as she walks ancient and modern African savannas, gathering wild cereal grains. These plant species whisper in the wind that sweeps across moonlit landscapes: 'Why have your people forgotten us? Why do they not dance and celebrate the promise of our harvest?' She wants to tell the people to remember that wealth is in the land, that they are still the richest people on the Earth; that in their genes, they possess this great indigenous knowledge of how to be great trustees and workers of the land. At night she started to plant sorghum, African rice, tef, fonio, pearl millet, finger millet seeds and wild yam. She knows that this harvest of African renaissance will help and strengthen families.

How to Unlock Your Family's Genius

Indigenous African Food Wealth

Foods	Energy (Kcal)	Protein (g)	Thiamine (mg)	Niacin (mg)	Calcium (mg)	Iron (mg)
Millet	341	10.4	0.3	1.7	22.0	20.7
Sorghum	340	9.4	0.25	3.7	45.0	8.8
Fonio	332	7.1	0.24	1.9	40.0	8.5
Bambara nut	365	18.8	0.47	1.8	62	12.2
Yam bean	350	19.2	0.69	2.3	55	10.5

Writings of an Educationalist

Wednesday is my counselling day; the day worried families brave the cold and arrive at my office with a sneaked chill under their coat, but still with a polite smile that is often the mask of sorrow. I have seen over 6000 of these masks, and the parents that have the courage to do so and removed them they would see tribal marks that reveal that their worries must be addressed through their culture; through a scientific ritual we have to call education. ADHD, exclusion, bullying, underachievement, homeschooling and family break-ups; these are some of the many problems that the parents arrive with, having already phoned and poured out their hearts as they desperately fight for a way to educate, protect and love their child. They insist on seeing me, as if it is a life or death situation, and in many ways it is: their child, their family, is under attack but they do not understand this attack, because they do not understand their history; the journey that their people have taken and how their arrival at my office is part of that journey; yes, they are being called to be warriors in the same spirit of Nzinga, Amy Garvey, Asantewa and Nefertari, and strapped to their backs are the children of an entire nation. They have, in truth, been travelling for over two thousand years, when the education centres of Africa began to close; burnt down, destroyed and ransacked. I romantically tell myself that these were the women that crawled out from under the smouldering boulders, saved their children as they escaped the gaze of foreign invaders, and have been walking to safety ever since. I have learnt to listen to these women; what they say is far more revealing than most people would think. They tell me that: 'the headteacher almost laughed in my face!', or, 'they accused me of being threatening when I challenged their report', or, 'I didn't want no assessment, I didn't want him labelled, and this label passed on..' Each parent, though not explicitly is saying that the school has accused them of being mad; is about to label their child with another pseudo-scientific label of failure, a kind of psychological disturbance.

When mental illness appears in a family, often the family do not know what to do. Some parents have told me, 'well I just go to church and I prayed for him.' Others have sought help from their pastor, or relative, or doctor. Those that seek help have to know the journey of the Blacks; the journey from the first kingdoms of Ta Seti in Africa, to ancient Egypt (Kamit), to Mali, Songhay, Ghana, to West Africa and then the slave ships and to the swamps where the Marroon communities resided. So great a journey, so great our spiritual disturbance that the family often underestimates the illness, and are unaware of their own hidden illnesses one that can only be addressed through cultural methods of healing. Sadly, this is compounded by negative experiences of trying to organise in the community but failing, and, as a result becoming cynical towards any attempt at Black self reliance and empowerment. The two are related and to understand mental illness, its roots and dynamics, one has to delve into these areas. So let's start our therapy, our healing; let's perform purification, let us perform libation, and let us ask the African faculty of Healing to help us as we prepare.

If we trace mental illness in the Black community we have to first start with a precise description of what is the mind according to African people. We might say that the mind is the brain and nervous system, the conscious mind and the subconscious/spirit. The understanding of this mind by Africans was understood through cosmology (the understanding of the universe), which is the model for understanding the human condition and the world. To live with this rich knowledge, and in accordance of the laws that were discovered from this intuitive investigation was to live by the laws of Maat, that is, natural law. The horrendous and violent invasions that Africans have had to endure, from the Hykos, the Romans, the Greeks, Arabs and the Europeans have all meant the violent imposition of another world view that has denigrated 'Black Africaness'. They, the Africans, had to accept, understand the world in circumstances of oppression. Violent enslavement, rape, whippings, lynching, branding with hot irons and torture. In all situations of oppression the African has had to develop survival techniques, and these techniques resulted in plantation types, with complex behaviour patterns that are still apparent today. Below is a summary of these types:

Personality type	Animal characteristic	Personality contradictions
Type A Weak and confused	Hyena	- appears docile - dreams of freedom - Would like to destroy every thing Massa has created but is scared to
Type B Weak, confused and jovial	Poodle Loyal to 'Massa'	- appears loyal - seeks own interests - would like to destroy everything Massa' has created
Type C Weak, confused and seething	Sheepish	- spiritual, outwardly loyal - secretive - dreams of the love of the rebel
Type D Rebel and strategist	Lion	- spiritual and secretive - healer and hidden - would like to destroy everything Massa' has created - Is prepared to take action

What we see is the formation of personality types under situations of extreme oppression. To understand these behaviour patterns further we have to ask questions on each personality type and speculate as to how they would behave in certain situations.

Type A

1. If Type A heard about a slave rebellion being secretly planned by other slaves would he/she:

    a) Join the rebellion
    b) Do nothing
    c) Tell Massa

Type B

1. If Type B had the opportunity to become an overseer and beat his own people, would be:

    a) Beat his own people and feel bad about it?
    b) Pretends to beat his own people when Massa was not looking?
    c) Beat his own Massa and escape?

Stage Seven

115

Type C

1. If Type C was sexually harassed by Massa would he/she:

   a) **Carry on as usual but be hurting inside?**
   b) **Slit Massa's throat when he/she is asleep?**
   c) **educate the next generation to strive for their freedom**

Type D

1. The Rebel has escaped and is in control of a Maroon community in a remote region of the country that is inaccessible to the slavers. Would he/she:

   a) **Set up a community of slaves based on a traditional African way of life?**
   b) **Establish a community of free slaves living the same as their masters?**
   c) **Establish a community of free ex-slaves and launch attacks on other plantations to free other enslaved Africans?**

Perhaps we have to ask if these personality types and behaviour patterns are at work in Theo's home. Subtle and almost hidden, these patterns can play havoc in relationships and perhaps they did with Theo's parents who we are quick to judge, but where could they go to? What marriage guidance counsellor could take them on this type of *Sankofa* journey to heal the pressures in the marriage? Yet there is a journey that they have to take to bring true love and respect back into their marriage.

In 2007 African communities in the UK marked the bicentenary of the abolition of slavery. Much talk was made of what happened as if it was an event that had finished, but the economic and psychological oppression continues, therefore the behaviour patterns continue, though in a slightly different way. One of the activities that people of African descent engaged in was the area of genealogy, which is the study of family history, family lore, oral history and written records. On television we saw Black people searching civil registration documents, looking at census records, parish registers, wills, marriage licenses etc. But there is a need to go further back into the past, especially when the lies one is told about Africaness is so brutally racist and a key part of continued oppression. Genetics is our history book; our genes with its X and Y chromosomes demands that we visit our biological essence, and go deeper still. There we find mind, spirit. The families that come to me, their spirit has been broken to an extent. The same spirit needs nourishment. They want ritual, African therapy; they want me to rid them of all these behaviour patterns that flare up in the home like demons. It is just the two of them in the home, but there are these other types; these plantation monsters that come and tell the spirit, 'just work harder', or, 'we just have to try our best and get along with everyone', 'it's wrong to think too Black because we'll alienate ourselves'. These behaviour types create turmoil within the home and undermine all relationships within the family.

So what counselling can we do to rid the spirit of these monsters that are so ingrained in the habits and thinking of the parents who come, and in the community at large? I try and show them that their parenting style is based on servitude and this is one of the reasons for their child's behaviour pattern, underachievement, learning difficulty etc. They, and we, need African therapy to celebrate self love, self identity. We need to hear the djembe drums again to call down the intelligence systems that can rid our minds of these monsters; we need to pour libation again and call our ancestry to help and remind us of our genius; we need call the names of the rebels who fought a million undocumented battles without which we would not be here today. The father needs to wear the loin cloth of the lion to outwardly show the testosterone we need to build community institutions; the child needs to be sent out into the 'bush' to develop survival skills, self-reliance and the understanding of nature, and to gaze up at the stars and wonder, and speculate as to the effect these celestial bodies have on their biological light of melanin. As a family they needed to perform a modern day sacrificial ritual and in front of a bemused community, 'slaughter' these behavioural monsters once and for all and in doing so, return their consciousness to that of genius. We could go so far as to say that these monsters lived in the house with Yvonne, Sebastian and Theo, but no one knew they were there.

Notes on Building Family

The family values, the standards of behaviour that a family applies to itself in pursuing its goals is key to its success. This implies that a family is aware that it will reap what it has sewn and our study indicates that a family will also reap what its family tree has sewn. This investing in family therefore has been performed by generations after generations, in circumstances of extreme oppression and difficulty which further implies that there has been great sacrifice by many. So what has been the mental state of those that have sacrificed, that have given so much, that have held onto these family values? It has simply been one of pure love; the giving and seeking of nothing in return.

So far we have looked at our family tree; our parents, grandparents and great grandparents and we have briefly looked at their skills, their sacrifice and the values and beliefs that they held onto as they fought for freedom. To understand family learning to a greater degree we have to realise that traditional African systems of learning viewed the intelligence that permeates the world as having different aspects or principles and these principles were studied and applied to daily living. These were our role models.

This understanding of these principles, its interconnectedness is what family learning is really all about and not simply families learning about literacy and numeracy etc. These systems of sub-intelligences is what has guided the family trees when faced with such horrific experiences like slavery and colonialism. From this knowledge of African family learning we can extract family values of honesty, justice and love; family values based on true experience and study of a great system of learning that has been fashioned by those of the family tree to build family and community.

These family values are part of the family capital, capital which produces family wealth both material wealth and wealth of knowledge. A whole cultural science was developed to study and apply this knowledge. The destruction of the African Tree of Knowledge and Learning through invasion, enslavement etc has seen the fall of family.

Both Yvonne and Sebastian are in many ways guilty of abandoning this cultural technology and science for ideas of individualism and a materialist view of the world. There was a time when their home was strong; when they home schooled Theo, when Yvonne made extra money by baking, by sewing and teaching other children, and when Sebastian fixed cars and sold Black books at cultural events. Then they had a strong home, that had sources of multiple incomes, and saw them pour libation together and live with no credit cards. They

Stage Seven

117

made a modest living but the home was strong. The break-up began when they stopped home schooling Theo, when they both went out to work, and when Sebastian got made redundant; when they started arguing about money and when the people at work started to tell Yvonne that she should 'find herself' another man. Unemployment, and debt both became triggers for self hate. They both gave less and less to the community and therefore received less and less from the community. They stopped their susu, they stopped visiting friends, they stopped attending cultural events and even helping out this cousin, or that friend. Their life no longer had their family tree or the African Tree of Knowledge as its reference point.

So Yvonne and Sebastian, like so many, needed to realise what their family capital was and what it could produce as long as they lived by the values of their ancestry. This is also why Amma is in the fields where indigenous crops grow. Perhaps she is reminding us to make sure we work the land so that we can reap a plentiful harvest and that it is this working the land that is the place for Theo and his parents to engage in real family learning.

Family Wisdom
On Relationships

- **To love unconditionally, to give unconditionally and understand unconditionally is to see the untainted flowering of an unbelievable family.**

- **Friends remind you that your family has a family.**

- **The relationship you have with yourself is the relationship you have with your family and the relationship you have with both are the gifts you'll carry to heaven.**

- **Create harmony in your home with the discrete use of furniture arrangement, flowers, colours, laughter, dance, art, music and sound. Always remember that the placement of care and love, especially at the door,is what creates a welcoming home.**

- **All family members should be treated justly but justice will only return when there is honesty.**

- **Truly there is no depth to the lover's love.**

Stage 8

Family History and the Family Tree

Themes of Inquiry

- The role and future of the black graduate
- The family plan for community success
- The structure of success

Gye Nyame: the supremacy of God

Gye Nyame reminds us of our immortality. It is the symbol that reminds us of the supremacy of God.

Family is always working towards the understanding of this great intelligence that permeates the world, an intelligence that humans possess and therefore each and everyone of us have this great power in kind but not in the same magnitude as God.

Stage Eight

Theo's Diary

Got sent to see the careers man today. Told him I wanted to be a detective so that I could find out who has been killing off all the members of my gang. He didn't understand me and kept looking at me funny like that fat arse Dr Seamus. Anyway, I told him that Biko, Malcolm X, Toussaint, have all been murdered. But I'm a survivor. They can't kill my spirit, that's why they keep sending me to see that nutcase Dr Seamus. He's killed so many children with his reports, assessments and little visits. When I become a detective I'll arrest him, then the Headteacher; run down to the pupil referral unit and free up all the children. I'll charge them all with attempted murder. This is serious stuff! I've got all the evidence. The fake assessments, school reports and all that. We should have some kind of trials; you know, crimes against children's humanity because that's what it's all about. We couldn't even celebrate Black History Month without them calling it racist then getting a whole set of Irish people to take over the place with their fiddle, and dancing and stuff.

It's time for me to stop writing now. It's time for me to stand up as a revolutionary and just mash up the whole school with my genius. Tomorrow I will go in and write some lyrics about revolution in my history book. I'll play my saxophone like John Coltrane. I'll walk into the art class wearing an African mask; I'll recite some rap in the English lesson. It's time to get serious. I'm a revolutionary! I can't wait for mum to stop brooding, or dad to come back home. I can't waste my time waiting for them. It's my time; it's time to plan.

So Theo has a plan and so must we all. We must plan our family's development, and this development must have a framework. African culture has used a framework based on the five major initiation systems, which, Professor Manu Ampim (African Business and Culture magazine June 2006) informs us are birth, adulthood, marriage, eldership and ancestorship. Training was giving to children, young people and adults in order to prepare them for a new phase in life, and this training was accompanied by various teachers and mentors. It is clear that if we look at Theo's family, they had no training. The father could just walk out of the home and act as if nothing major has happened. Did Yvonne or Sebastian have any kind of initiation before they married? Most probably they had a stag do, a hen night; perhaps got drunk, turned up the next day at the church and hoped for the best. This is a recipe for disaster and this is exactly what we are seeing right now with so many broken and casual relationships in the Black community (and other communities). There is little thought on the affects on the children, and the progress of the community as a whole, and what affects this behaviour will have on the community in the future. So let us see how we can apply this traditional system of personal development to our present day situation.

Initiation Type	Traditional	Modern Application
Birth	To determine the personality, life mission and human characteristics a chart would be made and the child's name determined to remind them of their incarnation objective.	Family should seek consultation from trained experts in the community who are able to determine the characteristic of the child; their purpose for coming to earth and advise parents on financial plan to facilitate the child's achievement. Parents should undertake courses, such as, *How to Unlock Your Child's Genius*, from a qualified and licensed trainer.
Adulthood	Training is given in social, moral and sexual behaviour. The young person is instructed in the behaviour and responsibilities that is expected of them when they become adults.	Youth development training workshops in subjects such as sex education, media literacy, youth culture and lifestyle, financial literacy etc should take place in schools, youth clubs, churches, mosques.
Marriage	Though there were and are many systems of marriage, generally spea king the young couple would consult elders as marriage was seen as two families marrying. Both young people would also be instructed in behaviour around marriage from those who have successfully been married.	Modern couples need to consider whether they should keep up the tradition of stag and hen nights for something more meaningful such as the gathering of mentors and advisors who can give them advice and training in making their marriage a successful one.
Eldership	A system for electing elders was established to access their wisdom and experience. They functioned as arbiters in disputes and local matters. These elders helped in the development of leadership capital in their society.	Councils of trained elders should be established in all our community institutions to advise and guide those in need. They should also play a role as community teachers, that is, supporting parent teachers and classroom teachers.
Ancestorship	This is someone who made great contributions to their community during their lifetime and not just someone who died.	We need to see their role as good community practice and acknowledge this in community gatherings. Their work should be studied in the local or national context. Training should be given to the elderly as part of our work and care for the elderly.

How to Unlock Your Family's Genius

The Clan System

The above initiations took place with the clan system. The clan system was a political grouping, consisting of different family groups who claimed descent from one or more ancestors. It was and is a subdivision of the tribe and its main purpose was to ensure prosperity, justice, order, continuity and harmony. To belong to a group was through birth and the real function of a clan was to ensure mutual help and support, so it operated as a kind of welfare system. It usually had a head figure but there were a number of checks to stop any abuse of power.

Part of the knowledge that was passed down was on health care; indigenous knowledge that was inherited from one generation to another based on good practice and results. So far we have heard little about Yvonne's mother, Theo's grandmother, who, had she been more included in the marriage might have been able to offer the couple some words of advice, but individualism has been sold to so much of the Black community that they no longer believe in the group, the collective. This is why poor old grandma, with her fading eyesight would stay up at night and read Yvonne's letters; read between the lines and she would reply with kind supporting words, all the time trying her best not to pry but why should not a mother pry into the breaking heart of her daughter.

So we now continue our strategic family plan with another look at our health.

Health Plan (Part Two)

We can follow the line of therapy that Dr Seamus and the education establishment have followed in looking at issues around Theo's learning, but our holistic approach means we have to look at lifestyle patterns in the home. Again we have to look at health, and good practice around health and learning/living. So let us consider how families should ensure good diet which will impact not only on educational performance but behaviour patterns within the home.

The Benefits of Water

- Water should be the first and last drink of the day (cleansing of kidneys).
- Water moistens the lungs to aid in the transportation of oxygen
- Water helps maintain sodium-potassium pump. Each of the 100 billion neurons in the human brain has a pump which assists in the transmission of messages. Therefore fruits like bananas, oranges and apricots which are rich in potassium should be eaten.
- Water assists in intercellular activity, that is keeping the cells healthy.
- 6-8 glasses of water to be taken daily (spring water).

Nutrients

- The most important nutrient for the brain is glucose.
- Glucose is the fuel of the brain.
- We get glucose from the carbohydrates we eat (slow releasing carbohydrates like wholegrains, vegetables and fruit).
- To have good 'brain health' you need omega-3 and omega-6 in your diet (makes the brain work more efficiently). Omega-3 can be obtained from flax, walnut and fish oils; omega-6 can be obtained from sunflower and sesame.
- Phospholipids, which are also known as the 'intelligent' fats are important to take. Lecithin (peanuts and wheatgerm) is a good source of phospholipids

Key Neurotransmitters (messengers) in the brain:

- GABA calms you down after a stressful situation
- Seretonin maintains and promotes happiness.
- Acetylcholoine improves your memory and keeps you alert
- Tryptamines keeps you connected and maintains biorhythms (e.g. melatonin).

Vitamins

- The B-complex vitamins are essential for good mental health and brain chemistry. B6 and zinc have been found to be lacking in people with ADHD, autism and depression.
- Zinc deficiency has been associated with schizophrenia, anxiety, hyperactivity, depression and delinquency.
- A good quality multi-vitamin and mineral should be taken daily to maintain good brain chemistry and supplement nutrient deficiency from food grown in poor quality top soil.
- Vitamin C should be taken to limit the damage done by the activity of free radicals which undermine the health of cells within the body.

Tips on Maintaining Good Brain Chemistry

- Drink spring water 30mins before you have a main meal.
- Eat a breakfast rich in fresh organic fruit.
- Eat a lunch with a large fresh salad.
- Exercise to keep the blood oxygenated.
- Drink lots of water (6-8 glasses or every 2 hours) to keep the body cleansed.
- Eat a diet which consists of 70% plus of raw organic foods.

Breaking Bad Habits of the Bad Diet

- Avoid eating acid forming foods which disturbs the alkaline state of the stomach like fried foods and citrus foods which inhibit digestion. Too much acid in the stomach can cause heartburn and gastritis.
- The caffeine in coffee can over stimulate the nervous system, creating stress in the body.
- Avoid eating too much mucus forming foods like cheese and mushrooms which can cause the build up of mucus in the nasal and bronchial tract.
- Rich spicy foods cause the build up of stomach acid and therefore should be avoided.

The Science of Breathing

Breathing consists of two phases; inhalation and exhalation. The air we breathe travels via the nostrils, throat, larynx, trachea and the alveoli. Breathing and respiration should be distinguished as breathing is the movement of air in and out of the lungs and respiration is the exchange of gases in the lungs. Whilst our everyday breathing is involuntary, that is, it is performed automatically without us consciously having to focus on breathing, breathing can be performed consciously and therefore we are able to improve the whole breathing performance and its benefits to us.

Breathing is really about liberating energy for the body through deep breathing and to avoid stress related illnesses. There are different types of breathing exercises aimed at eliminating stale air, improving the performance of the whole breathing apparatus, calming the mind and producing energy.

Inhalation:	the intercostal muscles and diaphragm contract, so the volume increases and the pressure decreases allowing air into the lungs.
Exhalation:	the intercostal muscles and diaphragm relax, volume of air in lungs decrease and the pressure increases so the air is forced out.

Every system in the body is dependent on oxygen and the diaphragm is the most important muscle in the breathing process, with exhalation being the most important phase in the whole breathing phase as it eliminates stale air from the lungs. The whole mechanics of breathing allows for the massaging of the internal organs.

When we breathe 'normally', often doing 'upper chest breathing' we only exhale three-quarters of the air, but when you use yogic breathing (slow deep breathing) your exhalation is far more efficient which is important in older people who need three times more oxygen than younger people.

Movement and Yoga

Yoga means to unite and is a way of life that includes physical movements and postures (asanas), breathing, concentration and in some cases chanting of mantras. The most popular form of yoga in the West is Hatha yoga (*ha* meaning sun and *tha* meaning moon, therefore yoga brings about balance) and this form of yoga has many benefits for the family in maintaining good health, flexibility and relieving stress. It is easy to say that Yvonne and Sebastian would have benefited, but they would have and much of the arguing that went on in their home was stress related.

The benefits of yoga are:

- Yoga massages the internal organs of the body.
- Yoga improves the circulation of blood and lymph.
- Yoga helps support the immune system of the body through relaxation.
- Yoga assists in correct breathing by developing the respiratory system which in turn eliminates toxins (carbon dioxide from the body).
- Yoga helps develop the muscular system of the body through stretching.
- Yoga helps in the maintenance of good posture, and therefore knowledge of the muscular and skeletal systems. Poor posture is linked to back and neck pain and constipation.
- Yoga helps develop balance and relaxation which allows the brain to be in the alpha state (the optimum learning state).

The Plan for Knowledge in the Black Community

The dream for many immigrant parents was to see their children get a good education; to go to university, graduate and have their picture framed and hanging on the wall in the living room, amidst the then fashionable doilies and biblical pictures. This is what Yvonne and Sebastian wanted from Theo one day. It was also customary for pictures of the proud graduate to be sent back home to relatives, who would also make copies and give it to neighbours. I remember when I wrote my first book my mother sent it to every aunt I had, and when I returned to Carriacou, people would come up to me with a curious squint and say, '*Is you dat make ah book?*' Announcements of our achievements would be sent via blue airmail letters, and later retold on well swept Caribbean and West African verandas, as friends and family gathered under the evening sunset to muse proudly on the achievements of 'family'. They had watched the journey of us immigrant children from when we stood in school photos in grey V-necked jumpers, grey socks, black caps, pleated skirts and well ironed blouses. We had a responsibility to achieve, and if we did not we got the belt, and shame and had to learn our tables, and made sure we said our prayers and did not 'cut-our-eye' in any kind of disgruntleness. So we dutifully went to these old Victorian schools that fed us cold milk and mass education that had ruined the potential of millions of white working-class children. Yet, we were expected to succeed. Perhaps our parents did not quite understand our journey and we did not quite understand theirs.

I, like many children of immigrant parents studied hard, but I was in an education system where it wasn't a level playing field. It did not matter how hard you studied you weren't getting into the top class. Things were blatantly segregated then. The form years went from A to G; A being the top and G the lowest. Form A was full of white boys, except one Black boy who had come from Jamaica and was so far ahead of everyone the teachers could not dare put him in a low class. G form was full of Black boys and one or two Turkish or white working class boys from the local estate. Our education was, as the Brazilian educationalist Paulo Friere would call it, 'banking education', we simply sat there and listened as information that totally excluded us, was 'banked' in our mental deposit box. We were expected to listen, to behave; not to question or discover, but simply do as we were told. All of us, the children of the Windrush generation; the ship that brought 498 Caribbeans to England in 1948, studied hard. Many years later, I managed to get some qualifications to get onto a degree course, and there I sat in a large lecture theatre being educated, yet knowing that something vital was missing. This was never more apparent than when I studied a subject called Western Intellectual Tradition. We learnt about Socrates, Plato, Pythagoras, and were told civilisation started with the Greeks but deep down, though in awe of all the learning I was expected to perform, I knew there were questions I had to ask. My elder brothers and sister had attended Black Power meetings in the early 1970s. In afro shirts, afro's, flared trousers, beads and chains, and wearing Free George Jackson (The Soledad Brother) badges, they went to lectures and brought home books on Black history and culture like Walter Rodney's Groundings With My Brothers, and The Autobiography of Malcolm X and the writings of Angela Davis. Everything was neatly packed: The Greeks started it all, then came the Romans, then came the European Renaissance and now the Western world. I had to counter this intellectual assassination during my three years studying for a degree by almost taking a second degree by reading everything I could lay my hands on on the subject of Black culture. When I graduated it was with relief. I could not take another lecture on Virginia Woolfe, or D.H Lawrence, or Shakespeare. I could not take another boast, another 'they were the first', another classic text, another quote from 'the greatest philosopher.' I had been imprisoned in an aggressive institution of Western propaganda, and it had ruthlessly excluded, not only those of its race but a different class, but the entire world. What I came to know of this Western intellectual tradition was that its foundation was: pessimism, materialistic, segregative thinking, racial hierarchy, the concept of progress and Eurocentricity.

Many many years later, I travelled to Crete on a cheap holiday, not knowing that I would once again confront the Gods of Western knowledge; see propaganda passed off as history. This was the land of King Minos, who built the Palace of Knossis. When I arrived at the airport I was picked up by a tired and argumentative taxi driver, before then driving me to my apartment in a popular tourist area, Hersonisos, but thankfully not far from traditional Greece that would keep luring me back to questions of truth. I booked into the Piskopiano hotel, which was in a once small fishing town near the coast; a small district given added historical depth by the many wells, old churches and old women in black who displayed stoic faces until you greeted them and then they offered you a warm genuine smile. To the east of the island is an old abandoned leper colony, where stands a large old Venetician fort that formed part of the leper colony. It was here that people were brought who suffered from leprosy: children, women, men and the old; here, segregated from the rest of the community and even one another. Walking around the fort the mix of courage and cruelty was still very tangible, and the untold stories lodged between the stone and wooden architecture, were still there, patiently waiting for the curiosity and compassion of the next generation to unearth. There were no curators that I trusted, no libraries, just an urge to once again confront my miseducation that I now saw in so many young Black graduates entering the teaching profession, who would eventually lose their way. I began to dismantle this false worldview that I saw destroying the future Black intelligentsia.

Those that taught me, those that control knowledge say that Greece emerged from Indo-European speakers from the north. Martin Bernal writes in Black Athena;

> *Greece had originally been inhabited by primitive tribes.*
> *Pelasgians and others, and had been settled by the Egyptians and*
> *Phoenicians who had built cities and introduced irrigation. The latter*
> *had brought the alphabet and the former had taught the natives of the*
> *gods and how to worship them. The earliest royal dynasties were*
> *supposed to have had both divine and Egyptian descent.*

However, this model was discredited due to what Bernal calls romanticism, racism and the concept of progress. The Black graduate, unaware of the manipulation to uphold the superiority of this tradition, they, like I did, enter university vulnerable, naive and with a hugely limited view of where their intelligence can take them and help their community, both local and global.

I started my degree in 1979, and the first thing I noticed was that it did not include me, yet Africa was everywhere, though hidden. It reminded me of when I worked in the reading room of the British Museum, just before I started university. A big building with colonnades and dark corridors off limits to the public. Treasures, artefacts and old books from all over the world, but I was the star of the show though no one told me. I used to go to the canteen at break times to get a coffee, and on my way I would go past the Rosetta Stone which Champollion used to decipher the hieroglyphs. It was just another artefact to me which marked where I would turn to find the staff entrance to the canteen. Later, I would take note of it; take note of the artefacts of the Black civilisations of ancient India, of Sumer, of the Middle East, and of Ancient Egypt (Kamit). Tourists from all over the world came to see me, my people, but they did not tell us, and they would disguise our glory. There was a reason why this happened in the museum; it was the same reason as why it happened in the university; it was to maintain the relationship of power: that is, one group who feels superior, and one group who feels inferior. For this relationship to be maintained, the consciousness of the exploited has to be carefully manipulated. It is here that the Black graduate must make a decision. A deep subconscious choice is made by the graduate. Do they buy into this western intellectual tradition (WIT) or do they search for a tradition that gives them ownership, and celebrates their own cultural genius. After a few years of joining the teaching profession, the new young Black teacher adopts a yoyo mentality. They blame racism one minute, then their Black community the next. Their ego needs an outlet for this WIT. They are never seen in our Saturday schools. Eventually, a few of these Black graduates do get to positions of 'power'; they are in senior management, they are headteachers, they are principals, and once again they feel they have been allowed to join a club, a kind of pagan religion. They worship Plato, Socrates and Pythagoras. But this worship inevitably comes to an end. A restructuring takes place at their institution, or they are undermined by the staff they line manage, or the racism from seniors. A few years would have passed now. They are in their forties, or early fifties, and the system has broken and ruined them. It is at this point they remember their community. They have no where else to go. It is here that they might go along to some community or grassroots organisations to help, to explore their culture. You will often hear them say: 'I want to put something back into my community'. Those that have come to me are sometimes in a dead end in terms of their careers. Their health is bad, they are angry, confused, perhaps, even venturing into alternative health. Ironically, they are the ones who need healing, but it is difficult when you have lived with such high expectations from others to admit you need help. In a sense, they have made themselves the lepers of their community. Now, looking back, I realise that I had escaped this fate, simply because I had an alternative; I had the opportunity to investigate learning, investigate my community and most importantly of all investigate myself. I had destroyed the illusion of the European tradition.

The trip to Crete reminded me of the illusion; the waste of thousands of our young people, lost in an education system that cannot equip them to be themselves, therefore they *cannot* put anything back in their community, unless, with true honesty and compassion, they re-evaluate this whole illusion of the centrality of European knowledge and the total displacement and invisibility of not simply African indigenous knowledge but their family tree too.

How to Help and Support the Black Undergraduate

Awareness	Prepare young people going to university by making them aware of university life, required study skills, financial support, institutional/academic racism
Vision	Encourage young person going to university to have a vision; guidance on how to maintain the vision by use of affirmations, meditation and breathing
Mentor & confidant	Encourage young person to have a mentor to support them not only with academic life but social and personal issues. It might so happen that at least two people are needed.
Cultural awareness	Encourage young person to have cultural awareness
Community/voluntary service	Encourage prospective undergraduate to gain some form of community service to help others who strive for a better education
Work experience	Encourage prospective undergraduate to gain work experience in chosen field
Financial support	Try and maintain some kind of financial support whether it is saving scheme, or part-time job

Writings of an Educationalist: Education and Development

On 20th October 2007 I arrived in Dakar as part of a British Council project on leadership in Africa and the UK. Senegal has always been special for me for it is the birth place of Ousmane Sembene, the great filmmaker who made Africa's first great film Xala (1985); it is the home of Cheik Anta Diop, the great African historian and Baba Maal the magical Senegalese musician. Though Dakar is in darkness, there is light that still glows in this ancient country; the light of ancient Egypt from whence came these people and their wonderful Wolof language. So I enter this stage, a minor actor in a complex landscape of greatness, slavery, colonialism and now, perhaps, rebirth. I am travelling with nine other participants from England, and we are met by officials from the British Council, a tall woman who speaks quickly as she greets us, ushers us to the mini bus and instructs the driver. There is the usual chaos. Our bags are hoisted up on the bus, precariously positioned by the driver who seems to know what he is doing but the sheer weight of the luggage gives many of us cause for concern. Before our misgivings can become substantial the old bus bellows smoke as the engine roars, and we head off to our hotel, meandering through the streets of this puzzling Francophone city with all its colourful and sometimes sad contradictions.

How to Unlock Your Family's Genius

Our arrival is bizarre; it is a scene from Sembene's Xala; in the reception of the Five Star hotel there is a grand banquet taking place; beautiful and elegant Senegalese women parade the plush foyer, accompanied by Senegalese men in black suits, the same suits that I saw the new government officials in Sembene's Xala wear. Were these men mimicking French style of dress? We had cocktails, we chatted, looked on at the pageant. I would soon discover, like so much of Africa and the Caribbean, this hotel, with its air-conditioning, its lavish meals, its fully equipped meeting rooms, its smartly dressed attendants, its swimming pools and pool side meals, its bar and satellite television; that this hotel, is surrounded by desperate poverty. Later, I would walk through a refugee camp and be taken not by the squalor but the ingenuity of a people who have the genius, but not yet the resources, to get out of an economic and psychological mess. In that moment I imagined Negritude to be a woman; a beautiful woman with long black braids, wearing African dress, proud of her Wolof tongue; and I imagined that she was in this grand function surrounded by these men in black European suits and each one had to dance with her and after each dance she would give them a kiss, and from this kiss they would return to a state of mind that gave riddance to the colonial mentality and its legacy of self-denial.

Two days later the leadership training started. The large meeting room was full of participants from some thirty or more African countries, keen to embrace a course that would address burning issues; government corruption, government transparency, new development paradigms, poverty, gender equality and empowerment, health care, education for all, investment and leadership. I soon discovered that the course, which was devised by Africans and delivered by Africans before the British Council came along as the main sponsors of the training programme, is hung around Neuro Linguistic Programme method. So we had to undertake tasks such as focusing on the me, visualising, addressing difference, diversity, appreciative inquiry. I found the course itself not that unique, but what was unique were the many conversations that I had to engage in; and in each conversation I learnt so much, because I had to listen to the passion of someone from Ghana, or Nigeria, or Uganda, or Tanzania, or South Africa, or Botswana, or Malawi. It was these conversations that inspired me, that made the trip worth while. I met a brother from Botswana and I had a conversation about education in his country; I met a sister from South Africa and I had a conversation about youth empowerment; I met a brother from Sudan who told me about the ancient greatness of the people who now found themselves persecuted in Darfur; I met a sister from Ethiopia who told me about her project working on gender equality; I met a brother from Nigeria who told me about publishing and literacy in his country; I met a sister from Zambia who told me about rural development in her country; I met a brother from Ghana who told me about indigenous banking systems in his country. In these conversations I met Queen Nefartari of ancient Egypt, I met the courage of Yaa Asantewa who fought the British, I met the spirit of Queen Nzhinga, I met the determination of the Mau Mau, I met the wisdom of Nkrumah, and I realised that I had been led to the African Tree of Learning, and here I would sit with Ifa, and elders under a tree, and share kola nuts, and contemplate leadership and the role family had in all of this.

Visit to Goree Island

After the course finished at 5pm we would have a break for a couple of hours and then be taken out of the hotel for a social event. On the second day we were taken to Goree island, a small island off the coast that was once colonised first by the Portuguese, to protect their commercial interests, and then by the Dutch. We are told that there is an old slave house there where enslaved Africans were kept before being taken across the Atlantic, and that this slave house is now a museum. We arrive and sail past the old fort, that begins to assume its sinister haunt as the sun goes down. We are ushered to a restaurant where we eat, drink, and talk and listen to local music. Some of us wait for the visit to the museum but it doesn't happen. A few hours later we are ushered back on the boat, and that's it; that's our visit to Goree island.

When we came back many of us were annoyed that we hadn't had the opportunity to visit the museum, pour libation, say prayers or simply be with the spirits of the Africans who had lost their lives in such barbaric conditions. The honouring of ancestors is fundamental to all African life, so it showed a big lapse in thinking of the organisers that it was omitted. So called 'ancestor worship' is really about the relationship we have with life and death; it's the engagement of the collective minds of your people that put together the good practice that you now live by, and this relationship must be continued, questioned and upheld. This is central to any leadership training. I could not leave Senegal without returning to Goree island and respecting those that perished.

The next day we took a yellow cab to the pier to catch a boat back to Goree island. The taxi driver spoke no English and understood little of my badly spoken French. Almost comically I was forced to draw a picture of the island and a boat which he at last understood. When I arrived I foundd that the next boat across to the island was not for another one hour. I was immediately spotted by an unofficial tour guide who befriended me with a grin and accompanying handshake.

'You need guide? I give you guide but boat not come yet. Have a drink and wait.' I'm irritated by missing the last boat; don't particularly want a drink, and the growing heat seems to be menacing. 'Come,' he says, 'you buy things; cheaper over here.' I follow him as we walk back up a main road to where women with babies strapped to their back squat over a mix of bracelets, chains and other jewellery. I'm tempted to buy but don't, but further up the dusty road it turns into a kind of shanty town. I continue to walk, curious as to what is at the other end of the road and see what appears to be a kind of mini makeshift refugee camp. I ask the guide if it's okay for me to walk into the camp, and he nods that it is. As I walk I see families living under old and weathered umbrellas, children wearing tattered clothes, men loitering, workless men; litter and rubbish everywhere, and amidst all of this I see brand new motorbikes. I look at the guide almost bemused. He tries to explain, telling me something about how they use them to earn a living, but I look away. There is so much to take in. The refugees are from neighbouring Mali. A sense of guilt comes over me especially when I look at the children. This was just another tiny glimpse I get of Africa; one of its many faces, yet this is a heroic continent, having endured invasion after invasion, from Arabs and Europeans, yet there is enough energy and ingenuity to see that Africa will one day rise up. The question is how soon, and for me, what will the role be of the diaspora.

By now I have walked away, I've been met on the pier by other participants of the course introduce me to another guide that they have acquired. Suddenly we have two guides, and I'm forced to part with my one, but not after he squabbles about being paid. I take out some local currency from my pocket and he walks away happy, yet another fleeting character in this complex but beautiful tapestry that makes Africa.

We sail for less than twenty minutes and arrive on Goree island, this time more solemn and respectful, and this time with a bottle of water with which to wet the earth upon where so much blood had already been spilled. But there is another problem; the slave house (museum) is closed for about two hours. This is no accident. Local restaurants want business; they know that we tourists will have to eat, have to drink something in the searing sun, and they are right so we go to a small food place on the beach and have a meal. Soon, having ordered from a menu that seems to specialise in fish dishes and not vegetarian, a kora player comes over. His melodies flirt with the women in our group, and he sings in Wolof, delicately plucking at the strings of his instrument and the growing giggles of the females. Eventually our food comes; we offer some money to the kora player and he accepts and soon departs to another table where he flirts once again, with the same routine of song and sweet lyrics. It is time, time for us to confront Goree island and so we leave, trampling through the sand to the stern brick building with its canons still pointing out to sea at enemies that it has already slain.

How to Unlock Your Family's Genius

On the door to the museum it reads, 'Maison De Esclaves'. The guide tells us that the economy of the island is based on fishing, tourism and art, but once the economy was based on slaves. He takes us to the weighing room where slaves were weighed. If a slave was less than 6 kilos they would be put in the fattening dungeon were they would be fed on local beans to increase their weight so that the slavers might get a better price. The health of male slaves was judged by their teeth and those of enslaved female Africans by the size of their breasts and their virginity. As we walk he tells us that 25% of the slaves were children, then he points to another low but long dungeon where the enslaved children were kept. We try and imagine what it must have been like; imagine the crying, the wailing , screaming, abuse and silence of those children so traumatised that they can't speak. I estimate that the size of the dungeon must not have been bigger than 14 x 12 x 4 feet. There is no sanitary provision. Only some water for the women who the soldiers required to be clean before they raped them. The guide, a willowy Senegalese man with a piercing voice, leads us into more dungeons, before we head out into the courtyard and visit the church, like Elmina castle, stands above the dungeons where centuries of abuse and human cruelty took place. Our guide informs us that it's the same church which the Pope apologised for the role the Catholic Church played in slavery, and points to one of the cells that Nelson Mandela looked into and wept as it reminded him of what happened when he was imprisoned on Robben Island during the Apartheid years. And soon we all be near tears as the guide brought us to the gates of no return; that gates where the slaves would be led to the boats to take them to the big ships and never to see Africa again. We all climbed the wall and looked out and watched the sea, apparently not willing to tell any stories, well, not until the moon came out and gave her permission. One of my colleagues passed me the bottle of water, and I stood at the gates and poured libation saying the words: 'For all those that have gone before, and for those that suffered during slavery; for those that perished in the sea, for all those abused, for all those who died on the journey, for all those who were separated from their families, for all those who died on the long arduous journey to the slave dungeons, for those who were cut down by disease and malnutrition, and for those who the history books will never recall, we offer this libation in your memory and to heal the pain that still lingers.' I called the names of the Akan people, the Ewe, the Yoruba, the Hausa, the Igbo, the Ashanti, the Fulani, the Ga. But then we were disturbed. A tourist, a black family push their way to the gates of no return and the daughter poses; the father takes out his camera and takes a picture, as if at a beauty spot. We look on incredulously, but carry on. My fellow travellers also pour libation, before we walk back to the courtyard where we interrupt another guide, this time the actual curator who is addressing another group of tourists where he is in mid flow, telling them of the horrors. He speaks through a softly spoken interpreter who explains to the English speaking tourists, but when the curator finished, almost wiping his mouth like a lion, a hand went up from the listeners and voice said, "Can you tell us about the role Africans themselves played in the slave trade.' It is the question that some Europeans ask to deflect any serious apology or atonement. And it is a question full of violence because it accepts no responsibility, not only what happened but to look into one's soul for answers and atonement. The curator, a giant of a man, took one big step forward and started giving his storm of an answer in French. The gist of his reply was that during the Second World War, the French had traitors; those that worked with the Nazi's but European history does not brand French people as conspirators. A great cheer went up from the majority of the listeners making one sense that they too are tired of this question.

We sailed back to the mainland, emotionally tired from sun and history. The programme was over and so was my visit to Senegal, yet it started something in me; a quest to know more about Great Africa, and the long term effects of having families having gone through *The Gates of No Return*; almost all never to see their families again, never to see Africa again and some never to see the New World they were being taken to.

Notes on Building Family

The family values, the standards of behaviour that a family applies to itself in pursuing its So family is subject to change but not random change and we therefore have to look at the natural cycles and rhythms that families go through and the planning they need to undertake so that these cycles and rhythms are understood and utilised to the benefit of family and community. We also have to look at the synchronisation of this multiplicity of cycles which is really key to families learning about family. If there is ignorance about these changes then there is fear, poor planning and break down of family.

What are these cycles that permeate family life? There are many but we can mention a few: the woman's cycle, the water cycle, the lunar cycle, the solar cycle, the human cycle and even the economic cycle. How have these cycles affected Yvonne and Sebastian. Did they prepare, did they put in place a structure that allowed for these cycles. Is Yvonne preparing for her mother's passing or will it just happen and she'll be in a state of grief. Has Sebastian prepared for his role as an elder, or is he simply seeking positions of power outside of his community unaware that he should have had the training to play a key role in the development of his community.

Though he has no teacher to teach him about these cycles taking place in his family, Theo, by trying to rebel against the school system is studying revolution and is beginning to understand that to have something new and vibrant and young you have to understand the death of the old, which is simply another transition.

Family Wisdom
On Cycles of Life

- **Realise that the cycle of death is an achievement and a beginning.**

- **Nature is nothing but millions of wonderful cycles, each with its own magic and beauty, so we should all take time to observe this glory especially when our minds are mad with anger.**

- **Each family should plan for the arrival of a new soul and the departure of an old one with the same joy despite the tears.**

- **It is said that before a soul comes to earth it agrees the path its life will take and each moment there are hints of this path with revelations we call incidents.**

- **Planning is living in the moment which is all the preparation we need.**

Stage 9

Family Counselling and Wisdom of the Elders

Theme of Inquiry:

- The sharing and embedding of wisdom in the family and community.
- Understanding higher education

Ntesi: the symbol of wisdom and knowledge

Ntesie is the symbol of wisdom and knowledge and reminds us to meditate on information in order to gain insight.

This symbol is useful to our inquiry as it encourages us to reflect on family and education, and to make this reflection and meditating central to our learning.

Theo's Diary

Mum and dad have broken up for good I think. I've lost contact with Biko, Toussaint and Malcolm; and the others can't even remember their African names. It's all sad.

The dreams don't come anymore. Amma has gone.

On the news they keep showing boys being killed. I see it here every day. I see boys excluded. Sometimes their parents take them back to Nigeria so that they can get a better education and be away from the knives and guns. Sometimes they just take themselves way from school and just never come back.

I've decided to get my gang back together again. I remember dreaming about Amma and seeing her make a kind of altar and she kept singing to the altar until it gave her her wish. I'll do the same.

Started studying hard now that I realise that I'm going to be a different kind of revolutionary. I'm going to teach children about Toussaint, and Biko, and Garvey, and Lumumba and all the others. I'm so excited now.The teachers don't know what has come over me. I realise that I have it all in me. I realise that I can fly like Amma. I realise that I am a genius.

On Wisdom

It was wisdom that Toussaint, Garvey and Biko tried to instil in the people that followed them, but for now we have to use a more limited definition. The Concise English Dictionary defines wisdom as *accumulated learning; knowledge; the thoughtful application of learning; insight; good sense; the teachings of ancient wise men and women.* This definition is useful to us as we continue our inquiry in unlocking the genius of the family and community. We therefore now have to look at how we can embed wisdom into the community so that resolution of conflict, the ability of the family and community to resolve all issues is possible, but for such an achievement to be the reality, this wisdom and higher learning must be embedded in all aspects of life and taught to the community in stages, depending on age, maturity and willingness to learn. Later, we will look at eastern Nigeria and how this sharing of wisdom was/ is conducted. This sharing of wisdom was at critical interventions; times of birth, adolescence, adulthood, marriage, eldership and becoming an ancestor. There was a framework which in effect meant that the home was the first training ground, the village square the second and the community the third. The wisdom of the community had to be imparted in a variety of ways; many entertaining, some not. Proverbs, stories, songs, epic tales, heroic poetry, praise songs, dance, theatre and masquerade: all were used. The wisdom,

the guidance meant that each family, each community knew what to expect from each man, woman and child. It informed all behaviour. Before we look at Onitsha in Nigeria, let us look at a popular type of education: family learning and philosophy for children, both of which are being promoted in schools, but both of which will only have limited impact as the school system is not really integral with the community, therefore education, guidance and wisdom are always external.

In the Black African community I see arguments, ignorant stances, breakdown of relationships, leadership betrayals and so on due to the framework of wisdom not being in existence and this framework of course starts in the mind. Sadly, we do not see this and so when a family is about to break up we don't go to an elder, we go to a professional; a marriage counsellor, a lawyer for a divorce. There is little intergenerational learning, sharing; forums that allow the most experienced in the community, the elders to pass on their skills, knowledge and wisdom to the least experienced in the community. In the case of Yvonne, her mother is simply a spectator who reads between the lines each time her daughter writes to her or they speak on the telephone. Yvonne's mother's wisdom is an accumulation of good practice that needs to be inherited by the next generation. This is self-sufficiency. However, we can look at a few models that can raise our awareness, allow us to develop these programmes in our homes, churches, mosques and temples, and start putting up the scaffold of this framework.

What is Family Learning

Family learning is when parents, grand-parents and children learn together, or when parents engage in parenting workshops, or any learning experience that involves family or family learning about family. These sessions can be held when the parents and children are in the same class, or work independently and then come together to share a learning experience. These workshops are best delivered informally, in an open space free of the traditional cluttered classroom that often does not allow for physical exploration. Whilst family learning is growing in popularity models of typical practice are normally presented to the Black community in terms of white middle class literacy and numeracy workshops. The success that we have had in family learning has been the complete opposite. We have based our family learning on the book *How to Unlock Your Child's Genius.* The literacy and numeracy, which are of course useful, are embedded, but the main themes are diet and learning, educational management in the home, how your child learns etc; these are presented within a cultural context. The approach to family learning that I favour is as follows:

1. Learning is for family and community development
2. Learning is theme based rather than subject based
3. Learning is through group and individual inquiry
4. Learning is interactive and culturally rich
5. Learning has a sense of cultural heritage
6. Learning promotes critical thinking

A little while back I was asked to deliver a family learning programme at a school in north London; one of those schools that are under special measures, that have a mix of hard working staff and staff that blame the estates, homes and poverty from which the children come. When I first arrived at the school and walked into the building there was a sense of tiredness. It was a school tired of emails from senior officials, targets, strategies, training, meetings, paperwork, inspection reports, specialists. It was a tired and untidy school, but with a few staff who cared, and I would later learn that it was a school that was saved by parents who, deeply cared about the achievement, development and dreams of their children. The officials had got it wrong. This was not an underachieving school. This was a fabulous school that had an underachieving system of education imposed on the community. Sometimes, when a system continuously fails the families with children who so badly need a good education, parts of that same system blames the families. In the workshops the parents read stories and the children listened; the children read stories and the parents listened. They drew family portraits, they did arts and craft together; the parents talked about their school life when they were growing up; the children questioned them. They did movement exercises together, we all shared plates of nutritious food and each week the families told me how things had changed for them.

They visited the library more. They purchased more educational and cultural resources for the home. They read together more. It was not only the children that were free; the parents seemed to excel in being able to simply talk to other parents and soon I noticed that other teachers on their way out of the building as they set off home would hang around, watching curiously. One teacher, who would look on with a critical smile, eventually came up to me and asked about the approach I was using. When I explained she bought one of my books. But not everyone is impressed with the Genius Method. Often, observers will question why I teach neuroscience to children, diet and nutrition, financial literacy, Black history, parenting skills, emotional literacy. In recent years I have noticed how this approach is being adopted more and more as the more innovative Headteachers try to engage in teaching about learning more. By the end of the course, we had achieved 85% retention, excellent attendance and the school asked us to come back and run the same programme. Since that time I have been a great advocate not only of parenting programmes (parents only), but family learning which allows parents not only to work with the children but build an even more supportive relationship with their children. These opportunities have to be routinely created in the home, church, mosque, youth club, in the school and in the community for intergenerational guidance to take place. When we have arrived at the this point then we need to consider organising of this family learning and implementing it effectively so we achieve high quality teaching and learning.

However, we must remember that real family learning is about families of the African Diaspora learning about families of Africans on the continent, and vice versa, and what we can both do to help one another. This is central to our inquiry and is what we are partly engaged in.

Family Games: Oware

Oware - The African Strategy Game

It is thought that Oware originated from Sudan (Upper Nile) 3600 years ago when African accountants and engineers made mathematical calculations, using tablets that had depressions in them. Writers have even called Oware the first computer.
Oware is played in many parts of Africa. In South Africa it is called Ohoro, in East Africa it is called Mankala and in West Africa it is called Oware or Ayo. Oware came to the Caribbean in the 17th century during slavery.

Not so long ago I had an interesting conversation with a woman who runs one of the main Oware societies and she told me that each time she visits a school to conduct a workshop on Oware with the children she finds that the Black child who is underachieving, with so-called behavioural problems, is almost always the one who is best at the game. It is as if something happens to them spiritually when they have to concentrate, plan and strategise. Perhaps it is because they are being asked to think in such a way that demands something of them and they immediately recognise that they have ownership of the game. For me personally, the Oware games are works of art; they are African sculptures and every African home should have one.

How to Play Oware

- The main object of the game is to capture more stones/seeds (48) than your opponents.
- The board consists of six cells, or holes. Each player owns a row. Sometimes there are two extra cells to keep captured seeds/stones.
- Each cell has 4 stones/seeds.
- The game starts by one of the players picking up all the stones/seeds from a cell on his/her side, and moving anti-clockwise, dropping a seed into each consecutive cell.
- The players alternate.
- If a player has many seeds and they go right round the board and return to the original cell, then the cell where the seeds were picked up from is missed.
- When a player creates a cell with four seeds, they capture those seeds by picking them all up.
- The game ends when a player finds that he/she has no more pieces to move, that is no more cells of four can be made, or all of the cells are empty. The pieces are added and the player with the most seeds is the winner.

How to Unlock Your Family's Genius

Oware: A Mathematical Mind Game

Oware is a useful mind game because it:

1. Develops concentration skills
2. Develops thinking skills
3. Develops problem solving skills
4. Develops mental arithmetic
5. Develops patience
6. Develops visual strategies

The benefit of family games are enormous as they promote conversation, a sense of togetherness as well as teaching thinking skills. Many of the computer games targeted at children isolate them from the family, don't develop language skills and of course do not involve any movement skills or convey any cultural knowledge. Perhaps even more than this is the intergenerational learning that oware promotes. Last year (2007) Ebony Education was at the Nigerian Carnival at Burgess Park in south London. We had our usually prospectuses, flyers, books and information sheets spread out on the table, but for decoration I had brought along some Oware boards. Every family that went past our table, young or old, immediately smiled calling out 'ayo, ayo' or one of its other names, reminiscing about their childhood as they grabbed the 'seeds' and, with no invitation, began to play. As they played I would start up a conversation with them and they would tell me how they used to play with their grandfather, grandmother or parents. This is family learning in the home.

In an article that appeared in *The Guardian* newspaper (25.3.08)) headlined, Board games 'boost early maths skills', it notes that researchers Professor Seigler and Dr Geetha Ramani of Carneighie Mellon University, found that playing numerical board games with low income nursery children improved the children's performance in mathematics. Whilst the research is with numerical board games we can see that the mental counting and subtracting in Oware may well have similar effects. This study is also important based on earlier research which shows that the differences of children in the first year of school continue into secondary school.

There is art, skill and joy in these family games, and we deskill and de-culturalise the home when we leave it to the television or computer to baby-sit or child-mind or entertain the family. Not only this, the skills needed for the family business, the socialising skills and the people skills are developed here and we should not allow them to be lost.

One day Theo, like thousands of other children, will leave school. Will he be a child with a mind schooled in strategising, problem solving, or will he just think in a reactionary way? Family games are important in developing thinking skills of the family and creating opportunities for family learning.

Teaching and Learning

Essentially teaching and learning comes down to the relationship between learner and teacher and what philosophy the teacher and community bring into the place of learning. It is this relationship where trust, respect and motivation are built and such qualities can only be truly brought out when education is matched to family, culture and empowerment.

What is important in the learning experience?

1. Although planning is key to any lesson, be prepared to improvise if the learners take the lesson in a completely different and unexpected direction. Follow their interest and thinking and learn from it.
2. Draw from your own and the learner's experience.
3. Draw on and stimulate the learner's and your own imagination and creativity by introducing, or accommodating, the unexpected, the unusal.
4. Make the session learner centred, that is, respond to their learning needs which is not always easy when you have a narrow curriculum or you are preparing the learner for exams, tests, assessments and more.

The Lesson

General and obvious aims which are not always obvious to the learner:

The lesson structure:

1. An imaginative introduction, perhaps with something tactile or a kinaesthetic experience like role play.
2. Questions and answers that naturally flow into a group discussion
3. A mix of group and individual work using varied learning styles, and vary the learning pace which can be done through the encouragement of excitement and reflection.
4. End the lesson with group reflection that also acts as a check for learning.
5. Encourage independent learning, and self-directed learning depending on the learner.
6. Homework might encourage family support/involvement in some way, like the learner questioning their family on a topic or their experience. This extension work is important in making the rest of the family not in the session feel that they are included and that the curriculum is for the community.

Ideas for teaching:

1. Make the lesson interesting, fun and challenging.
2. Make the learner and teacher think during the lesson, with not only straightforward question and answer sessions but with discussion and reflection.
3. Make the learning space a community space whereby parents, volunteers and family can come and contribute to the whole experience of learning.
4. Try and encourage group support and peer assessment, so you end up with a class of teachers and learners.
5. Differentiate between learners and use this as a way to develop group support, that is, a more confident learner might be able to support a less confident learner, and the camaraderie that this builds then lends itself to an important life skill. Learners learn from one another and peer teaching can be effective depending on the mix of the group. What is key is that we emphasise the sharing of knowledge. Currently, there is too great an emphasis on individualism and personalised learning in education; a trend that everyone seems to mimic with little thought. Communities that have gained power over their own destines have done so through collective action; this is one of the things that should be at the heart of teaching and learning.

How to Unlock Your Family's Genius

Teacher reflection:

- Did I manage to draw out the leadership skills in the learners?
- Did I really manage to make them think, and think critically?
- Did I vary the pace of learning according to their natural learning pace?
- Did I allow them room to learn and explore the topic or theme in their own way in their own cultural context?

Resources

Resources can be key in helping to inspire the learners when they are used as stimulus materials. Additionally, resources are an important part of teaching and can give the learner that much more independence.
Do not over rely on resources because they have a habit of not working at key moments, and the human interaction between teacher and learner is of much greater and longer lasting value than a student working at a computer.

It is also worth noting, that whilst the education industry has gone mad with new technology, natural and everyday items can also be used to aid and stimulate the learning experience. For example, in the teaching of science, plants, insects, nature walks are inspirational. Personally, I have found imaginative storytelling the best teaching resource you can have. However, not so long ago I attend a seminar in South Africa on the underachievement of disadvantaged groups in the country, and one small teacher stood up complaining and lambasting the government official about the lack of resources, that is, computers. Yes, computers are important but to raise achievement you need the will, the correct philosophy and a true commitment for the learner and the community they come from and that means understanding family.

Philosophy of the Community: The Modern Griots

There are now many initiatives all over the country in both the UK and America and elsewhere where children are being taught philosophy and being encouraged to develop their critical thinking skills. This recent trend is a very old system of youth development, but is being increasingly adopted to counter the traditional education approach that just 'banks' or 'stuffs' information and facts into the minds of children without allowing them the opportunity to learn through inquiry. Edward De Bono, Mathew Lipman and Carol McGuinness have advocated the teaching of thinking skills in the modern classroom, with a view to improving creative thinking, critical thinking, proactive and reactive thinking and emotional intelligence, that is, how emotions affect thinking. For Theo and his 'gang', their thinking was increasingly on how to survive; how to out smart Dr Seamus and escape being labelled. The dominant emotion affecting this thinking has been fear. It was a pity that the parents of these children didn't see the long term benefits of mind games like Oware, and didn't realise that they, as parent-teachers, had an even more important role than that of the classroom teacher in teaching their children not only survival skills, but thinking skills that would make them thrive as young men in the world.

Children of the Square

In conversations I have had with elders in the Nigerian community, it has been pointed out to me that the traditional education system, which was replaced by the colonial system of educating children and young people, was that youths were educated holistically. In Eastern Nigeria, in Onitsha, children are divided into 'age-sets' and it is in these 'age-sets' that the children are educated, often being referred to as 'children of the square' and these children must keep the village square clean as well as performing other communal duties. At this age, six or so, these age sets also go hunting lizards, learn wrestling, fighting, and learn how to stand up for their rights, how to take criticism and how to take praise from their elders. The children increasingly learn independence and as they grew bigger they have to build their own hut on the outside of the village, which is known as, 'the Kings House'. This initiation begins at about six years and is normally complete by the age of fifteen years. In these 'age-sets' the youths learn the secret knowledge; they have to take part in festivals, burial processions, organise meetings and as they grow older learn the arts of argument and oratory.

It might be said that Theo and his friends have not gone through any such initiation system but there seems to be a natural need, a natural inclination to create temporary families during key and strategic transitions in life. The outside world has little insight into the lives of these young Black boys as they brace themselves for adulthood.

The Griot and the Harp

We also know that these children, and the community at large, were surrounded by teachers in different guises; parents, immediate family, extended family, teachers, uncles, aunts, but very visible in West Africa are the griots. Griotees and griottes were/are historians, advisors, geneaologists, messengers and praise singers. On occasions, they have been called living libraries. Griots perform many functions in traditional and modern African society but one can say that their role is to make people think about their history and prepare for the next generations. Legend has it that Fasseke Kouyate became the first griot in 1235 after Soundiata had become King (who later went on to found the Mali Empire). With their harp, or another instrument, they sing about moral issues or they counsel the community or an individual or even warn an individual.

In Ousmane Sembene's classic film, Xala (1974) on post-colonial Africa, we see an attempt to carry on the tradition of the griot in modern film, for Sembene uses the oral tradition of the griots with its hidden meanings; his characters are types rather than individuals, e.g., the trickster type. Like the griot Semebene focuses on greed, selfishness, vanity and waste which are common themes in African tales. In Xala, as with the work of the griot, the serious is presented as comedy, whilst songs and proverbs are used. This makes the work accessible to the masses. Franz Fanon, in his great work, *The Wretched of the Earth* , writes about the role of the Black artist in the African struggle of liberation:

> …the oral tradition, - stories, epics and songs of the
> people – which formerly were filed away as set pieces are
> now beginning to change. The storytellers who used to relate
> inert episodes now bring them alive and introduce into them
> modifications…From 1952 – 3 on, the storytellers, who were
> before that time stereotyped and tedious to listen to, completely
> overturned their traditional methods of storytelling and the
> contents of the tales (p195).

Clearly we can see that wisdom has to have a context for the people, it has to be in a form that is accessible and in a narrative that is of the people. Such an artist who has achieved this and who was and still is, a griot of the people, is Bob Marley.

Stage Nine

How to Unlock Your Family's Genius

The Chair of Bob Marley: Professor of Healing and Music

Bob Marley was born Robert Nesta Marley in St Ann's Jamaica in 1945 on 6th February to a black mother and white father, though he didn't grow up or know his father. During the 1970s and 1980s he was to become the Caribbean's biggest international music artist and one of the greatest singer-songwriters of all time. Many have written about Marley, but when we venture into the spiritual fight of the Africans of Jamaica, we begin to understand that the genius of Marley's work stems from a collective experience of a people fighting oppression; psychologically, physically and spiritually. His 500 compositions were from the rebellious experience of the militant Maroons, and from the incredible courage of Jamaica's hero Paul Bogle, and from the infectious Black nationalism from Marcus Garvey and the inspiration of the Rastafarian movement. Whether Marley was conscious of this or not, this might be why he wrote *Natural Mystic:*

> *There's a natural mystic blowing through the air,*
> *If you listen carefully you will hear,*
> *This will be the first trumpet,*
> *Might as well be the last,*
> *Many more will have to suffer,*
> *Many more will have to die – don't ask me why.*

So if we look at Marley's life, not in the typical genre of autobiography, we begin to see what crystallised in his work was this collective spiritual experience; that he is in many ways the traditional and modern griot; the awakener of the masses, the teacher, the storyteller, the poet.

Marley first grew up in rural Jamaica amidst the knowledge of African-Jamaican folklore and folk-medicine; amidst a people that healed themselves with bush-tea and bush-baths and proverbs. I am not Jamaican, but I have grown up amongst people of Jamaica and I have always admired their spirit of rebellion that manifests itself in many ways. To me, all Jamaicans are Maroons; those escaped slaves who fled to the most remote and inaccessible regions of Jamaica. From these remote settlements they launched guerrilla attacks on plantations and freed enslaved Africans, and took food provisions. From these remote areas they kept a look out for the British Redcoats, and when they saw them they blew their abeng horns to warn the Maroon communities, and then they attacked the Redcoats and chanted Marley's future lyrics: *Ambush In the Night*, which they sang with wicked irony in their voice as the great Nanny of the Maroons laughed with a spiteful cackle in her voice. This abeng horn was heard by Toussaint L'Ouverture, Shaka Zulu, Marcus Garvey and the spirit of Marley.

Though the Maroons fought gallantly and enslaved Africans of Jamaica won their freedom, they were still left in poverty under colonial rule. Their conditions were harsh. So, in 1865 Paul Bogle and many more Blacks marched to Morant Bay on 11th October to protest to the colonial authorities. Baron von Ketelhodt, in charge of the colonial government, ordered that they dispersed, but they refused. The Baron ordered his forces to fire at the crowd. Seven of the protesters were killed. Bogle and the others then fought back, killing Baron von Ketelhodt and other whites. A massacre then followed, leaving 450 Blacks dead. Later, 600 Blacks were flogged; a thousand huts belonging to the poor were destroyed and Paul Bogle was hanged at the Courthouse. To understand the rebellion in Marley's lyrics, to understand Marley's militancy, his hollering, you have to understand what made Paul Bogle, who was better off than most Blacks at the time, march to the Courthouse. You have to understand the persistence of this *natural mystic*: understand what possessed Marley at night as he watched Jah-Moon and the Dogon stars. Surrounded by the ancestors Marley would write *Small Axe:*

If you are the big tree,
We are the small axe.
Sharpened to cut you down,
Ready to cut you down…

Marley was born under the 'Jah-Moon' of the Rastafarians. His cradle, the thick tangle of Akan traditions; Marley, born at a time when the great Pan-Africanist leader, Marcus Garvey, had supposedly fallen. But the energy of the Universal Negro Improvement Association (UNIA) was still strong. In 1929 Garvey prophesised that a Black King would be crowned. Many people in Jamaica saw the crowning of Haile Selassi (1898 – 1975) of Ethiopia as this king. In 1940 Howell founded a Rastafarian community in Jamaica. By the time Marley became more inspired by Rastafarianism, Garvey's talk of self-pride, self-reliance was joined by the militancy of Malcolm X and the vision of Martin Luther King. It was Marley who kept these voices alive when he sang *Redemption Song:*

Emancipate yourself from mental slavery,
None but ourselves can free our minds,
Have no fear from atomic energy,
Cause none of them can stop the time…

It was these great heroes and heroines that informed Marley's work; in each line he wrote are the African-Caribbean proverbs, folktales, folklore, rituals and beliefs. Let us not only create the Bob Marley Chair of Music, but let us rediscover so many great ancestors who gave so much which we have forgotten. Let us use their examples of courage and plant their wisdom in our home and community; let us be up beat and sing Marley's One Love song and call out the names of our heroes: Toussaint L'Ouverture, Paul Bogle, Nanny of the Maroons, Nat Turner, Denmark Vesey, Harriet Tubman, Sojourner Truth, Marcus Garvey, Paul Robeson, Claudia Jones, Malcolm X, Martin Luther King, Patrice Lumumba, Kwame Nkrumah, John Coltrane, Robert Sobukwe, Steve Biko, Rosa Parks, Nina Simone. Let us teach our children about the wisdom that these great people struggled to learn. These are our griots, so our children like Theo should not have to start from scratch in putting together Black History programmes that can truly empower youth, gender and family.

Family Counselling: a time for healing

A long time ago, a good friend of mine who I studied with, took his life. Talk at his funeral said that he had everything ahead of him; had studied hard, had a steady partner, but for some reason became more depressed than people realised and hanged himself in his own home. I remember him laughing, cracking jokes at my 21st birthday party where he was the DJ whilst chatting up the girls that flocked around his music deck and good looks. Then there was another friend, this time not so close who took his life when his business went bust. After him an ex-teacher; a once strong Black woman, who was passionate about helping our youngsters, took her life and crushed the dreams of her mother and many friends. An English teacher who accepted no nonsense from the children and so I had naively assumed that she took no nonsense from life. I was wrong. These are sad stories of family members who needed help; and we all have these sad stories, and in quiet moments we wonder what we could have done. These are extreme cases, and often family members drift away after an argument and sometimes never return, or bad feelings linger for much too long. There needs to be someone in the family, or a close friend or relative who can heal these wounds, whether it is of grief, broken relationship, divorce, or the stress and strains of debt, of unemployment. There needs to counselling at different levels, at different times depending of the seriousness of the situation. When we need help few of us cry out. We try and be brave because people think we are doing well; people think we are strong, successful and so we present ourselves to the world with this 'brave' facade.

Stage Nine

How to Unlock Your Family's Genius

Families have to be brave and deal with breakdown of relationships or any other problems that occur. We can of course run to experts and I am not advising against this, but there are experts in the community who can help, but often this is not the case because there is no framework, there is no family network to fall upon in the bad times and good times, so we ignore this great family capital that can support and enrich our family. The family network is simply other families and support groups that may be linked vertically and horizontally, which can offer guidance and help in a social framework where genuine relationships can be built up. Traditionally family counselling focuses on relationships, parenting, emotional disorders and supporting families that might have experienced some breakdown or disturbance. These families will normally seek the expert, who, in the typical counselling session would give 'expert advice'. With the family network, this expert is a member of the family. They might be an elder, or someone who has accumulated years of experience in the family, who know the family politics, cultural protocols and experience in dealing with the family. It might be that their expertise is in not being the classic expert, but show the family their own strengths in addressing the issue. Often, when a family come to see me on an educational matter I notice other dynamics within the family. On a few occasions the child, normally a girl, hates the parent because the parent has made them feel that they are ugly. Ugly in this sense is really referring to their skin colour. The child now hates themselves and the parent, yet they are really also calling out for love. I find that when I am doing workshops with families there is something deeper going on. The workshop is really for families to rediscover love, to have the opportunity to love. This is not of course to say that Black families do not love, but the everyday pressures do not always allow that space. Here counselling is not the classic setting of a few family members and the 'expert' but simply a carefully worked out workshop that allows families the opportunity to explore themselves in a play/learning environment. What I have found that works best is for there to be an initial interview where the family talk. Usually the parent does most of the talking and the child simply listens uneasily. I then allow each one to talk with me on a one to one basis then bring them both back together. Whilst I can recommend strategies for a more harmonious relationship, what I do is to invite the parent, and sometimes the child to a workshop that I run which allows them to explore home life supported by other families. The feedback that I get is that the sharing of experiences with other families is what helps them heal; gives them strength and most important of all, simple and practical strategies to improve the home life which is normally associated with family health, family wealth and family love.

Often in the media they will loosely use the term Black-on-Black violence; this term does not pinpoint the real issues that leads to a young Black man taking the life of another. Before this stage is reached there is a total falsification of reality that a young person is confronted with. At the heart of this false reality is self-hate which is almost systematically delivered to Black families, and those who do not deconstruct this reality of self-hate end up acting out behaviour patterns in their homes that destroys their families, their relationships and leads to an almost permanent state of confusion and inner turmoil. To address this, there needs to be an inquiry into Black family life in an individual and collective setting, and in a culturally enriched environment. Theo's parents, Yvonne and Sebastian, were unaware that they had, during their own marital tussles, created a home of self-hate, hurt and argument, offering Theo no strategy to deal with it.

On Elderhood

Recently, I have had to attend the funerals of my parents' generation: uncles, aunts, cousins, old friends of the family. I have sat in a cold church, amongst relatives, and listened to eulogies on old Caribbeans who came over on the big cargo ships; took the worst jobs and abuse, and raised families on pitiful wages, some of which they sent back home to more families who did not travel to England. The plight of so many elderly in the community is wasted. They retire and we assign no special role for them, so their skills, their knowledge, their wisdom is lost. Some I have spoken to feel bitter; they feel that the community has not appreciated what they have gone through to raise a family, to work, to put food on the table. To have survived in such hostile circumstances. How can

we change this situation, so that this wisdom is a key part of our community development? Well, we might consider some of the following:

- Establish elder committees in our churches, mosques and community groups
- Provide additional training to elders when they retire so that they might provide a more social or entrepreneurial service to the community if they so wished
- Encourage and invite our elders into our Saturday schools, home clubs, schools; for example, to help children in their reading or maths.
- Establish befriending schemes and food cooperative services as loneliness and poverty are, unfortunately, major concerns to the elderly, especially those who have been abandoned by their sparse families
- Establish health and fitness workshops in our communities to maintain and improve health and health awareness
- Help our elders in preparing or updating their wills and financial arrangements for increased healthcare

Many years ago when I went to Grenada I stayed with an elderly woman who had been very close to my mother when she stayed in England. She was a determined and intelligent woman, who, despite a hard marriage had always maintained her optimism in life which was epitomised by her sweet beige hat and handbag that she wore to church that she dutifully attended every Sunday morning. One particular Sunday however, she did not go to church, but stayed in the house. I sat on my bed with my notepad having listened to the heavy rain fall and was half waiting for the muse of the house to return when I over heard this old woman praying. It was full of a kind of humour, dignity and sweetness that reminded me of how people lived close to the land, a poem that could have easily been written by Theo's grandmother.

Of Rum and Water

I first started thinking about eldership and ancesterhood when I saw my father, uncles and other men from the islands, take a drink, and watched them do a little ritual that I would later find out was called, "*Wetting the Ground,*" where they would say, 'for all those who have gone before' before pouring a little water and rum on the ground, then swigging back a glass of Jack Iron (local strong rum). This little ritual would be performed at stone feasts when the head stone was laid a year or so after someone had died, or at the 'Parents Plate', or when visiting a grave. It was a respectful display of remembrance, of honouring. But there was more to it than this. Implicit in the way they handled themselves, in how the whole community accepted their authority was governance. Clearly, their roles, their routines, stemmed from Africa, but they managed to function in this way even in colonial times and before, when as men, they would have seen their women beaten and raped and they too would be beaten and mutilated in front of their families. These were deep scars that were healed by a dance called Big Drum, where all the villages of the island, some of whom would have certain tribal dominance, would gather and sing songs, and beat their drums. Both here in England, and back in Carriacou I watched these elders pour their rum and water; I watched the elder women cook food in the big pots. I watched them arrange proceedings on the 9th and 40th night after someone had died. I watched them dance The Callendar, (Congo),The Cud (Igbo) and perform Stick Fight Dance. They led their families. They had a role. Years later, in England, I would see the elderly of my parents land, sick, weak and often lonely. Some would be crippled by strokes, poverty, high blood pressure, diabetes; illnesses that so cripples the African-Caribbean community. Perhaps more than these illnesses is that they have no role; no leading of the family, no formalised eldership.

There are two special relationships that the elders have; one with their grandchildren and the other with the ancestors. In the Buddhist and Kamitic traditions they both have literature which details the journey that the elders take when they die. These books are known as The Tibetian Book of the Dead and The Pert Em Heru (The Egyptian Book of the Dead). Both books give guidance to the elders or anyone else on the journey taken at the point of death. They detail the withdrawal of consciousness, the handling of the body, the journey of the spirit, the confrontation of the negativities of the mind, the brilliant light that guides the spirit, the world beyond, rebirth; the interconnection of life and death. In the African tradition at all stages of life, birth, puberty, adulthood, marriage, parenthood and eldership, individuals are prepared, they are trained; they are informed of their responsibilities. One of these responsibilities is their last wish which might be expressed in a will.

The Family Will: planning for the future

The will is about your last wishes, how you, hopefully, want your family and community to prosper. Also, the will can be about how the deceased wants their surviving family to keep the memory of the deceased alive; how to maintain the standards that the deceased built the family on and this is traditionally done in Black communities by regular visiting of the grave, maintaining an altar and burning candles at key times of the year in memory of the deceased. Once, in the Caribbean, I was taken to an old cemetery for research purposes, only to find many groups of relatives still cleaning old gravestones; still talking to old Tantie, old Uncle and to this and that cousin. This wasn't morbid. It was part of the healing process, but also it was keeping something alive: perhaps the family values that the deceased nurtured.

Family Feuds

When someone makes a will they have to be mindful that they could actually be leaving behind a document that sets the family fighting each other. Many family arguments or feuds stem from families fighting over property; fighting over who will inherit the family business or land, which then leads to jealousy. All this happens at the absolute worst time for the family when there is grief, shock and deep sadness, and sometimes regret, with the family members often not realising that they are still grieving when it comes time to read the will. In reality, what has happened is that the family has lost its anchor; that authority that they have had all their lives. So their needs to be a kind of succession plan and for the family to discuss who will take on certain roles that will give the family its anchor. If possible it is advisable when making a will to be fare to all the children and share the estate out equally.

Yvonne was unaware that these thoughts were what were going through the mind of her mother who wanted to leave something for her children and grandchildren. The little piece of land that Grandma had was important to her as she wanted Theo to come over to Jamaica, to get up early in the morning as the cock crowed and feed the chickens, and move the goats and watch the morning sun. She simply wanted him to experience nature; to understand the cycles of life; the magic of Nature's seasons, and all the education that this would bring. For her she wanted to leave more than instructions in a legal document, she wanted to a real gift of life that would help this troubled family.

Have Pity

Lord, me is a good woman
Me soak me peas,
Me season me meat,
Feed me fowl,
And sleep never catch me in church yet!
Lord, have pity 'pon me soul.

Lord, I still keep mummy picture on me mantelpiece
To remind me to inherit her wisdom;

Yes, mummy, who you graciously take;
Mummy who quarrel still in she grave;
Telling children not to steal from mango tree
If dem want pick fruit from Tree when dem big.
Lord, pass some pity 'pon me soul.

Lord, is I that teach dem rascals in church,
Use family shame to give them licks,
Take my splashing young frock to dry dem eye
When I catch dem naughtiness and dem start cry.
Is me, frail Miss Betty, so leave me some pity please.

Remember who carry fresh food to dying Tantie,
Who bring crumple dollar for preacher;
Who sing two hymn at harvest service,
Who walk to church with sick foot,
Is who?
Forget 'bout your pity!

And when me breath finally done;
When only weeds and old friends trouble me stone,
When me humble memory just conjure smile,
And people me help remember me good;
Well, let dem say:
Lord, have pity 'pon she sweet soul.
Amen.

Writings of an Educationalist Who Went to Robben Island

I flew into South Africa on Thursday 12th June 2008 to attend the Cape Town Book Fair. The city was already tired; people were preparing to sleep and the sea front was cluttered with boats and yachts that already closed their eyes for the night. I had booked a booth with other Black publishers from the UK, and it was there that I networked for four days; talking to librarians, booksellers, wholesalers, distributors, families and journalists. Opposite our booth was a large children's area; decorated with balloons, colourful toys and teddy bears. There were numerous activities that took place; storytelling, singing of well known nursery rhymes, only a few being traditional Xhosa or Zulu. Authors of children's books also came and spoke and read from their books, often tantalising the children with their tales. One lady came who was from some k ind of organisation that were organising Nelson Mandela's 90th birthday. In a school teacher's voice she told the children about Mandela; that he was a very kind man who loved them, who loved all people of the world, that he had a very kind wife and so on. Slowly I began to realise that they had made Mandela into a kind of Father Christmas; completely depoliticising the whole liberation struggle. Yet, what this woman was trying to do was what large sections of the country seemed to be doing; talk of the real struggles that were still going on were often whispered about. No mention of Apartheid, racism, brutality, death squads, or even Steve Biko. All parents will tell you that there comes a time in the life of a child when they discover for themselves that Father Christmas does not exist. The children of South Africa will come to this moment and will they be prepared for the truth?

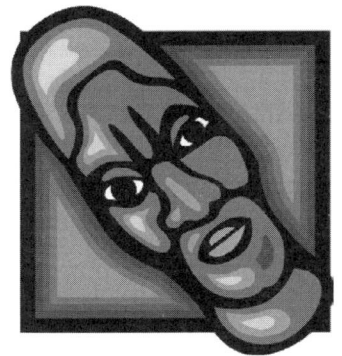

How to Unlock Your Family's Genius

It seemed that I had a million conversations with a million people, all of whom seemed to give me insight into this staggeringly beautiful and tragic country. I spoke to an old white returnee who told me that he had been a member of the ANC for over forty years but he was disillusioned with the party. I spoke to an Asian woman, who, forgetting that I was Black myself because of my English accent, made slightly derogatory comments about Black men. I spoke to people who were just interested in working with me to take advantage of the governments Black Economic Empowerment initiatives. I spoke to a Black South African woman who told me that the ideology of Apartheid was rampant but hidden in the country. I spoke to a white librarian who told me proudly of her universities work in archiving Black literature and oral history from all parts of Africa. I spoke to a Cape coloured who was angry at the rise in tuberculosis in the country. I spoke to others about unemployment, about the new so called black middle class; I spoke to another Asian woman who claimed that reverse racism was now operating in the country because blacks were being given jobs to hit quota figures. I continued to talk to people; to taxi drivers, hotel staff, lecturers, teachers, doctors, artists and business people. But sometimes you have to stop talking as truth has a way of revealing itself in the secrecy of silence. This happened to me when, the book fair now finished, I became a tourist again, and did what all tourists do when they come to Cape Town, I went to the infamous Robben Island where the racist Apartheid regime kept political prisoners.

I sailed on the Susan Kruger boat, as the rain and wind kept annoyingly sweeping across my face, with some sixty other tourists, who huddled over their digital cameras as they prepared to take that one important shot of Nelson Mandela's cell. In some ways it is here that our story starts, for on this same boat, political prisoners were actually taken, sick, not from the rocking vessel, but the rottenness that saw the small white minority, through violence, had held onto power. Finally, after some forty minutes or so we arrive on the island which, in many ways lives up to its name, for its landscape; flat and barren, is both austere and secretive. There is no bigger secret in what happened on this island of imprisonment which stretches back to the imprisonment and enslavement of the Indonesian people, than the imprisonment of Robert Subokwe (1924 – 1978), first political prisoner of Robben Island and the leader of the Pan African Congress (PAC) who led the fight against the oppressive anti-pass laws. Our guide was a well mannered ex-prisoner of the island whose smile, in the end, did not make his insight into the horrendous ordeals that the prisoners went through any less harrowing. The first stop on the tour was of Subokwe's house; a green house where, apparently, he lived under house arrest in total isolation. He had already distinguished himself by becoming Sough Africa's first Black university lecturer, but his political work saw him arrested. A touching story around his arrest is when he would be seen by other political prisoners, and on seeing him they would wave, make a salute with clenched fists, and he in return would pick up some earth from the ground, let it trickle down his fingers, a sign to the other prisoner that they are the sons of Africa. Later, fascinated by stories of this almost forgotten hero of Africa, I would speak to people who knew him and they would describe him as charismatic, brilliant and explain that he was the prisoner that the racist Apartheid regime could never really free. Known as *The Professor* to his followers, he died mysteriously aged fifty-four in 1978.

We continue our tour. Just like in Elmina Slave Castle and Cape Coast Slave Castle of Ghana, there is a church on Robben Island. Whilst people of one race suffered torture, imprisonment and near starvation, those of another race prayed to their god. This happens in places of imprisonment. We soon learn that these men had to be family to one another. The old prisoners helped the young ones and the young ones helped the old. They went on hunger strike together, broke stone in the hot sun together and took beatings together. It was in the quarries where they broke stone, or sewed, that the dust and glaring sun caused permanent damage to their lungs and eyes. Together they had to construct a whole system of psychological and physical survival. Their oppressors would build walls so that the old prisoners could not communicate with the young ones. They would be watched so that they could not smuggle food to one another, or write letters to their loved ones, or have any political meetings. Of course they were men of different political backgrounds; African National Congress (ANC) men, Pan-African Congress (PAC) men; coloureds and others, and they argued and disagreed. This family of revolutionaries renamed Robben

Island *The University*, because they learnt so much from one another. Remarkably some of this learning took place clandestinely in a filthy cave; the cave situated in the big stadium-like stone quarry, where, as far as the prison wardens were concerned, they went to relieve themselves. Unknown to these wardens, who wouldn't go near the cave because of the stench, the men taught one another literacy and numeracy and other subjects. There are hints that the real education that went on was on lifeskills; how to cope with daily imprisonment, emotionally and physically.

It is winter in Cape Town; there is a chill, and the persistent rain will not stop even for our growing astonishment of the whole organisation of the island, which in truth was a concentration camp. Hard labour, rotten disgusting food; denied writing materials or conversation; hunger strikes, few family visits, filthy mats and mattresses given to sleep on. This is the life we are shown. We continue and now arrive at Nelson Mandela's cell where he spent his first years imprisoned. Everyone gets their cameras ready for the all important shot. The cell is remarkably small. It has so little in it. A mat or thick blanket to sleep on; two small pots, a bucket for a toilet. The cell is no more than five by six feet, with heavy bars. Mandela and many others lived like this for years, decades. We, the visitors, file pass and take our one shot. When this is done, our tour guide waits patiently for us to finish, then asks: 'Are there any questions?' There is only silence. No one says anything. No one can. The real horrors of Apartheid; the death squads, the murder of Steve Biko; the tortures, have not been mentioned, but everyone wonders about the extent of the cruelty that took place. There is only silence.

Notes on Building Family

To avoid repeated arguments, to have a home where the family can resolve their conflicts and support one another when one of the member's behaviour is found wanting, demands that family members learn to listen and respect the other's view point.

The root of this resolving of conflicts and having a home that is not full of arguments is in one's ability to resolve the conflicts within oneself. This of course is not easy but when situations of stress and conflict arise in the home then it is important to detach oneself from these feelings, monitor one's breath to see if one is breathing from the upper chest (hyperventilation) and therefore creating more stress.

If we are serious about creating a peaceful home then we have to programme the home with wisdom, that is, use art and music that supports this sense of peace. Space clearing might be considered; the throwing out of old clothes, items in the home that might be associated with a bad relationship and of course the removal of all negative thoughts.

When there are times of great change, then family meetings, where everyone can have their say is important, and the support and advice of a respected friend or cousin of the family can help give good counsel in times of turmoil.

Stage Nine

Theo sees conflict coming from the whole school structure that is constantly assessing, testing and monitoring the boys and giving them labels of underachievement. He forms a gang, not to create conflict within the school but to protect himself, to support the other boys and give them hope. He is trying to resolve things in his mind by writing his diaries, and this opportunity to express himself is important to all family members. It is just unfortunate for Theo, and his gang, that this self expression does not take place within school and is not encouraged.

As for Yvonne and Sebastian, they need friends to support them, they need time to be quiet and reflect on their marriage. What they both have to realise is that there is no problem that cannot be resolved. We all have this great intelligence in us; this intelligence that makes our heart beat each second, that carries out the processes of digestion whilst we're watching television, or heals a slight wound when we are focused on something else. This great intelligence, if it has enough quiet, can allow ways to intuit solutions.

Family Wisdom
On Intuition.

- **Intuition is your family's best friend because it always visits, especially when the home is quiet.**

- **Treat your family meetings like an old grandparent that loves to give good advice and a little mischief.**

- **The spirit within is the great counsellor; it listens without condemnation, it gives advice and it writes your inevitable autobiography.**

- **Treat the hidden wisdom in all your family members with respect and remind them of this quiet and guiding conversation that goes on in them each and every day.**

- **If you could see your intuition it would have on the oldest of clothes and the most welcoming smile.**

Stage 10

Family Reunion and the Gates of No Return

Theme:

- **Growth and abundance**
- **Family and inheritance**

Sunsum: the symbol of spirituality

Sunsum is about the soul, that is, the essence of the human being which is non-material, and that this essence survives after death.

It is said that all children are given sunsum before birth.

This symbol is important in that it reminds people of their true spiritual self which is eternal. This soul must be nurtured not only through prayers and rituals, but a way of life that acknowledges spirit in all things.

In our inquiry into education and family we seek to acknowledge andunderstand this soul as it is where genius resides.

Stage Ten

Theo's Diary

Life has changed so much now that I have a vision in life. Of course, the careers officer doesn't take me seriously, but Grandma believes in me, and mum too, and perhaps Dad.

I still believe in revolution. I believe that the boys in the school, the teachers, the parents and everyone must believe that we can revolutionise school; that, we can make it a place for family, and community; a place to examine every prejudice in life that we secretly hold.

And it's given me hope that one day mum and dad will get back together. I understand dad now. He's lost, even though he's surrounded by people who keep patting him on the back; even though he's big in politics, he is still lost and I can see it in his eyes, and I know deep down he doesn't want me to end up like him: a fake! When I meet up with old Garvey, and Biko, and Toussaint and Shaka they all tell me the same and they wonder why we make our gangs when they are so vulnerable. Life is a battle; a battle against those special needs people, a battle against the police, against some of our parents and against ourselves when no one takes the time to tell you what is going on around you and inside of yourself. Life's just one big maze.

Got up today feeling much better. Amma came in my dream and told me that Toussaint, Shaka Zulu, Biko, Lamumba and Tupac are not dead. She sent me back over to the Kora man and he played and he talked and he showed me the world of Spirit and there I saw Toussaint, Shaka Zulu, Biko, Malcolm, Garvey and Lamumba. They were sitting down at a table planning to take victory, but there was one seat empty. I kept wondering who should be sitting in that seat, and as I wondered they all turned and looked at me. At me! I'm not mad. My gang is real. They aren't dead!

The African Family Reunion

So far we have looked at the family, the compound family and the clan system but now we have to reflect on the African family especially when we consider the African diaspora and the relationship that it needs to develop with itself and the continent of Africa. The role that the Diaspora can play in Africa is critical. The Diaspora family consists of millions Black Africans, and their survival, both economically and psychologically, is tied to the future of Africa. To reconnect with your African family you have, as I have indicated in this book, to first make a psychological decision to live your life based on African principles of the African Tree of Knowledge. The mind, and then the home has to be transformed. Once the mind and home are made powerful, this radiates to the community. This family structure is what made Africa great and will make it great once again. But we have to take certain actions for this great African Family reunion to happen.

The Unseen Family Album

If you are going back to this family reunion, metaphorically speaking, the chances are that you cannot remember who is this or that uncle or aunty. Perhaps you should look through your family album. You will see pictures of your African family. You will see: Africans from the east, north, south and west with the same nose as you, the same lips as you, the same hair as you. This is your family, but you might not be able to speak the same language; their food might be strange to you and yours to them, and they will wear clothes that you have been told not to wear, and they will have customs that you may not be familiar with, but their spirit is the same as yours. If you look into the real family albums you will see the real family traits. You will see yourself ploughing the land; you will see yourself in a circle of other Africans at night under the moon performing a healing dance; or you might see yourself in another photograph as an activist with your grandmother's cutlass under the African Tree of Knowledge protecting the fruits as it falls. You turn the page again and this time you see yourself with wings and you can see your heart and it is as light as a feather, and of royal African women with braids. And you cry, for you begin to realise that you are looking directly into the wonderfulness of your spirit. People begin to surround you; they sing praises to you for they know how hard it was for you to go through *The Gates of No Return*. They too were branded with a hot iron. Some of them were raped, and captured. They sing because they are so glad that there is a reunion. These pictures are only strange to you because you were separated from your family.

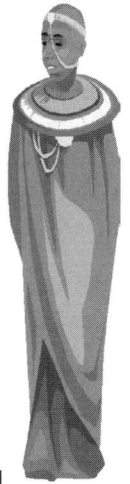

When Yvonne looks at her family album she will see pictures of the Massai warriors wearing great ostrich feathers. She will see pictures of a mother shaving the head of her son as he enters a new stage in life but she will not quite know that they are her family; and she'll look in the family album and see pictures of Benin heads of Nigeria, of bronze castings; pictures of Akan necklaces, and pictures of royalty wearing ceremonial Kente cloth but she will not realise that they are family. She will see Dogon women wearing jewellery that reflects their rich and complex cosmology; pictures of granaries, of Wodaabe men and women as they prepare for courtship and pictures of Zulu people, of the Ndebele, but she will not realise or recognise who is part of her African family. This is why we have to study our family tree so we know who is family and the power of family.

The Pilgrimage

All African families should make a pilgrimage to Africa to set foot back on the continent, having once gone through *The Gates of No Return*. You will return, and you must return as a defiant African who brings gifts back to his family in need, and these gifts must be ones central to African liberation. Of course your spending on your trip will help the local economy but you should come with a game plan. This plan is based on what you have put into action in unlocking the genius of your family which is of course a development plan. You are simply transplanting your development plan to another part of Africa. My experience is that it will need permission, altering, but essentially it is the same. The needs of Black Africans in the Diaspora and the Continent are the same; they want self-determination and self-reliance which can only be achieved through culture.

The Gates of No Return

African history started way before slavery and the slow demise of the greatness of Africa may well have started when we adopted the influence of others and were not vigilant in maintaining and further understanding the African Tree of Knowledge. To return to this great family reunion, to go back through the gates of no return needs courage. People will ridicule you; call you mad whilst they sit in front of their plasma televisions and absorb the viewpoints of people who do not have Black people's interest to heart. But real madness is when you live in an illusion of happiness when you are really in a crisis.

How will you present yourself in this reunion? To get to the family reunion you have to go through these gates of no return. It is not easy. You will face ridicule from other family members who still have the behaviour patterns of the slave mentality. Who still eat slave food, who still shop like slaves.Unfortunately, at that precise moment you will not be able to bring them with you. If you did, they will try and go through these gates, but the Ancestors will stop them; or at least strip them naked, lash them again until they had the courage to scream: '*I am African!*'

Your Family's Wealth & Inheritance

There is a new scramble for Africa; a scramble amongst the Chinese, India, US and other Western nations to take Africa's wealth due to the growing economies of China and India and the economic difficulties that the US and many Western nations find themselves in

So what is being taken in this new scramble for Africa and what can we do to prevent this exploiting of our family wealth? Africa's wealth consists of oil, diamonds, gold, gas, timber, copper, uranium, titanium and bauxite. Africa has about 90% of the worlds natural mineral resources, but this is not its main resource. What we have seen so far is that Africa's greatest resource is its people and the African Tree of Knowledge. It is this system of teaching and learning that allowed the Black Africans of Kamit to develop the sciences, astrology, medicine, architecture, music etc. This has to be taught to Theo. This is his inspiration

Why Our Trees Can't Grow: Environmental Education

This education system that I am presenting, is the ultimate environmental education. A little boy plays by the tree. He is unaware that his life opportunities are tied to this tree and that the very existence of his species is dependent on whether this tree will receive the sunlight it was designed to receive. Given this holistic education this child has the ability to become a genius; to transform their family, their community and their nation, but those in authority in his now 'independent' African state have simply adopted the colonial education system. There will be a sudden disaster in this African state; a mass flood, war and external financers will impose economic conditions that will further stifle the countries development, and this child will not go to any kind of school, or may even be recruited into an army to fight in a regional conflict.

The Ozone Layer

Ozone is a form of oxygen, a gas, and is part of the upper atmosphere where it shields us from ultraviolet (UV) radiation. It has been in place for over two billion years. Some say the ozone layer is destroyed by the use of chlorofluorocarbon (CFCs), or other means, and damage to the ozone layer can lead to skin cancers and the killing of plankton in the sea, disturbing its role in removing carbon dioxide from the air. Somewhere in Asia a little child sits under a tree, where they think the shade will lessen their burden, but the effects on their environment will see the tree die. There will be drought. Her parents' cattle will die. The child's parents will become scavengers, then feeble migrants, then corpses for the peck of starving birds that will circle even the bony face of the child as she stares up at death. This child is too weak to take from their indigenous Tree of Knowledge. There will be a sudden disaster in this family's country. A sudden rise in food prices, or oil, and unbeknown to this family the government will take an international loan and be told to cut spending on education, on health and privatise all state owned services. Not only will this child, this family have no prospect of a real education, but they will witness the daily undermining of any kind of a philosophy of self-reliance and self-determination. The family will be destroyed and the Western financers, and the puppet leaders will send their children to the best private schools in Europe, and give their own children big cars, and big wedding receptions.

War and Weapons

There is another child and their family, perhaps in South America, who is missing a limb. They live in a land where arms dealers trade. The child sits aimlessly looking out on a world that has forgotten it. The land mine that exploded when the child was simply playing, was made by the same company that makes bombs, guns, missiles, bullets, explosive devices, and more guns; and this company, like the rest of the arms industry, is part of a heavily subsidised industry. This child, that sits under a tree, rarely plays now; he is still traumatised; he does not know that the people who made the landmine that blew off his hand and leg, will make more. Their governments will arm wicked dictators, and give arms contracts to these people who make the weapons. It is too far for this little boy to hobble to school, so he sits under the Tree wanting to learn, but what should he learn? Who will teach this child about how to stop people planting landmines in his village, instead of trees? Suddenly, in this family's South American country, there will be a coup, and a new regime will take over, and they will put the central bank in private hands; they will use the national budget to buy arms to suppress political opposition and they will cut spending on education and health. This limbless child will, with their parents, scavenge a living in rubbish heaps or grow plants to make strange cigarettes that the children of those who now own the central bank and sell the arms, smoke in the top universities of the West.

Debt

The heat of this country is fierce. When left alone, though struggling, the people are happy, but happiness has its limits. They are in a south American country that is in debt; part of the 'family' of debt nations that owes billions, and cannot sell their goods which would allow their family billions in lost earnings because those 'rich' nations that have contrived this debt put up trade barriers. So this child that plays in the dirt, dreaming of new trainers, of an ipod and mobile phone, can only dream under the lazy shade of the Tree. There is no way out except they plant not trees, but seeds that will grow to plants which they will smoke in the filthy prison they will languish in having been caught selling marijuana. Theo, when walking through the streets will walk past a dealer that sells the plants that were grown by this same young boy of Columbia.

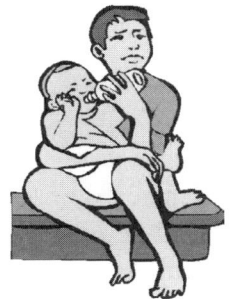

Poverty

This child of poverty should have been the star of a Bollywood film, but his skin is too dark. He belongs to the original inhabitants of India, the Dalits, the Black Africans that migrated to India thousands of years ago and built the magnificent Harappa Valley civilisation. That grandeur has gone. This civilisation once grew acres and acres of food to sustain itself. Invaders came and put a caste system in place after they conquered, massacred and enslaved the indigenous people. The business of modern agriculture now destroys their environment especially the biodiversity. More people are hungry in the world than ever. This Indian child and their family are hungry. Those of us that eat this mass produced food, if it is not organic, have to consume food contaminated with herbicides, pesticides and fertilisers. Somewhere in India, there is a little Indian child; an untouchable child, whose parents can no longer make a living from the land. A large industrial company pollutes the local streams and there are few fish in the local rivers. This child now has to go and work in a squalid little factory making trainers with other poor children who work ten hours a day for pittance. They will never meet the hero of our story, but Theo will crave and eventually wear the trainers that this poor child has made. They will never meet but they will both suffer.

Then there is the family that lives in London; Theo's family, who watch the television and see these other families living in such poor conditions, and the propaganda that they watch tell Theo and his family that these other families are poor because they cannot create wealth for themselves. Ironically, Theo's family is just as poor, though they might have modern gadgets; they are poor because they do not have the indigenous knowledge of their people to create wealth for themselves. Since their libraries belonging to their people were burnt down knowledge has been controlled. The media that they watch simply tells them that they and these other families have contributed nothing to world civilisation.

So you see, our Tree of Knowledge cannot grow because of environmental devastation caused by people. Yet, we have it in us to cultivate the soil once again and allow our tree to grow, perhaps as part of an orchid, or as part of a rainforest, or in a local park, or in an African village giving shade to elders as they cut kola nuts and dispense good governance and research on laptops. We need to build grassroots libraries, reading clinics, Saturday schools, homework clubs, research and development centres, full time schools and nurseries, colleges and universities. We will have to put in place an education centred around the family; one that leads to community development, and for this to happen the education system will look different; it won't be a pen and test paper examination system; time has to be invested, work experience, apprenticeships, home schooling, blended learning (a combination of these). A new philosophy of education has to be implanted in all families around the world in order to mobilise the whole community to help unlock their genius.

Writings of an Educationalist

In the eyes of African-Caribbeans, Ghana has always held a great deal of romance. It is the land of the Akan people, the land of Yaa Asantewa the great woman warrior; the land of Kwame Nkrumah, of the god Shango. The hand of Ghana, drapped in wonderful kente cloth, has always seemed to be outstretched to the African Diasporeans, whose hearts, whether they know it or not, have sought a spiritual return. Many of us still bare Ghanaian names: Cudjoe, Quashie and so on. I was asked to deliver a teacher training workshop in Ghana in 2006, similar to one I had delivered in Grenada, but the efforts of the Sonibron Trust, a non-governmental organisation (NGO) meant that the whole event had government involvement and brought teachers together from across the region. Again the training was based on *How to Unlock Your Child's Genius*, and I was once again made aware by the initial interest that there is a quiet, growing awareness across the globe that people themselves need to put in place a different type of education system. One lazy Friday, having left the guest house, I set off to a nearby school to deliver a whole day teacher-training workshop. My brief was concise: deliver training to the teachers centred on the book and give them ideas how they might improve their delivery to the pupils. I was also informed that the teachers work on a ratio of one teacher to sixty-five students per class.

An unsteady car drive, in which I was tossed to and fro took place before I stepped out of the old car, and almost like a mountain climber, made my way to the colonial like school with its familiar brown and beige painted walls. On the way I see women on the side walk; selling food, washing clothes, preparing food, whilst dogs chase invisible spirits. The classroom I entered was big; no pictures, no artwork of the children, no evidence that this was the place that hundreds of young bright children, spent the best part of six hours in. The tables are old, the chairs are surprisingly sturdy. This doesn't help the unease I have about the training. Africa is littered with educational consultants from the West. I don't want to be another one; peddling Western solutions. Neither is it right to assume that just because I am Black I automatically have solutions. My unease builds a narrative in my mind: 'they have different issues – gender, health care, corruption, poverty. But this talk was soon interrupted. I was suddenly in a circle of handshakes: government officials from the local education authorities greeted me. I now realised that this wasn't just another training session; a great deal of importance had been put on the workshop. The circle of voices told me about the rote learning, the lack of training, the lack of resources. An official explains that the teachers, some with minimal training, have to copy lessons on the board for the children who then monotonously copy what was written on the board. Already I am in awe of the teachers. Who could stand for so long and copy so much? Who could carry on teaching year after year, lacking continuing teacher development on so little pay?

After my clumsy setting up, the formalities commence. A dignitary makes an short opening speech; someone says a prayer, and this is followed by another speech before I am formally introduced. These are miracle teachers; teachers of different grades, abilities, age groups and responsibilities. This is a unique event for them and I become a little nervous at the expectation which I am supposed to meet. When I start my presentation by telling them about how Ebony Education was started, all I can see are polite, but blank faces; dutifully and respectfully looking back at me and this only serves to unnerve me more. I would later be told that this is normal. Some of the teachers are not used to this type of training. It is their way. However, at the time I did not know this. I was desperate for some kind of reaction, so I began to tell them about my parents who inspired me to become a teacher. I told them about little Carriacou; about the villages, about how there still remains people of Akan, Youruba, Hausa; about how they come together to perform *Big Drum*, a kind of micro Pan-African festival; about how they make *Stone Feast*; perform their stick-fighting, about '*big-pot food*', about Shango, about *Nigger House*, about the candles in the cemetery on all Saints Night. They begin to warm to what I have to say. We now get into workshop but as we progress I sense that they want Western resources, Western solutions; they want me to quote Western educationalists. Are they any different from Black teachers back in the UK? I address this briefly head on. There are those in the training room that agree. So where are the solutions? We are now looking at the teaching of mathematics. I ask them: 'How many of you play oware?' All hands go up. I then ask, 'How many of you know that oware helps develop concentration skills, skills in strategising, mental arithmetic and prediction?' Again all hands go up. My final question is this: 'How many of you use oware in the classroom to teach children mathematics?' This time not one single hand went up. There was now a growing realisation in the room that the solutions to the problem concerning the education of children, not only in Ghana but all over Africa and the African Diaspora, lies within ourselves. Group work follows. Inevitably the history of African mathematics came up. The Rhind papyrus, was mentioned. I had a copy of the book, *Africa Counts*, but no one had seen it. The Adrinka symbols, and kinte cloth and their portrayal of spiralling living systems was mentioned. The word chemistry, that comes from the science of Khem (black) people was mentioned but not dwelt upon. It seemed the entire greatness of the Black world was hidden from not only all children, but Black teachers. It dawns on me that I am being naïve here. I can go to local museums and see weights and measures that black Africans were using thousands of years ago. I have books with drawings and photographs of convex and concave lens that Africans developed; I have pictures of medieval family manuscripts in Mauritania. By now I know that the teachers are beginning to think

Stage Ten

about African solutions. We turn to the teaching of literacy and we begin to piece together a framework. When can we get the words, the sentences, the texts to put together our reading schemes, our literacy worksheets, our poetry, our songs. A lady stands up and begins to sing a song. Others join in. They are now openly celebrating their Africaness. I prompt them as to where the stories will come from. 'We are a fishing village and there are many fisherman stories,' answers one woman. Someone else mentions that they can base problem solving questions on these stories and relate the learning directly back to the community. Suddenly there is noise in the room as possibilities are excitedly realised. We continue for another hour, by which time I am tired. What should have been delivered in three days I delivered in one. I have learnt more than anyone else. Sonia, from the Trust thanks me for attending. Wearily I head back to the guest house and throw myself on the bed. I am more tired than I realised. The travel, the jet lag had taken a lot out of me. A couple of hours later the evaluation forms are handed to me. When I read them a big smile spread over my face. Each one is favourable. I am invited back to deliver another training but there is a realisation that I have to be better prepared. I needed to have done more ground work, more primary research. As the night progresses I slowly question this. Is there any difference between these teachers and those in London, I ask myself. The answer is no. There is an urgent need for Black teachers to recognise that if they are going to play a critical role in providing an education that is going to address the needs of the people then we are going to have to establish alternative education provisions and challenge the existing education monopoly.

A few days later our hosts took us to see two incredible African Americans, who, not only settled in Ghana some sixteen years ago but have run several youth programmes for the local youngsters, as well as establishing a unique museum full of archives, eccentricity and a romantic love for their people. Their home, consisting of African chalets, a bar, a museum, main house and several cats, is a mix of the 60s Black Power, the spirit of Nkrumah and the radicalism of the Rasta movement, for there, tucked away, is an old dread; a boat builder who, with pictures of Marley on his wall, chisels and hammers away as if making the biblical ark. As a couple, they seemed to have gone through various stages in their settlement: romanticism, anger, joy and peace. As I sit with them, sipping a cold drink, listening to their story, I realise that their home is a retreat. Its beauty is shared between tropical shrubs, artwork and their single-mindedness. The boat-maker, who journeyed from Jamaica, is part of their extended family. They have a compound-family. It has not only helped them but the local community. In their great adventure of returning to Africa, they have done something so simple, yet so significant; they have addressed the brain drain; they have given, not just their talent, but their soul to their community. It is said that 80,000 highly skilled professional Africans leave Africa each year, and amongst these are 23,000 university graduates and 50,000 are said to be at the professional levels. More than this, when this mass of talent leave they take Africa's hope with them. They cannot work the fields of learning and harvest another generation. In order to stop Africa's brain drain we first have to become conscious of the need to invest our talent, our time, our genius into Africa. We do not have to do what this admirable couple did in returning, although this is a feasible option for many, but we do have to learn from their example by devoting resources, both intellectual and material, to Africa. When I walked into the training room in the school in Elmina at first I thought that the issues regarding the educational needs of Africans on the continent and those in England were different; but they are not. They are more or less the same. Being good community-teachers, we have to make that initial assessment; we have to essentially teach self-love, self-reliance and self-determination. This education starts and end s with the family.

Notes on Building Family

In the case of Yvonne, Sebastian and Theo we could have a family about to break up permanently, but this family has to perform one more task and that is to go back through 'The Gates of No Return'. Here people like Dr Seamus have no role to play but it is the psychological journey that all African families have to perform. The Johnson family did not just arrive before us. The family of their ancestors was broken, then reshaped to suit the economic interests of those who forced them into slave ships. Yvonne, Sebastian and Theo have to all be brave and come to the realisation that their true self cannot come to the fore in a family structure that does not give them access to great teachings about humanity that are thousands of years old. Family is the social organisation for this practical realisation to happen. They therefore have to prepare themselves to go back through these gates with a pride and inquiry that is truly in search of truth, truth as to their true identity as human beings and not one which has been given to them by oppressive sources.

How many African families are prepared to take this journey? How many are prepared to eat African food, wear African clothes, take African names, speak an African language and learn the science of the great African Tree of Knowledge.

There are those who have partly taken this journey before; these are our revolutionaries who were once abandoned by Sebastian and then reclaimed by Theo: Toussaint L'Ouverture, Steve Biko, Robert Sobukwe, Marcus Garvey, Malcolm X, Yaa Asantewa, Queen Nzinga, Amy Garvey and Sojourner Truth. Those families that are prepared to take this journey will, with compassion, see how they have been taught to hate themselves, hate their family tree, but the love that radiates from the true self will be enough to rebuild their family. Now it is time to see if this is possible with Yvonne, Sebastian and Theo.

Family Wisdom
On Intuition.

- **Life is the artist that paints your true portrait on an old canvass and finally leaves you with a picture that you can only marvel at if you have lived a life of helping and giving to others.**

- **No one knows your true name except that inner light that truly and sincerely wishes to guide you home.**

- **The true you, the real I is the only oneness which has put up with your ego, and emotions, and anger, and remained there, waiting for you with compassion; the true you that you did not even recognise.**

- **Our true potential is to realise that we are part of this greatness and beauty we call life, which is achieved each and every moment by the smallest to the largest creature by simply being themselves which nature intended.**

Stage 11

Family Journey to Sankofa

Theme of inquiry: Peace

Gye Nyame: the supremacy of God

Gye Nyame symbol of supremacy and supreme power of God; that God is omnipotent, omniscient and omnipresent.

On Leadership

Leadership means everything – PAIN, BLOOD, DEATH

HON. MARCUS GARVEY (Pan-Africanist leader)

Theatre and Education: Reaching the People

So far we have had our case study family in the background but it is now time for them to take centre stage; to tell their story and take us on a journey that can give us further insight into family, and the rebuilding of family.

Voices of the Estate

By David Simon

Setting and characters

Set in 2008 in south London on a local housing estate.

The Main Characters:

Madame Sankofa	An elderly Nigerian woman who claims to have psychic powers. All her life she has pursued a variety of careers and has been unlucky in her five marriages.
Yvonne	A Jamaican woman, in her early forties, who came to England in her teens and is prone to be a little melancholy at times yet possesses a strong temper if provoked.
Sebastian	A confused man who is in search of answers to what has happened to him in his life. He is in his mid forties and is desperately trying to hold himself together, as he tries to rebuild his life.
Theo	A twenty-one year old young Black man who wants to do good for the community but who is still unsure which route he should take in life. He desperately wants to live outside of the system, yet, is slowly realising that he might have to go into the system in order to reach those in his community that need his help.

Act One
Scene One

(Seven years later. Thunder and lightning are heard. The strong sea splashing against the shore is also heard and finally calms. Lights go up on a moonlit silhouetted collage consisting of Elmina Castle that has two canons on either side and a housing estate. At the bottom of the Castle is a dungeon where DJ Teacher Theo sits in a pirate radio studio. At the front of the castle is a triangle drawn on a school hall floor., In the middle of the triangle is the old desk of the headteacher, a chair with her coat on it, her glasses, a photograph of Ms Maudsley on the desk, a pair of shoes and couple of boxes with the words 'lost property box' pinted on them. In the background are two gates; one the gates of no return of Elmina Castle and the other of the school gates of the now derelict school. Yvonne is there pacing up and down. She is reading a letter that she wrote some ten years earlier to the headteacher. Madame Sankofa is there with a small dust cloth having wiped down the desk.

The people of the estate perform a song about their protest against the Local Authority's proposal to knock down their estate. Monique and Ray-I are seen holding placards, whilst M Sankofa builds the shrine of self-hating items that the people of the estate have been indulging in, and sings as she puts items around the desk.)

Yvonne.	(*shaking her head*) No, I'm not doing it!...(Yvonne *ignores her*). Don't need no therapy. (*Pointing to herself and taking a few steps closer to* Sankofa) ..Yvonne is okay. (*opening her bag and throwing things on the floor*)..Here, you can take back your incense and herbs and spells and charms..(*Suddenly jumping in fright*) What's that! (Yvonne bursts out laughing)
M. Sankofa.	Say hello to Ms Maudsley. (Sankofa *gets up and strokes the picture*) Glad to be back at school?
Yvonne.	(*pointing*) You de one that needs therapy..
M. Sankofa.	She remembers you.
Yvonne.	Never should have agreed to...(Yvonne *turns quickly and begins to walk out but stops suddenly*)
M. Sankofa.	(to the picture) Say hello to Yvonne. You two used to be such good friends. (Yvonne spits at the picture)..I've told her why we've come.
Yvonne.	(*accusingly*) Came to you for help; now you talking to some picture. And what's all this (*pointing to the 'shrine'*).
M. Sankofa.	It's what you people of the estate have been worshipping; what they are really fighting about, not the council knocking down the flats.
Yvonne.	And this is my treatment; what am I spending my hard earned cash for.
M. Sankofa.	My ad said it all. Therapist; confidant, counsellor; lay preacher and educationalist. (*she half laughs to herself*) Please, God sent me to help you.
Yvonne.	(*Again stepping backwards to the door. Takes out her purse and starts throwing money on the floor.*) Here take your money, an' your therapy and let me help my son by myself.
M. Sankofa.	(*holding a letter*) I've got the letter...About Theo.
Yvonne.	(*be coming weak*) No.
M. Sankofa.	(*to the picture*) We've been talking haven't we.
Yvonne.	..de one I wrote..all those years ago?
M. Sankofa.	Please, understand that his rebellion is his misguided journey. He doesn't know how to escape the plantation. (Sankofa *hands her the letter.*) You'll understand..
Yvonne.	Not interested in our people; your people. What people helped me when me husband left; when Theo take up in gang. Which people we talking about! (Sankofa *hugs the picture as she now takes on the character of* Phillipa Maudsley)

M. Sankofa.	The ships haven't stopped, have they Ms Maudsley. They sail into our community with drugs; sail out with our young people taking them to prison; sail back in with guns. The triangle is still there. (*pointing to the triangle with her finger*)
Yvonne.	(*getting angry and scared*) Not going on no journey with no mad..
M. Sankofa.	..You've already been on a journey.
Yvonne.	I'll heal myself; cook up some gunga pea soup, drink some fresh coconut and..
M. Sankofa.	Look at you! (*teasing*) Soon you gone write in the lonely hearts column. (mocking) Lonely miserable Jamaican woman seeks gorgeous man. (*change of mood*) What gorgeous man will look at you with your self pity?
Yvonne.	Then tell me what's happening to my life?
M. Sankofa.	..they made you go through the gates of no return; they did something to your mind..
Yvonne.	(*not listening*) Why is everything around me falling apart…
M. Sankofa.	D'you know what happened when we went through the gates; when we were dragged from the dungeons..
Yvonne.	…(*still not quite listening*) …they're even gone knock down de estate and I don't feel anything.
M. Sankofa.	…they made you hate yourself.
Yvonne.	…and everyone is campaigning, protesting to the council except me because everything I touch just fall apart..(*grabbing* M. Sankofa)…Madame Sankofa help me….(M. Sankofa *just looks at her*)
M. Sankofa.	We need to settle the finances. I will accept cheque with credit card if you don't have cash.
Yvonne.	I've got a post dated cheque.
M. Sankofa.	Post dated? Please, d'you want me to post date your therapy? Make you walk all over the high street like a mad person! Will your depression wait for a post dated cheque to clear? Please, I feel cash will be better. (Yvonne *pauses and then takes out some money and gives it to* M. Sankofa)….You see, you feel better now. It's important that money must circulate in the Black community.
Yvonne.	Circulate to your bank account.
M. Sankofa.	(*half disgusted*) Look at you; the way you dress; your perfume, your hair.
Yvonne.	Is you who need therapy?

M. Sankofa.	(*holding her outstretched hand to* Yvonne) You came to me with your big crocodile tears. (*mocking*) Oh Madame Sankofa; what's happening to my life; make me into a new woman, a strong woman. You think I'm going to give you breast implants; botox, suction and blonde wig. Is that kind of new woman you want to be? A cosmetic black woman. (*sympathetically*) …Come. I'll help you.
Yvonne.	How many journeys me must take..(M. Sankofa *suddenly pulls her and twists her arm round her back*) Read the letter! Before I beat you.
Yvonne.	(*desperate and hurting*) This is about Theo, not me..
M. Sankofa.	(*almost sympathetic*) I know. They're preparing to take Theo away. We'll follow the ships to Brixton, Feltham and Scrubs prisons…Read. (let's go of Yvonne) (*Sounds of school can be heard.* M. Sankofa *begins to hum. She picks up a map and studies it then goes to and sits behind the desk as* Ms Maudsley).
M. Sankofa.	(*as Philippa*) Let's live and forget.
Yvonne.	(*Opening the letter. To* Ms Maudsley) So many letters I wrote to you
Yvonne.	D'you remember this? (waving the letter in her face).I want you to listen; 'cause you didn't listen last time..
M. Sankofa.	(*as Ms Maudsley and totally exacerbated*) Please, Ms Johnson, I told…
Yvonne.	Listen…(Ms Maudsley *begins to sob.* Yvonne *reads.*)
Theo.	(*In Freedom FM's community radio station.*) This is DJ Theo, your local community teacher on Freedom FM the radio station that takes you on a journey of discovery..
Yvonne.	(*To the presence of Theo. Screaming.*) I want her to listen; just for once!..(pause)
Theo.	Tonight's show is on moving forward in your life. Can we as a people move forward in the 21st century? Has our past left baggage that we have not dealt with? What strategy do we have as a people? Do we even have a vision? (he laughs)
M. Sankofa.	(*as Ms Maudsley*) We did all we could for Theo…(gesturing as she remembers)…got him a psychologist, his own social worker.
Yvonne.	Dear Ms Maudsley..
Sankofa/Phillipa	(*hopelessly distraught*)..please..he had behavioural problems..

Yvonne.	Dear Ms Maudsley, now that de tears have stopped drop from me eye I just want to say a few words. You see, it God that did give Theo to me so me can't just abandon him like you…
Sankofa/Phillipa.	I didn't abandon him…our psychologist assessed him…twice!
Yvonne.	..you call it permanent exclusion, but we call it abandonment. You see, when you bring a child into dis world; you suckle dem, you wipe sleep from them eye, watch dem likkle foot start to walk; you can't abandon them. Theo get exclude because de teacher keep pick on him. Pick on him because of de way he keep him hair; de way him walk, de way him wear him uniform; until he just explode.. (Madame Sankofa *signals that* Yvonne *has to go and stand at a certain point of the triangle.*)
Theo.	…. Also on Freedom FM tonight we'll be taking calls on the Mad Woman that everyone is talking about who has been carrying out bizarre things in the community. Stealing coconuts, food, two suitcases. Pure madness. Do you know this mad woman, and if so can you make sense of her actions? Apparently 'Mad Woman' has nailed debt bills on the doors of banks and insurance companies, and the British Museum. What debt is she talking about? (in accent) Mad woman, if you out there give Freedom FM a ring and talk to the people. Also, we want to hear from you on the estate; those of you stopping the council from knocking down one half and developing the other half for some yuppies in the city. We want calls on all this mad gun crime taking place. Is Gun Boy who the police are hunting really the culprit or is this just to distract us on the estate from the real perpetrators of crime. Anyway, more later; let's play some old school tunes..
Yvonne.	..De teacher is supposed to be a teacher not a policeman. (*pause*) We as parents blame ourselves 'cause we believed you. Believed your school reports; believed your educational psychologist; believed that Theo was really underachieving. I kept running up to de school to see you; hoping that you would even understand me as woman, because you is woman too. We different yes, but we woman still. You keep your hair perm, whilst me wear braids; you wear tweed skirt, me wear jeans; you eat roast beef, me eat rice and peas; you read T.S Elliott, I read people palms; but we is both woman; we breathe de same air, live under de same sky. Woman was put on this earth to give life, not mash up de dreams of a little black boy. We believed you Ms Maudsley.
Sankofa/Philippa.	Theo was a lovely child…but he was dyslexic, and had other problems, and there were language issues…
Theo.	…(*turning down the volume*) A tune I'd like to play for someone who is still mad at me for dropping out of university; I didn't want to be no middle class classroom teacher. (*remembering*) For you beautiful listeners new to the station I was training to be a teacher, but each day I would hear about someone being shot; someone being knifed, someone going to prison. So I, along with others, decided here to set up Freedom FM and become a teacher of the street; teach the yout's about how to survive; how to avoid all dem bad t'ings. But my decision has broken someone's heart. Mummy, this tune's for you..(he puts on a cd which can be heard very low in the background). Sebastian sings from the estate.

Yvonne.	(*to* Ms Maudsley) Was? He is not dead Ms Maudsley. (*pause*) Let me read on. (*she reads*) You say that him start keep bad company; that he take up with a gang. But you have gang too: your psychologist, your social worker, your special education needs teacher, your chair of Governors; dem all gang up on Theo and agree that him should be excluded; them was all your gang! Especially when you keep your school play. We would come along excited; clutching our video camera, wanting to see our precious child on stage, but as we keep watch him, he don't say anything. All de main characters was for de white children. Them parents would be videoing, and clapping, but Theo and de other Black children have no lines to speak. Them dress up as donkey, as pig, and stay at the back and do some silly little dance….(*dancing*)….Piggy, piggy. You even excluded him from the school play. And after the play you and de teachers were celebrating; you was wearing your Marks and Spencer trouser suit, drinking champagne, and you had your friends of de Earth badge on. I kept wondering, you is not Theo's friend, or my family friend, or my community friend.
Sankofa/Phillipa.	(*mocking*) I am, I am, I…Remember we had Black History Month; jerk chicken, rice and peas, jellof rice and chin chin, and…
Yvonne.	Ms Maudsley, we taking Theo to a new school. We hope that him ambitions is not totally destroy. We as a family is not angry, just disappointed in you, in de whole school system.
Theo.	So my beautiful listeners, has anyone got any baggage that they would like to share with DJ Theo, your pirate school teacher; baggage which is holding them back from simply being beautiful..Call Freedom FM now and let's all start the journey to unlock the genius that we all have…
Sankofa/Phillipa.	(*totally distraught*) Let me go…please…
Theo.	(V*olume of Freedom FM gets loud. Rapping.*)

…And the texts are coming in. Marcus from Hackney says we're still living on the plantation; our relationships with one another are still that of a people on a plantation; our family break-ups; the food we eat like pig tail, and cow foot; the names we give our children: Thomas, Sally, Shantell. Listeners, is there a mental plantation that we need to educate ourselves out of? Do we need a new type of teacher in the community to teach our children? Why are we always complaining and not doing? Ring or text Freedom FM Radio. And listen, especially all of you fighting against the council on the estate…(begins to rap)

As a people we can't see the slave ships, as a people;

As a people, when the hot iron of the slave master brands us conservative, socialist, environmentalist or any other ist-ist we can't see that we are still in the slave market; as people.

As a people we can't see the slave ships bringing in guns and drugs, and drink, and disease to the estate; as a people.

As a people, we can't see that we are still in the same plantations where our grandmothers gave birth to light-skinned babies, as a people.

As a people we can't remember going through the gates of no return; can't remember the capture, the beatings, the rape, the dungeons, the passage, the hymns and the baptism. No, as a people..(radio jingle is heard)

This is Freedom FM, London's number one pirate station. *Next,* we'll talk about educating our children. And whilst we're on the subject, I drove past my old school the other night and there was a light on; the building's been derelict for years; in fact I've been wanting to knock it down myself . A place that gave my poor mother so much grief. Talking of my old school, let's play some *serious* old school music.

Yvonne.	(quietly) Yours sincerely, Mr and Mrs Johnson. (long pause then music is heard)
M. Sankofa.	(taking off the Ms Maudsley wig and shoes etc) Good. Now our journey can start. Pack your things. Say bye to the old Yvonne, to the estate. We going to Africa. To eat some yam; drink some palm wine. Going, on a kind of slave ship. In a few days we gone set sail. (Madame Sankofa's radio advert is heard)

**Act One
Scene Two**

It's late evening. It is now one week later. Images of enslaved African women are seen with extracts from early slave narratives and the rundown housing estate. Sankofa is in the school hall singing to herself as she beats a small drum. Next to her is an old suitcase. Enter Yvonne gingerly. She pauses waiting for Sankofa to finish.

DJ Teacher Theo is seen in the pirate station studio taking a call.

Theo.	…My oh my; have you the listeners been going crazy with your texts. What vision do we have as a people was the simple question I asked you last week. I received a text from Ray I de Rastaman. (in accent) Ray I says, burn down Babylon. Dr Tunde, says that we have to educate ourselves about power. How we once had power and dominated the world for over 3500 years and how we fell. Then we had a call from Mrs Thompson who said we should all study the bible. Thank you Ms Thompson. Amen! Now, Ray I de Rastaman rang back again and said that we have to stand up and fight; fight the council people trying to knock down part of the estate – and by the way there's a tenant's meeting at the town hall so get down there and fight. You know, no one can tell me of a single thing worthwhile that Black people have got without fighting for it. So, if you have something to say ring Freedom FM, the only community station that gives the Black community a voice then..(picks up one of his many mobile phones)
Monique.	(*Monique seen at right of triangle*) I'm here Theo.
Theo.	Is that babymother Monique?
Monique.	Live and kicking from the estate.
Theo.	How's the little one?
Monique.	He's fine; getting big now, and troublesome.
Theo.	And when next you coming in here to give us a live track. Anyway, so Monique, what you got to tell us today?
Monique.	Been listening to the other callers and I just want to say it's hard being a babymother, bringing up a child by yourself. It's lonely on the estate too. My child's babyfather don't give no maintenance; just hangs out with his crew; he can't teach our son to be no man…

Theo.	But don't you agree someone has to?
Monique.	(*interrupting*) Luckily my child has his uncles, and grandfather to look up to as positive role models. His babyfather walks round Hackney with his crew as he calls it acting like some bad-man; how can he teach my son anything? When I see pictures of how Black people behaved back in Africa, I don't see no Pharaoh walking out from a pyramid leaving his woman to bring up a child by herself. Don't see no African Egyptian woman pushing pram to go and sign on the dole. Something mentally has happened to us. We don't know how to fight; fight with some kind of strategy. Look at what's happening on the estate.
Theo.	Monique, I'm hearing you, and I see you're involved in the campaign to stop the council knocking down...
Monique.	(interrupting) Just fed up with people walking all over us. I know I shouldn't say it but I'm glad they aint catch Gun-Boy; if it's him that tried to burn down the old school and council office then good, because they aint for us!
Theo.	Anyway, how d'you feel we can keep family together?
Monique.	Well, for me, and all the baby mothers and fathers have to step forward; we have try and educate our children ourselves, 'cause in school they just give up on them once they see your child is from single parent family.
Theo.	Monique, thanks for your call. Keep believing in yourself; the record deal is going to come soon; (*in a Caribbean-English accent*) your voice too good; it too sweet!
Monique.	(*interrupting*) One last thing; I think the mad woman that you was talking about last week yeah; I think she aint mad, 'cause I hear she walk in to an Indian man shop and take some yam, and rice, and plantain. Next, she cook one big pot of orange rice and red stew and come to the estate and start feeding people who on benefit. This is what we need in the community.
Theo.	(*shouting jokingly*) Yeah? Mad woman, save a plate for me! And on the subject of this mad woman; I get some serious licks you know. People say me sexist. Why? Because I say mad woman mad, and a whole heap of Black woman ring in and say why is it that when Black woman stand up and do something unusual we call her mad. Well all you women who start cuss me I want you to tell the mad woman, I mean the African Woman, to come to the studio: go live on air and say what she's doing on the estate.
Monique.	Know what; I start cook up some African food; cook some orange rice business and all my boys' allergies just dash 'way. And he start do better in school.
Theo.	Gonna have to leave you there Monique.
Monique.	Just wanna say big-up Freedom FM radio, and can you play something for my son Omar. Okay bye.
Theo.	Hello; we have a new caller.
Sebastian.	Theo. (*Sebastian is seen on the angle of the opposite side to where* Monique *was*)
Theo.	Hello caller; your name?

Sebastian.	It's me; dad! (*pause*)
Theo.	Dad?
Sebastian.	I'm back on the estate; trying to change things.
Theo.	Dad, please; leave me and mum alone.
Sebastian.	I've changed Theo.
Theo.	You haven't; you never will.
Sebastian.	Listen…
Theo.	(*remembering he's on air*)..a little domestic confusion people. Let's play some more music. (*music is now heard in the background*)
Sebastian.	Hear me out Theo. I'm working on a project; it's on the estate; trying to help the youth.
Theo.	Another project. What happened to the last one? And the one before that?
Sebastian.	I made one mistake Theo. One!
Theo.	Only one? You mean one big, gigantic, enormous mistake.
Sebastian.	Don't judge me Theo. Until you walk in another man's shoes don't..
Theo.	What else can I do? Eh? Look, I've got a show to finish. (Theo *hangs up on the phone. The music continues to play and Sebastian sings a little as he takes a small bottle of drink from his jacket pocket. The phone rings again and Theo answers*)
Dr Tunde.	Hello.
Theo.	Dr Tunde
Dr Tunde.	You're welcome.
Theo.	I hear there's a new book on the way.
Dr Tunde.	Yes, and it's based right here on the estate where we've been having so much trouble.
Theo.	You mean with Gun-Boy?
Dr Tunde.	Gun-Boy; poverty, crime, drugs. But these people deserve better. They are people; our people! I spoke to Ray-I de Rastaman. You know him.

Theo.	Yeah, me and Ray-I go way back to school.
Dr Tunde.	He started the campaign to stop the council people knocking down the estate.
Theo.	They can't do it. Just because of one little shooting, and it wasn't even on the estate. Blame Gun Boy. How come they're not chasing the drug dealers, the pimps, the crack people and those selling the guns? Make sure you put the truth in your book. And how come no one ever publishes your books?
Dr Tunde.	Never mind that. I tell you Mr DJ the people are tired of the media coming down here whenever there is trouble and stereotyping. However, I hope my book will help. And one last thing. We need to transform the estate into an African village. When I say this people laugh at me, but a real African village is sophisticated, democratic and civil. Let's knock down the estate in our minds and in our minds build a modern African village!
Theo.	Village! Isn't that going backwards.
Dr Tunde.	Living on an estate with guns, crime, povery and unemployment is backwards! Do we really understand progress? Our people need to understand their oppression. Realise that when they watch tv, soap opera, reality tv and news programmes that they are being lied to. Gun Boy does not exist as such. They've created him so that we can hate our own youth!
Theo.	Well doctor, always good to talk to you. Anyone doing anything positive is welcome on Freedom FM, the people's station. Okay doctor, we'll speak soon.
Dr Tunde.	Bye, bye. And play something nice for all de people of the estate to cheer them up.
Theo	Will do. Time for commercial ads. Back in two minutes. (*the Madame Sankofa advert*) *Are you happy with your life? Are you tired of putting on skin lightners and wearing European clothes to find the man of your dreams? Have you forgotten how to cook jelloff rice, moi moi and agussi soup? Come to Madame Chief Sankofa, Nigeria's leading therapist and counsellor. My rates are very reasonable and I'll accept payment in Nira and pound sterling. Let Sankofa take you on a journey of self discovery. Ring me on 08788 151 25588*
Act One Scene Three	*Lights go up on front of stage. Sankofa is sitting on a chair with one suitcase next to her and another suitcase next to the other chair. Yam, green bananas, bags of ground rice, black eye peas are seen by her.*
M. Sankofa.	(*stopping suddenly*) Have you brought everything? (*she carries on singing to herself*)
Yvonne.	I think so.

M. Sankofa.	Ring?
Yvonne.	Yes.
M. Sonkofa.	Album?
Yvonne.	Yes.
M. Sankofa.	Wedding dress?
Yvonne.	Yes.
M. Sankofa.	Scissors?
Yvonne.	(*unconvincingly*) I couldn't find….
M. Sankofa.	(*shouting*) Scissors!
Yvonne.	It's all I have to remind me of…
M. Sankofa.	Stop clinging to bad memories. This is about your journey. That is why you came to me isn't it?
Yvonne.	(*defensively*) But I was once married; have a child; still have a home and…
M. Sankofa.	(*insisting*) Cut the dress up woman!
Yvonne.	…This is my wedding dress, my veil, my ring and…
M. Sankofa.	(*turning to the picture*) You're right; you're absolutely right…(*to* Yvonne) Did you hear that?
Yvonne.	(ignoring Sankofa and seething with anger) Stop talking to her!
M. Sankofa.	(*to the picture*) She's scared.
Yvonne.	It's answers I came to you for. My marriage break up; my son didn't graduate, my hair's falling out and..(exacerbated) answers.
M. Sankofa.	(*to the picture*) Yes. (*walking to Yvonne*) The veil.
Yvonne.	(*puzzled*) What?
M. Sankofa.	The veil. Put it on.

Yvonne.	Just told me to cut it up.
M. Sankofa.	Who is to guide you through this journey. Put it on! (Yvonne *slowly puts on the veil*) ..On your knees
Yvonne.	(*beginning to realise*) No.
M. Sankofa.	Time to take new vows.
Yvonne.	(*pointing to the picture*) Not in front of her.
M. Sankofa.	D'you vow to love yourself..do you?
Yvonne.	(*whispering*) yes.
M. Sankofa.	Louder.
Yvonne.	Yes.
M. Sankofa.	Unconditionally.
Yvonne.	Yes.
M. Sankofa.	And to forgive yourself?
Yvonne.	Yes.
M. Sankofa.	To be merciful to yourself?
Yvonne.	Yes.
M. Sankofa.	And to love and cherish yourself.
Yvonne.	I do, I do, I do
M. Sankofa.	(*pointing at the picture*) And to forgive others who have sinned?
Yvonne.	(*half screaming*) No!
M. Sankofa.	Why?
Yvonne.	I can't…(*taking off the veil*)
M. Sankofa.	You can!

Yvonne.	Leave me alone.
M. Sankofa.	What kind of woman are you? (Sankofa *suddenly slaps her across the face*) Feel better now..
Yvonne.	(*Jamiacan English*) But wait. You slap me?
M. Sankofa.	'Cause your face look like it need a good slap.
Yvonne.	If you ever slap me again…(Sankofa *slaps her*)…(*in Jamaican English*) What! You playing wid your life..
M. Sankofa.	Try and slap Madame Sankofa..Come.
Yvonne.	(*in Jamaican English*) If me slap you you dead.
M. Sankofa.	Woman like you who grow up on chips can't beat me.
Yvonne.	(*holding her fists up and ready to hit* M. Sankofa) Cornmeal porridge is what my mummy feed me.
M. Sankofa.	Chinese style eh? Ground rice (*now circling* Yvonne *with her fists held like that of a boxer*)
Yvonne.	Dumpling and ackee.
M. Sankofa.	Moi Moi .
Yvonne.	Green banana.
M. Sankofa.	Agussi soup
Yvonne.	Plantain
M. Sankofa.	Yam
Yvonne.	Salt-fish
M. Sankofa.	Well come Ms Saltfish (Sankofa *slaps her face again. This time* Yvonne *goes to hit her back*)…Wait….Good….Now breathe…Save your fists to fight the battles within you as we go one this great journey. You are going to walk back through the gates of no return; are you willing to go within; to re-enter the Church of Sankofa? And forgive? (*long pause*)

M. Sankofa.	(*with compassion*) Yvonne, you have to learn to fight. I had to learn to fight. This stage of your life is about fighting for what you believe in. When I first established The Church of Sankofa in Nigeria, they all came to destroy me..
Yvonne.	(*interrupting*) They?
M. Sankofa.	Archbishop, Deacon, Iman and even a nun with one big smile! I had to fight all of them.
Yvonne.	(*disbelieving*) Not literally?
M. Sankofa.	Literally! First, the Bishop ran at me. He was an Igbo man from Onitsha, in the east of Nigeria. He laughed, then charged at me saying my church was fake. He tried to punch me like this, then like that, but I gave him one big upper cut. He dropped straight on the floor.
Yvonne.	No?
M. Sankofa.	Yes. Then the Deacon came and charged at me like a bull. I picked him up and threw him over my shoulder. The only one left was the nun. Luckily, someone had told me that she had done her bible studies in Thailand so I knew straight away she would come with her kick boxing business. She threw one foot up at my head, then another foot, and another foot. It was like she had three legs. All I could see was foot, foot, foot! So I grabbed one and I bit it. She yelled then fell down on the floor. She looked up at me and begged me to help her. (Madame Sankofa *gets down on her knees*) So I spared her her life.
Yvonne.	You've really seen some trouble.
M. Sankofa.	Yvonne, I have had to learn to fight. We have to learn how to fight strategically as a people.
Yvonne.	Been fighting all my life!
M. Sankofa.	But with strategy? That's the key; you must have a strategy! (*turning suddenly and pointing*) The lost property box.
Yvonne.	What?
M. Sankofa.	Oware…Ayo…Mancala. Get it!
Yvonne.	(Yvonne runs over to where the lost property box is) What?..Which one?
M. Sankofa.	The board game.
Yvonne.	(*taking out the oware game*) You mean this piece of wood.

M. Sankofa.	Wood! That's the oldest game in the world; that's the first computer in the world; that's one of the things we used to train our children on how to have a strategy to build and protect their communities!
Yvonne.	But it's just…
M. Sankofa.	Bring it! (Yvonne *runs back clumsily with the oware game*) You see that lost property box.
Yvonne.	There's nothing in there but old…
M. Sankofa.	Old what? It's full of our people's lost property. Lost culture, lost history, lost books, lost artefacts. (Madame Sankofa *suddenly gets up and starts to pray then dance as she cuts some kola nuts that she takes from her pocket*)…Ashe… (*looking at* Yvonne *questioningly*)…Ashe! Repeat.
Yvonne.	Ashe. (*she is handed a piece of kola nut*)
M. Sankofa.	You see Yvonne, the only thing that is going to heal you is not dreaming about your ex-husband, but loving yourself, loving your culture even though your culture has been made to appear ugly and not modern and hidden in lost property box. It will save you. Reclaim yourself and know how to fight.
Yvonne.	(*becoming weak and beginning to cry*) I can't….I'm so tired of fighting the whole world…
Theo	In the pirate station. Bob Marley's 'No Woman No Cry' can be heard sang by Sebastian.

Breaking news. Mad Woman has contacted Freedom FM. This is what she said: was Nefatari who ruled Black Egypt with Ramases mad; was Queen Zinga who fought the Portugese to stop slavery mad? Was Nanny of the Maroons Mad when she fought the British in Jamaica, mad? Was Harriet Tubman mad when she led Black people out of slavery through the underground railroad, mad? Was your own mother mad when she fed you before she fed herself? So let's big up mad woman. And listen to this, someone's text me to say that they saw the mad woman in the park with all mad people on the street; and she was teaching them to row; row as in boat and water. Next we hear that she did the same with the drunk man that always sleeping on park bench. (*In accent*) Where is she trying to take them? What journey is she trying to make the community go on? |
| M. Sankofa. | (*walking over to the items the* Yvonne *brought with her*) Take your album, your dress, and ring out of the suitcase. If its memories that you want to cling on to. |
| Yvonne. | You don't understand. |

M. Sankofa.	Your husband left you, but you haven't left him; haven't dealt with the break up. You still think about him at night. Wonder what might have been. Blame yourself. (*in Yvonne's voice*) Perhaps I should have done this different, or that… He's gone. Walked out on you. Yvonne deal with it.
Yvonne.	I can't…he was….. my everything. Always organising things. Reading books me never heard of before. In a room with people he would be the one with de biggest voice and opinion.
M. Sankofa.	Look, I know how you feel. I had five husbands. But I got them out of my system, as soon as the finances were sorted out.
Yvonne.	..but..
M. Sankofa.	(*with compassion*) Think back. Did you know when his journey started?
Yvonne.	(*puzzled*) Journey?
M. Sankofa.	Did you not see the lashes on his back; hear him calling out Massa in his dreams; or see him unable to walk because he had his foot cut off because he tried to run away from the plantation, from work? Did you really know your husband? What vows did you really take when you married him? (*pause*)
Yvonne.	(*remembering*) Met at a party. In '81. I was there wid me friends. Some sweet lovers rock was playing (*in the background, from Freedom FM, lovers rock music can be heard. Sankofa starts to 'wind-up' herself as the music is heard.*)
M. Sankofa.	Yes Mr DJ.
DJ Theo.	This one's for my mother whose going through a bit of a hard time right now; she doesn't tell me much, just says she's on a journey; some old school lovers rock, just for you mum. (music starts and Monique sings)
Yvonne.	He asked me to dance. First I refused. He come back. Me friends giggle. I accept and we dance, and we talk, and we dance a next tune..(*meanwhile* Sankofa *has picked up a coconut and is dancing with it*) …and he ask me out on a date and… (Sankofa *has stopped dancing and become serious again, and is holding out the coconut to* Yvonne *who suddenly looks at Sankofa in a puzzled way*) ….What's this?
Sankofa.	Your husband! Your man! This is what he was then, and now; a coconut! Uncle Tom, from the plantation.
Yvonne.	No.
Sankofa.	That's who you fell in love with.
Yvonne.	Him was different then.
Sankofa.	He wasn't. He was a boy. That's what they did to our men on the plantations. They broke them..

Yvonne.   Stop talking about plantations..(Sankofa *bursts out laughing*) My life is about the now; today, here.

Sankofa.   What was the name of the club where you met?

Yvonne.   The Cotton Club.

Sankofa.   What was Sebastian doing when you first saw him.

Yvonne.   Singing. Used to sing for a living.

Sankofa.   What was he drinking?

Yvonne.   Rum and…

M. Sankofa.   So you want this dancing, rum drinking, lovers rock, womanising Black man from the plantation to be a husband to you; keep the family together; be true to your marriage, and teach your son how to be a man. Wake up Yvonne.

Yvonne.   (*breaking down*) T'ings were different then. (*pause*)

M. Sankofa.   And who was the woman he left you for? (*pause*) Did you not lie in bed wondering about her? (*pause*).

Yvonne.   Hated her, though I never saw her…He changed. Became local councillor. Everyt'ing; him friends, him clothes, de way he carry himself; it all change. I became invisible.

M. Sankofa.   Did you confront her?

Yvonne.   I did smell her perfume; find her blonde hair on him jacket; receipts from expensive restaurants. Just drift away from us.

M. Sankofa.   And Theo?

Yvonne.   Did blame himself. Once, Sebastian turn on Theo; tell him to go school like ordinary child. That day Theo change too.

M. Sankofa.   And you?

Yvonne.   Became obsessed with her. Bought myself perfume; try and dress up, put more make-up on hoping that him would notice me. Do me usual Yvonne trick and blame meself. Made no difference. Next week him didn't come home. He stay wid her. Say he gone leave me and Theo.

M. Sankofa.	So you never confronted this other woman.
Yvonne.	Why should I? Would it make him come back?
M. Sankofa.	Ask the other woman why she stole your man from your home.
Yvonne.	My home is no plantation!
M. Sankofa.	(*pointing at Ms Maudsley*) Ask her!
Yvonne.	(*puzzled*) Her?
M. Sankofa.	Wreck your son's education….
Yvonne.	But..
M. Sankofa.	..and your marriage
Yvonne.	..she old; (*half laughing to herself*) him wouldn't look 'pon her.
M. Sankofa.	He more than looked Yvonne.
Yvonne.	(incredulously) Ms Maudsley; de headteacher? Sebastian?
M. Sankofa.	Yes Yvonne. Ask her. (*to the picture*) Ms Maudsley, Yvonne wants to know why you slept wid her husband.
Yvonne.	(*screaming*) No.
M. Sankofa.	(*running over to the picture and now pretending to be* Ms Maudsley) I was lonely.
Yvonne.	Lonely?
M. Sankofa.	(*as Ms Maudsley*) Didn't mean for it to happen. He just took an interest in me.
Yvonne.	After what you did to Theo.
M. Sankofa.	(*as Ms M*) *Never had an affair before.*
Yvonne.	..(*incredulous*) In de school teaching my child 'bout religious education, citizenship, and whole set of t'ings.
M. Sankofa.	(half mocking) Forgive me Yvonne

Yvonne.	Forgive!
M. Sankofa.	(*as* Ms Maudsley) Stress. I was suffering from depression.
Yvonne.	So you sleep wid me husband; what happen to paracetamol, an' valium. Depression!
M. Sankofa.	Want to go on the journey with you.
Yvonne.	'Bout depression. (*confronting the picture*).
M. Sankofa.	(*running back to* Yvonne) Good, good
Yvonne.	What you mean good; she depress so she jump in bed with me husband..
M. Sankofa.	(*interrupting*) No, no.
Yvonne.	What?
M. Sankofa.	Most Caribbean women I know would have run back to them Grandfather house; get the biggest machete they could find; fly back to England and, as you Jamaicans say, give her two lash in her skin.
Yvonne.	So I must murder now?
M. Sankofa.	Some women would. Him was your husband. She destroy your home; your confidence. Look at you. (*now stalking her*). When was the last time you bought yourself a new dress? Some shoes? When was the last time you smiled Yvonne ?(Pause)
Yvonne.	(*angrily*) I always smile.
M. Sankofa.	(*having gone and grabbed a mirror and holding it up to* Yvonne *who tries to dodge it*) look then. You call that a smile?
Yvonne.	Leave me alone.
M. Sankofa.	No. Not until you smile. So smile.
Yvonne.	(*exaggerated smile*) Happy now.
M. Sankofa.	No wonder your husband run and leave you. Call that a smile.

Yvonne.	(*looking at the picture*) Depression. D'you know what it was like to see your marriage fall apart. Friends you thought were friends just gossip behind your back. Spend five years staying at home homeschooling your child. Suddenly Theo at college, and I have no career. D'you know. I want answers; I want justice, and I want my life back; just want some love..
M. Sankofa.	(*pointing at the suitcase*) How can you go on this journey carrying all this baggage? Where can we fit love in. (*suddenly they hear a noise*)
Yvonne.	Who's there?
M. Sankofa.	Did you come with anyone?
Yvonne.	No! (M. Sankofa *takes up a Kung Fu stance*)
M. Sankofa.	If you value your life you'll come out. (Sebastian *slowly emerges. He looks a bit rough and has a small bottle of whiskey in one of his jacket pockets and a book in the other. He wears worn plimsolls and is carrying a carrier bag.*)
Yvonne.	Sebastian?
M. Sankofa.	Sebastian? You mean your husband
Sebastian.	Yvonne.
Yvonne.	(*to* Sebastian) What you doing here?
Sebastian.	I..
M. Sankofa.	Why you walk out on your family?
Sebastian	I've moved back on the estate.
Yvonne.	(*half pleading*) Don't want you in my …
Sebastian.	(*interrupting*) …Just hear me out; I've…
Yvonne.	You haven't changed. It's the same story; only think about yourself
M. Sankofa.	(*sniffing*) Smell as if you need a bath..
Sebastian.	(*ignoring* M. Sankofa) I'm doing a thesis; on the estate..
M. Sankofa.	Another one..(*calling out*) Dr Tunde you have competition.

Yvonne.	What business do you have on the estate; after you run off and go live in leafy suburbia..
Sebastian.	Helping Ray-I with the campaign; this is my roots..
M. Sankofa.	(*to* Sebastian) You're living rough.
Yvonne	Roots! Your roots start with your family. You left us!
Sebastian.	(*noticing* M. Sankofa) Keep out of our relationship..
Yvonne.	Relationship! We've been separated, humiliated, broke and you're living back on the estate.
Sebastian.	Because..
Yvonne.	Why?
Sebastian.	Because I know where Gun-Boy is hiding.
M. Sankofa.	My Goodness
Yvonne.	You have nothing to do with Gun-Boy.
Sebastian.	I do. He's from another estate. He's just a product of this urban mess we're living in. Look (*holding out his research notes but* M. Sankofa *who has sneaked around the back of him suddenly grabs him*)…Let go!
Yvonne.	Leave him!
M. Sankofa.	(*to* Yvonne) Get your cutlass.
Sebastian	Yvonne tell her..
Yvonne.	Just leave him alone..
M. Sankofa.	Kill him! It's your big chance. Revenge!
Sebastian.	Tell this mad woman to let go.
Yvonne.	Madame Sankofa?
M. Sankofa.	Why. You just said you don't love him anymore.

Yvonne.	..leave him..(M. Sankofa *lets go*)
Sebastian.	(*very emotional to* Yvonne) I'm back; I'm not asking for forgiveness, just understanding.. I'm back. If I could I'd help the council knock down this estate. Give the people some decent housing, some hope; another chance. Another chance Yvonne. (*He pauses*. Yvonne *begins to cry.*)
Yvonne.	Go, please.
Sebastian.	I was listening; I've brought some baggage too.
M. Sankofa.	Don't let him fool you.
Sebastian.	Look. (*he begins to take out some things from a carrier bag he has*) This is what is killing us. Trainers, fast cars, fast food; cheap make-up, mobile phones, music, the latest fashion. Look. (*he runs to the picture and puts the items down as if making a kind of shrine*).
Yvonne.	And what killed you Sebastian? What killed the man that was so conscious, so proud of his family, so proud of his son and wife?
Sebastian.	They destroyed me.
Yvonne.	They?
Sebastian.	I got elected. Only Black councillor that would say anything; that would stand up for our rights. They gave me stress..
Yvonne.	(*pointing to the picture*) Another one with stress. (*sarcastically*) Paracetamol where are you?
Sebastian.	So I started to drink again. You know I hadn't touched a drop since…
Yvonne.	Sebastian.
M. Sankofa.	(*to* Yvonne) If you give me one thousand naira…
Sebastian.	(*ignoring* Madame Sankofa) This is what we're worshipping; this is what's just making us blind…
Yvonne.	(*to* Sebastian) No…
M. Sankofa.	(*continuing*) I will go back to Lagos; to the market…

Sebastian.	…making us consumers of junk and junk ideas, and….
Yvonne.	Please…
M. Sankofa.	…and I can get you a husband twice as good and this hopeless one here…
Yvonne.	(*shouting*) Stop it Sebastian.
Sebastian.	(*half pleading and pointing to the shrine*) worshipping idols that's killing our minds….
Yvonne.	(*suddenly becoming forgiving*) Sebastian…Come (*she holds out her hand to him*)
M. Sankofa.	In the name of God you can't take this man back.
Sebastian.	..(*walking towards her thinking that she's forgiven him*)…I'll never hurt you again…
M. Sankofa.	Reminds me of my first husband…
Sebastian.	(*continuing*) thank you Yvonne (*he moves towards her slowly and goes to hold her singing as he gets closer to her*)…..remember our tune; how we danced the first time we met….(she pulls out a bottle of whiskey from his pocket)
Yvonne.	And what about this Sebastian?
Sebastian.	Give it back!
Yvonne.	Put this on your shrine.
M. Sankofa.	Drunkard!
Sebastian.	(to M. Sankofa) You be quiet! (to Yvonne) You don't know what they did to me.
Yvonne.	Always blaming someone.
Sebastian.	(*almost to himself*) ..could have made it in politics; they set me up, then they ruined me.
M. Sankofa.	(*to* Yvonne) Come. (*making her way to the entrance*)
Sebastian.	Yvonne. Please. (Yvonne *ignores him and leaves with* M. Sankofa *who hangs around a little. Sebastian goes to the 'shrine' and picks up the bottle and sits by the shrine and half attempts to take a drink then begins to sob*).

181

M. Sankofa.	In Africa there is a goddess Yemaya. She is the goddess of love. Perhaps, when your heart is ready to understand that love is not just for yourself she might come. (M. Sankofa leaves) *Lights go down. Lights go up on Monique. Monique sings a love song.*
Theo	The next day. And we have Monique in the studio who is going to give us a song to make everyone on the estate feel good. Come Monique. (Monique sings.)

Act One **Scene Four**	*In the pirate station. Madame Sankofa's jingle advert is heard. It says:* Are you having marital, or financial, or sexual problems? Then come to Madame Sankofa; Nigeria's top psychological therapist and life coach. Let Madame Sankofa take you on a great journey to discover your potential; let Madame Sankofa make your dreams come true. I will help you find your partner and true love; I can make you become a millionaire. 'Hello Black people of England. My name is Madame Sankofa and I have come to take you on a great journey so that you can realise your potential. Come to my church this Sunday.
Theo.	As promised listeners, we have in Freedom FM studio the one and only; the woman we're all talking about, the one who we called the mad woman but who is actually, Madame Sankofa….make some noise wherever you are.
M. Sankofa.	(*with humility*) You're welcome. Please, thank you.
Theo.	..some of you have called her, the mad woman; some have said she's a fraud; some have said she's on the run from the Nigerian police. (in accent) Big time rumours have been following this woman, but she's in the studio coming to you live and direct; so let's put rumours aside and say a warm welcome to our guest. Madame Sankofa welcome.
M. Sankofa.	Please, I am so delighted to be here. May God bless you.
Theo.	I'd imagined an angry woman but you are so calm; what's the secret?
M. Sankofa.	God has given me peace since the break-up of my five marriages.
Theo.	Five?
M. Sankofa.	The last one was particularly traumatic. A Jamaican man. Came to live in Lagos. Said he was a top fashion designer. Called his business 'Jah Fashion Studio.' Made me some red pea soup. Six months later we married, but he changed. Stopped cooking. One day I came home and found everything empty. My pot of rice, empty; my bank account and my wardrobe, empty; even my lingerie, all gone.

Theo.	Listeners, you hearing this?
M. Sankofa.	I tracked him down. Found him selling me leopard skin underwear in Portobello market. Gave him back him ring; took back my lingerie and a cousin of mine told him to watch his back. One week later he was found dead. Someone strangled him with his own underpants. I was traumatised. After this little episode in my life I opened the Church of Sankofa. Since then God has given me peace.
Theo.	Glad t'hear it. Now, what's with all this bills of debt; final demands of payments being nailed to the door of High Street banks; graffiti on walls saying, 'leave the plantation'. Madame Sankofa, explain.
M. Sankofa.	Before I start I would just like to say hello to my Aunty in Harlesden, my Aunty in Peckham and my great Aunty in Lewisham.
Theo.	(*in accent*) Big up de aunties. Oh yeah, Aunty Gladys I coming Sunday for me rice and peas and chicken…(*turning back to* M. Sankofa) Sorry.
M. Sankofa.	I have come to tell Black people that they are living on a modern plantation. A plantation of debt, and plantation of ignorance.
Theo.	Plantation? The estate! *Yvonne enters the school area with a mirror. She takes off her coat and begins to look in the lost property box. She finds a traditional Nigerian outfit, hesitates and then puts it on. She sits next to* Ms Maudsley. *She stares at herself in the mirror. She begins to cry.*
M. Sankofa.	The real issue on the estate is not whether it should be knocked down but how we change our thinking to make it an African village where families can flourish.
Theo.	Sound like Dr Tunde.
M. Sankofa.	Pardon?
Theo.	So your saying the estate is really a plantation and what we should pull down are the chains that keep us thinking like an impoverished people.
M. Sankofa.	Precisely and a psychological journey is needed. That's where I come in.
Theo.	Explain.

M. Sankofa.	Let's define a plantation as we experienced it when as in chattel slavery. A plantation is a place where you are dehumanised. Your real name is taken away from you. The food that you have eaten for generations is taken away from you and you eat pig-type food; a place where you are beaten, daily; forced to work for nothing; forced to be interested in only things the plantation owner is interested; and you're scared to be yourself because the plantation owner doesn't like you being your true self; he only likes you trying to be like him.
Theo.	So where are the chains?
M. Sankofa.	Please, they are in the mind. And that mind is controlled through alcohol, media, drugs, and school.
Theo.	Amazing. Now, who was it that brought you here? Were you invited? Are you here on holiday.. (*Yvonne slowly begins to adorn her face.*)
M. Sankofa.	I am a motivational speaker and life coach. I have come to ask the people what's your game plan? How will you create wealth? Do you have the health to create wealth because I see so many of you eating chicken and chips. You've forgotten your yam and banana and pea soup.
Theo.	And who is this woman whose sadness is so deep?
M. Sankofa.	That's confidential. She is at a very delicate stage in her life. I shouldn't, but perhaps I could leave her mobile number for you to ring. It's important that we talk if we want to heal.
Theo.	(laughing) Sounds like my mum. Anyway, and what's the game plan Madame Sankofa? Tell the people.
M. Sankofa.	I want everyone to stand in front of the mirror and tell themselves that they are beautiful.
Theo.	Hear that listeners. So do it.
M. Sankofa.	I want people to raise their energy; we have to create positive energy on the estate. We need our ancestral drums Can you hear them. (Drumming is heard) Come on people of the estate. Dance! (Ray-I *and* Monique *are seen and begin to dance*) Any you too Ms Mystery woman. (Yvonne gets up and begins to dance. M Sankofa shows Theo a few moves who then starts dancing and before she starts talking over the drumming)

Theo.	Come on people; let's start moving. We can't keep complaining. Move! To the left, to the right. Come on people. (*Everyone is now dancing/moving.*) Our joy will bring us health, our health will bring us wealth. Repeat after me: our joy will bring us health, our health will bring us wealth (*the chant is carried on by* Ray-I *and* Monique) We must be positive and we can achieve anything. It was your positive minds that built the pyramids; it was your positive thinking that developed hieroglyphs, it was our positive minds that built the first schools and universities. So we must be positive. Each morning I want all the people of the estate and beyond to get up and say I am the most positive person in the world, and thank God for it and for bringing me to Madame Sankofa's Church of Positivity. Praise de Lord.
	(*Everyone continues to dance and chant for awhile whilst lights flash.*)
Theo.	(*answers the phone as the music fades*) Hello, Ray-I?
Ray-I.	Just like to say Jah-thanks to Madame Sankofa. Never knew she was the mad woman too, because she's been on de estate helping us in our campaign to stop dem wicked Babylon people from knocking down our homes. We holding meetings, make placard, write petition but still dese people wan' to mash up our homes.
Theo.	Is that so?
M. Sankofa.	You're welcome. I keep busy.
Ray-I.	But I must ask somet'ing dat puzzle me. How come you bring dis African board game to de estate.
M. Sankofa.	Please Ray-I, we as a people have to learn to have strategy again. That game is known all over Africa. It goes back to Ancient Black Egypt. In Nigeria it's known as Ayo; in Ghana, it's known as Oware; in East Africa as Mancalla, and Jamaica as Babu! (*Yvonne is now seen trying to figure out how to play the oware game*)
Ray-I.	Why on de estate? We can't play game when we under attack.
M. Sankofa.	Game! This game teaches you how to have strategy. We don't have strategy. When people come into your neighbourhood and open shop and sell yam, ochre, plantain and sweet potato, they have strategy to take all your money; when the council knock down your housing estate they have strategy to build luxury apartment which you can't afford. Please Ray-I, Ayo will teach our people to have strategy and solve our problems. Knocking down the estate won't solve anything. We have to build up our strategy to prosper as a people.
Ray-I.	Jah Blessings to you, and give thanks. And by the way Theo, your dad is back on the estate.
Theo.	My dad left long time and I don't mind saying that on air.

How to Unlock Your Family's Genius

Ray-I.	Catch you later. *Lights go down on* Theo. *Lights up on* Yvonne.
Yvonne.	Dear Ms Maudsley, he wants me back you know. Him writing me letter, smiling when he see me on de street. But I want a man, not a boy. That's what the estate, I mean the plantation, has done to many of our men; made them into boys. (Shaking her head) I can't have him back. Him will just lie with me; touch my hair hoping it like your hair; touch my lips, hoping it like your lips; touch my nose hoping it is thin like yours…. (Monique hums then sings a little)
M. Sankofa.	She doesn't realise it but she cries not only for herself, but for those who went through the gates of no return…
Yvonne.	….how can I trust another man on this plantation. All I see is our people hating themselves?
M. Sankofa.	…cries for those who died on the long march to the slave dungeons; cries for those who died on the boats; cries for those who died fighting the slave catchers, those who died waiting in the stench of the slave ships anchored off the West African coasts; those who died of syphilis, gonorrhoea, malnutrition
Yvonne.	…am I still the woman of the plantation who can be raped; sold, beaten and be your nanny, your nurse? You took my husband for excitement. To break him. To humiliate me because I stood up to you?
M. Sankofa.	Please people I beg you listen. My journey is to show you how to build a relationship with God, how to make the estate into a village. Let us regain our science, our knowledge, please. *The silhouette of Gun-Boy is seen in the gates of no return.*
Theo.	And how can people sail with you; how can they become part of this journey.
M. Sankofa.	Well, they can contact me; or, if they have lost their way; they're doing bad things in their community then people can nominate them to come on Madame Sankofa's Journey.
Theo.	(*interrupting*) You mean people like drug dealers selling drugs outside our schools; and the people in the crack houses; and the coconut politicians we have like like….
M. Sankofa.	Yes, all are welcome. We sail on Sunday. Come early because we have 500 hundred years of baggage to check in that we will then throw them overboard once the sea calms down.

Stage Eleven

186

Theo.	Well listeners you have heard Madame Sankofa speak on Freedom FM, the people's radio station. Once again, big up Madame Sankofa. So why don't we as a community take this journey. Why don't we achieve the impossible; why don't we go back through the gates of no return and reclaim our greatness. Did they ever think that we would survive; attempt to go back through the gates; reclaim our names, history, culture and psychology? People, we all have to start this journey and stop pretending we is okay. (*in an African-Caribbean accent*) So Gunman, crack dealer man, and waste of time Black politician, come sail wid us, so that we can all confront those demons we pretending that don't exist. Black people, it's make your mind up time. It's Sankofa time. Anyway, let me ring this mystery woman and ask permission for us to join her on her long journey.

(*Theo rings and waits until Yvonne answers*.)

Yvonne.	Hello
Theo.	Who's this?
Yvonne	It's me.
Theo.	Mum?
Yvonne.	Theo?
Theo.	Sorry mum, must have phoned you by mistake. Listeners, this is my mum. Speak to you …
Yvonne.	(*shouting*) Listen!
Theo.	Mum?
Yvonne.	No Theo, there's no mistake..
Theo.	But?
Yvonne.	Yes Theo.
Theo.	The mystery woman; you?...No, no.
Yvonne.	I'm de woman going on the journey.
Theo.	No mum. What's the matter!
Yvonne.	Everyt'ing de matter. Your father leave us; you drop out of university, them done knock down our home and I just drifting…

Theo.	This journey's not for you, not for us..
Yvonne.	(*shouting*) ..course it is! We no different to anyone else from round here. We all living on estate. Slaving away to pay bills; in relationship one minute and out de next. Seeing our children fail; carry guns; some can't find work, and those that do good they just move out of the area. Both of us need this journey. Theo. (Theo has gone silent)
Theo.	Mum, I have to fight for a decent life on the estate. I love my history yes, but can't be dealing with no looking back in time business!
Yvonne.	So what you gone deal with?
Theo.	Look, we have parties; they say it's too loud. Yout's get together and just joke around, police arrest them. We need pest control to get rid of rats and dem yuppy private housing people who gone rebuild the estate into private flats. I want to deal with joy, and some love, and some respect.
Yvonne.	So why did you drop out?
Theo.	Didn't want to teach in no school.
Yvonne.	And who will save our children?
Theo.	Hear that listeners; even my own mum is calling me a failure..
Yvonne.	Didn't say that Theo; you know that!
Theo.	Let me tell everyone what happened. I stood in that classroom doing my teaching practice; training to be what they call a teacher. Kids from the estate, just like me. But I wasn't reaching them; not touching their soul or making a difference to their lives. I was having a lesson observation by some ball 'ead man. I taught them maths, maths that didn't mean anything in their lives. After the lesson, I decided to try something different. I taught them maths and art, maths in Africa, maths that they could use in their lives, and maths games like oware or ayo, and they loved it because it meant something to them, but you know what, that same ball head man fail my lesson observation. Hear that mum.
Yvonne.	No Theo.
Theo.	Fail me; fail the children, fail this estate because he say the maths I teach is not linked to National Curriculum. It's linked to their lives…That's why I drop out of teacher training college.

Yvonne.	You're scared. You hid away in your pirate station playing Malcom X. It's all fantasy Theo; like your father. (pointing at Ms Maudsley) D'you want people like Ms Maudsley to win?
	Enter M. Sankofa *with a shopping bag.*
Theo.	(*to the listeners*) Hear that people, my own mother is the mystery woman. And it's me…
Yvonne.	..no Theo…(Madame Sankofa *goes to* Ms Maudsley *and begins to comb her hair.*)
Theo.	…me who causing her so much trouble.
Yvonne.	Come Theo. Be part of this. Let's make this journey together. (pause)
Theo.	And Dad?
Yvonne.	It's too late for your father…Bye.
M. Sankofa.	(*smiling as she combs* Ms Maudsley's *hair*) You have to look your best.
Yvonne.	What you doing?
M. Sankofa.	Making her look good for the journey.
Yvonne.	What! She going?
M. Sankofa.	Ms Maudsley say that she feel sorry for what happened to Black people and she would like to come along for the ride.
Yvonne.	Ride! (looking around) Where me cutlass!
M. Sankofa.	She needs this journey even more than you. Look at her.
Yvonne.	Tired look at her.
M. Sankofa.	She's sorry for the condition of the ships; the chains, the filth, the branding, the beatings..
Yvonne.	Sorry!
M. Sankofa.	(to Ms Maudsley) Yes, I've got your shopping.

Yvonne.	Shopping, you think we going on a cruise
M. Sankofa.	(*reading from a list*) toilet paper, toothpaste, and soap for dry skin
Yvonne.	No, if she goes; she goes as we went. In chains, in filth, in shit, in fear, in blood… (*with sarcasm*) Okay Ms Maudsley, welcome to the slave ship. (*Yvonne goes and gets the chains and begins to put them around the picture of* Ms Maudsley. Meanwhile M. Sankofa *has picked up an oar, taken off her coat and has began to row on one side of the triangle*).
M. Sankofa.	(*she turns on her phone/mouthpiece and shouts*) Is everyone ready? Theo, tell your listeners its time to sail?
Theo,	Listeners of Freedom FM, are you ready; pick up your oars, bring all your baggage you've gathered over the last 500 years, cause we going on a big journey, or do you want to mentally stay on the estate?
M. Sankofa, Yvonme and Theo.	(*shouting and holding their oars aloft*) Sankofa, Sankofa, Sankofa. (They now all begin to row at the three points of the triangle)

End of Act 1

Act two **Scene One**	*Thunder and lightning are heard and seen. M. Sankofa and Yvonne are seen rowing in the school, whilst Theo, in the pirate station raps: Meanwhile, on the screen, news headings are seen on contemporary issues.*
Theo.	This is freedom FM giving you a report on our schools. Schools that sometimes fail our children, fail our family, but I'm not into blame no more. Earlier I was there in our old derelict school right here next to the estate, the one they closed down when we started to become governors, and organise, and challenge things, and question why so many of our children were in special needs, excluded, failing. People, our ship is sailing; I know that some of you have started already. We are about to arrive on the shores of Africa and our families are going to go back through the gates of no return. The real transatlantic journey has begun. Madame Sankofa is the Captain, her first officer is Yvonne, my mother. Are we ready for this journey…….M. Sankofa stops rowing and looks through her telescope
M. Sankofa.	(*screaming*) Africa is in trouble. Egypt, the beautiful land of the pharaohs has fallen…they're running; temples are being pulled down; our libraries ransacked; our priests slaughtered; the pyramids looted. The Blacks are falling.

Theo.	We have a historical newsflash now that some of us have chosen to take our families back through the gates of no return.
	(Radio news accompanied by musician drumming) Queen NZinga has launched another attack on the Portuguese forts along the coast of Africa. Western observers have again called her a terrorist, with the Portuguese slavers offering a reward for her capture. However, the rebel leader issued a statement claiming that she was a freedom fighter and one day her great grandchildren will rise up.
Yvonne.	(*to the picture and the items that have now accumulated around it*) Dear Ms Maudsley, me and Theo are going on a journey with Madame Sankofa. We taking de whole community with us. Even Gun Boy, and if you come then what will happen to you when you go back through the gates of no return? Will you feel remorse? Will you quote Wilberforce? Will you pretend nothing ever happened?
M. Sankofa.	Foreign people have come. I see great migrations of Blacks travelling to far places to escape persecution.
Theo.	It is the 1750s. More ships come; millions more are taken into slavery. We have another historical newsflash here on Freedom FM Radio.
	Thomas Clarkson and Olaudah Equiano, two controversial abolitionists have been compiling evidence and speaking out against the slave trade….Have we really dealt with our history
M. Sankofa.	(*looking through binoculars*) They're going deep into Africa. (turning to Yvonne) There's a big storm ahead. I'm going to get some rest.
Theo.	Once again people I'd like to hear how are you coping with the preparation for the Sankofa journey. According to Madame Sankofa she's picking up the ship today.(*Phone rings. Monique is on the line*) First caller of the day. Monique.
Monique.	Yeah well, I think it's good 'cause a lot of people dem don't know their history and are lost. And I reckon we should have another Abolition of Mental Slavery Act 2009 because the way I see my baby father just walk out on us and ……it aint right!
Theo.	And how are things on the estate?
Monique.	They still want to knock it down; I mean the council people. Police searching for Gun-Boy, I'm trying to get money to pay for studio time…same really.
Theo.	I hear Ray-I's got things delayed.

How to Unlock Your Family's Genius

Monique.	But for how long? We've been having meetings after meetings. Whilst we're just trying to make the estate safe police keep raiding, stopping and searching us like we're terrorists; saying they're looking for Gun-Boy, as the yout's call him. Gun-Boy weren't involved in no shooting from what I hear. We need people to stand up for their community.
Theo.	What d'you suggest?
Monique.	Well I know from my child that we need fathers to come back to the estate; we need men to teach our boys to be men; to teach them how to run businesses or something like that.
Theo.	Sound like you been on a real journey.
Monique.	It's the only way.
Theo.	Good speaking to you Monique. Stay strong.
Monique.	You too. Bye.
Theo.	This is freedom FM dealing with our people's issues. Now we have the man himself; Ray-I de Rastaman. Ray, man how you doing?
Ray-I	I'm good you know. Still in the firing line. Organising petitions, meetings; writing letters to stop them knocking down the estate; this is my journey as Madame Sankofa says.
Theo.	Respect. But do you feel you can win.
Ray-I.	We have to learn to win. That's why me was so glad when M. Sankofa come over and start teach the youth dem dat game she call Ayo and oware. It teach dem how to win; how to think, and soon all de yout's from de estate start playing it. But you know what?
Theo.	Tell me.
Ray-I.	Someone t'ief de game; t'ief it because is start teach de children 'bout dem culture. We would get some kola nuts and cut a little and taste it and play de game; plan we strategy and out think them; that's why de estate isn't knock down yet. Strategy works!
Theo.	Tell me.

Ray-I.	Someone t'ief de game; t'ief it because is start teach de children 'bout dem culture. We would get some kola nuts and cut a little and taste it and play de game; plan we strategy and out think them; that's why de estate isn't knock down yet. Strategy works!
Theo.	Who t'ief de game?
Ray-I.	Babylon; de police or dem council people! Now de estate full up wid crack dealer, poverty, drugs, derelict flats. Police still raiding de place looking for Gun-Bwoy as everyone call him, even though they know he innocent; it's pure madness.
Theo.	Ray-I, blessings to you and the estate. We gone catch up.
Ray-I.	Respect.
Theo.	We'll take just one more call.
Dr Tunde.	Dr Tunde here.
Theo.	How's the book going Dr Tunde?
Dr Tunde.	It's at a critical stage.
Theo.	Explain.
Dr Tunde.	My thesis has examined how the poor are being dispossessed. They have no land; some of their labour is of no use to the ruling classes so they are being incarcerated in prisons, in schools, in mental institutions and in run down estates. Children born on the estate will have little opportunities. But it is important that I interview Gun-Boy as they call him for my new thesis. You see, he tried to bring the gangs together; it appears that he realised how the people could come together and better themselves, but the gangs turned on one another. Why the police and media keep suspecting Gun-Boy is wrong, that's why he's in hiding.
Theo.	Just had Monique on the line. She thinks that much of the problems of the estate is to do with fathers playing their role.
Tunde.	Look, I live on the estate; I am a responsible father and grandfather. The difference between me and the fathers that Monique is talking about is that I was brought up in an African village. I had a million fathers disciplining me. I had a million mothers. This isn't romanticism. We had a practical and loving way of raising our children, our families. Poverty is spoiling this. I tell you, we have to go back to a village system to live.

Theo.	Doctor, it's been great…
Dr. Tunde.	No wait. Why I rang was about M. Sankofa.
Theo.	It's okay she's just about to come on…
Dr. Tunde.	She's a fraud.
Theo.	Fraud?
Dr. Tunde.	(*his mobile phone rings*) Just a minute I have a long distance call from my cousin in Nigeria, I will ring you back.
Theo.	We'll take a short commercial break. Stay tuned.
M. Sankofa.	(*a storm in the distance is heard.*Yvonne *is seen sitting at the small oware table trying to strategise.* M. Sankofa, *who has been sleeping on the floor/deck, jumps up suddenly. She runs and gets a pirates hat from underneath the table*) There's a big storm coming. Hoist the sails.
Yvonne.	(startled) What?
M. Sankofa.	Hoist the sails, throw some more cargo over board..
Yvonne.	What you talking…
M. Sankofa.	(*Pulling imaginary ropes*) You're on a ship; now hoist the sails woman! (Yvonne begins to hoist the imaginary sails)
Yvonne.	(*still a little confused*) I didn't realise…(M. Sankofa *stumbles as if the 'ship' has been hit by a big wave*)
M. Sankofa.	Oh my god, we're going to sink! Throw your baggage over board. We're too heavy. Now!
Yvonne.	No, I can't.
M. Sankofa.	Throw it. (*looking up at the sky*) the storm's getting heavier. (Yvonne *is now throwing her baggage over board*)
Yvonne.	I don't have anything else to throw. (M. Sankofa *is now at the helm steering the ship.* Yvonne *is half distraught*) You've made me get rid of everything. There's nothing left of me. Nothing!
M. Sankofa.	(*the storm is becoming calm*) The true you is what is left. You have a lot more baggage to get rid of Yvonne. (M. Sankofa *hands Yvonne her binoculars*) See if you can see the storm that our people face every day but don't know it, and then see if you can see those of us who strategised. (long pause)

Theo.	Another caller.
Ray I.	Ray- I man.
Theo.	Ray-I, you back.
Ray I.	T'ings rough. I did forget to speak about the journey. My journey start already. Me did wan' jump ship cause tings bad but me have to t'ink 'bout them yout'. We have to teach dem to have courage 'cause dem getting it bad.
Theo.	So no regrets 'bout starting the journey.
Ray I.	We must. We have no choice. We have to deal with mental slavery. We have to look for de Sankofa tree in our community too. Have to bring these heroes into our schools as teachers. Make dem live again! We have to bring back Queen N'Zinga, and Equiano and Toussaint and make the children understand that the first part of freedom was just to get rid of the chains, the next part is to get rid of the chains in de mind! We mind!
Theo.	Thanks Ray-I. Always wid passion. Respect.
Ray I.	Peace.
M. Sankofa.	(*helping Yvonne to see and understand what she sees in the binoculars*)..hunted and chased they hide; they go to remote places; into swamplands; they distrust one another, they try and rebuild…
Theo.	People, I like the fighting spirit I'm hearing. Remember, we had to fight for this radio station. How many times did they raid us? How many applications did we submit to get legal? We had to fight to sit on a bus, and we are going to have to fight to get our sanity back. So get ready!
Yvonne.	(*Yvonne goes over to the picture with a black doll in African attire and holds it up to* Ms Maudsley) Ms Maudsley, I glad you coming with us. I want you to meet Queen N'Zinga and all the African people who fight against slavery. You didn't teach about them? Only tell us about Wilberforce.
M. Sankofa.	(now looking throught the binoculars herself) Soon we're great again. We built Mali, Ancient Ghana, Songhai; but the Arabs now come to enslave us…..look!
Theo.	Listeners, I want you to imagine. Imagine that the school is open again. Exactly like it used to be. Can you hear the children playing; boys messing around; teachers scolding them, not understanding them. (*shouting*) Equiano, Toussaint L'Ouverture, you're supposed to be in here, not in no history book! Is part of our journey to make our children's learning real, to build family again?

M. Sankofa.	Again we fight back. We drive most of the Arabs out. But the Black man is weak. In the distance there is a small ship sailing towards Africa. A Portuguese flag flaps in the wind. It has goods, but they also bring guns, for one tribe, gunpowder for another, alcohol for the chiefs…..
Theo.	Garvey, Biko, Tubman, Sancho where are you? When we get to the gates of no return are we going to pledge that we will make these heroes and heroines come alive?
M. Sankofa	All along the coast of Africa are ships waiting, silently waiting with chains, and whips. And right across the Atlantic are plantations, waiting; waiting for our families.
Theo.	(*Looking through his binoculars.*) People of Freedom FM; I have a text from M. Sankofa who has secured a ship and will be returning for us all to board. The text reads: our heroes say we must all go on the Sankofa journey. There is no other way.
M. Sankofa.	But we fight back. I see Queen N'Zinga leading armies, I see King Truda, attacking and burning down forts, attacking slave castles. Suddenly, they lay down their weapons; they hear children,…they have something to say; tell the children…..(Equiano *and* Queen N'Zinga *appear*).
Q. N'Zinga.	(*in African accent*) Yes I fought, but I ask myself why. When I see our people living as they do. Why did we fight?
Theo.	Perhaps I should become Equiano; and campaign for the Abolition of the Mental Slavery Act. Perhaps I should do what I did in the late eighteenth century, and go around England campaigning in the Black community for the abolition of mental slavery. What say you Queen N'Zinga? *Equiano appears.*
M. Sankofa.	I see raids; their homes burnt; they're being marched across great lands.
M. Sankofa.	They're being taken onto the ships; each one branded; each one beaten. Some cry, some curse, some pray, some die in pain and agony. They are counted, and inspected, and taken down below into the hold, where they wait in the darkness; all stripped naked: children, women, men; some pregnant, aching from the long tortuous march, some on their cycle where they lie with no dignity….but there is one slave who is not of that era. He is tormented; broken hearted and with shame. Slowly, he picks up his pen and begins to write.
Theo.	(*phone rings*) We have a new caller. Who is this
Dr. Tunde.	Evening to you.
Theo.	Dr. Tunde, how are things in higher learning?
Dr. Tunde.	Very well thank-you.

Theo.	So are you getting on the ship when it comes?.
Dr. Tunde.	Well, let's wait and see.
Theo.	You're sounding mysterious.
Dr. Tunde.	You know I had my reservations about this Madame Sankofa.
Theo.	Go on…
Dr. Tunde.	Sankofa is a Ghanian name, it is not Nigerian. I should know, because I specialised in African Studies at Oxford.
Theo.	And?
Dr. Tunde.	So I hired a private detective in Lagos. He's my cousin and has solved many high profile murders amongst my relatives. His name is detective Emeka. He said he went all over Lagos; east, west, north and south, trying to find something out about this woman. Until he came to an old lady's house and he say, Grandma, have you heard of Madame Sankofa? Grandma said that the only M. Sankofa she had heard of was a cleaner from England who had retired and come back to live in Nigeria.
Theo.	Cleaner?
Dr. Tunde.	At a school right here in London.
Theo.	Cleaner? School? You don't mean Ms Abuja!
Dr. Tunde.	That's right. And Abuja is a name of a place in Nigeria. It's not anyone's name. They call her Aunty Ngozi in Lagos.
Theo.	You mean she tricked all of us into….
Dr. Tunde.	Travelling around the place; talking a ship; rowing around when there is only concrete. And people like Ray-I and Monique thinking that they can row their way out of the estate. Where is de water. It's madness. We need scientific revolution; not a rowing boat!
Theo.	No..
Dr. Tunde.	Oh yes. And I bet you she is on a ship right now heading back to Nigeria singing Sweet Mother with all the money that you people have given her.
Theo.	Mummy, are you listening…

Theo.	Mummy, are you listening…
Dr. Tunde.	I have to go to a church meeting.
Theo.	Mum…(*suddenly realising what* Dr. Tunde *has said*) By the way, heard you had some problems there.
Dr. Tunde.	Where?
Theo.	Your church. Heard you got suspended.
Dr. Tunde.	Well. There was a disagreement.
Theo.	Sounds like you went on a journey of your own.
Dr. Tunde.	In my thesis I began to document how we as a people are always portraying Jesus and God as white; and now we have started wearing white wigs, and putting white cream on our skins. Half the congregation are now white even though they are Black. It's confusing, because they are confused, and our children are confused. This would never happen in my village. I simply put it to the church committee that we should start worshipping God as Black and beautiful people. That's all! You know what they did to me? They suspended me!
Theo.	Perhaps you should pray for forgiveness?
Dr. Tunde.	But how should I pray. As an African with a blonde wig on my head?
Theo.	Anyway, hope you manage to work things out. Got to sign off now. Take care.
Dr. Tunde.	We are still a confused people. Okay bye for now. And watch this Madame Sankofa woman with her nonsense. (pause)
Theo.	Mum, if you are listening then get away from that woman. She's the woman that used to be the school cleaner and get into trouble for sitting in the cleaning room playing cards, drinking palm wine, and playing that board game…(*phone rings*)

(*Yvonne has been listening to the radio incredulously. M. Sankofa is at the helm steering the ship*).

Yvonne.	(moving towards her) Cleaner…. A school cleaner
Theo.	(to himself) …the Nigerian cleaner, and the Nigerian boys used to call her aunty, and she'd use to walk around, singing and eating chin chin.
M. Sankofa.	(*singing as she steers the ship*) Sweet mother, sweet mother…..

Yvonne.	(*pointing*) You told me you was Nigeria's first international life coach; (*sarcastically*) award winning motivational speaker.
Dr.Tunde.	…and when she came back to Nigeria she got a job in Lagos cleaning buses, one of which was an international coach company for tourists. So Cousin Emeka, the detective, tells me.
Theo.	Coach company, but my mum, and half of the estate thinks that she's..
Yvonne.	Cleaner…and what you 'ave to say for yourself?
M. Sankofa.	(*singing*) Sweet mother…sweet mother (She takes out her binoculars).
Yvonne.	What you doing, looking out for the police!
Theo.	(*half to himself*) No, let me phone mum.
Dr. Tunde.	It's a sad reflection on our people that I have a Phd and the people on the estate will not embrace my political philosophy and yet they are prepared to follow this cleaner.
Theo.	Mum, are you there? Pick up the phone.
Yvonne.	(*shouting*) Don't pretend you can't hear me.
M. Sankofa.	(*Taking off her head phones*) Why are you shouting?
Yvonne	You're a cleaner!
M.Sankofa.	Yes, I clean up peoples lives that are..
Yvonne.	Stop lying to me. You're Aunty Ngosi from Lagos, who worked in some place called Jah Jah Buja
M. Sankofa.	I'm not a Rastafarian.
Yvonne.	Cleaning coaches.
M. Sankofa.	Who told you that?
Yvonne.	Detective Emeka!
M. Sankofa.	Detective..

Yvonne.	Dr Tunde's cousin. Got your finger prints, witness statement to say that you're no therapist. And we have pictures of you in Lagos market selling ochre. We even have forensic evidence of your DNA on some yam and bush meat! Bush meat! And you said you was a vegetarian!
M. Sankofa.	So, he's started to spy upon me.
Yvonne.	Why? The journey, the suitcase, the lies, and my, my emotions…why (*pause*).
M. Sankofa.	…Please listen. Oh my goodness! Seventeen years I worked at that school. Saw how the Black boys were treated, and even some of the white ones too who lived on the estate. The school had no ambition for them; didn't believe that they could be anything, and so they didn't become anything. And the parents; trusting, naïve, and were scared to challenge the school.
Yvonne.	So you decided to come back after all these years?
M. Sankofa.	Once I saw Theo being told off for getting his sums wrong. The teacher sent him to the Headteacher's office. He was upset. I called him over and said, 'you can be brilliant at maths'. His eyes lit up. The next day I brought my Ayo game in. Each day he'd sneak in the cleaning room and we'd play the game. He became good. It helped his maths and confidence, but the teacher spotted us. Sent Theo back to the Headteacher's office and told me to stop my African nonsense. African nonsense!
Yvonne.	(*almost resigned*) So you came back to do what?
M. Sankofa.	These children need a different type of education that prepares them for life. After my fifth husband died I decided to come back. I had to!
Yvonne.	(*to herself*) A cleaner. Spring cleaning my life.
M. Sankofa.	God is my witness. I had to listen each day in that school as the boys were scolded, shamed, disrespected, failed. Soon the school was full of social workers one minute, police; psychiatrists and people who'd come to fail these children. I saw myself as a community educator. I had a right to help educate these children.
Yvonne.	(*shouting*) You're a cleaner for Christ sakes. (now mocking M. Sankofa and speaking in an exaggerated Nigerian accent) My name is Madame Sankofa and I am an eminent therapist, life coach and motivational speaker. (Yvonne begins to stalk M. Sankofa) Why you don't look after yourself. Why your five husbands run away and leave you? Why you don't dress better? Look at your hair. (sniffing M. Sankofa) And your perfume, it smell like animal urine.
M. Sankofa.	Please. (remembering) One day sports day came. Black children win most of de races. One hundred meters, two hundred. Them had the biggest smile on them face you ever see. Then one year the headteacher change the rules. She introduced egg and spoon race; and sack race, and pyjama race. Our children start to lose.

Yvonne.	(in her normal voice) Came to you for therapy when all you good for is to mop the floor.
M. Sankofa.	(*still reminiscing*) I retired. Went back home. At nights, couldn't sleep. Tried to live a good life; had just married my fifth husband. Thought I was happy. Spent my days eating moi moi and jellof rice. One day I just found myself walking in my night dress to the beach. Everywhere was splashed with moonlight. The goddess Yemaya appear and tell me to follow her. I took a fisherman's boat and began to sail, sometimes I could barely see. But I knew she was leading me back to England.
Yvonne.	(*sarcastically*) You sure this goddess didn't take you back to her house so you could wash de dishes.
M. Sankofa.	(*angrily*) Please don't mock Madame Sankofa. I am Nigeria's most eminent, and distinguished therapist and personal coach. (Yvonne *storms out*) Please don't mock me…

A news bulletin is heard about the campaign to save the estate.
THE LOCAL COUNCIL HAS POSTPONED THE REMOVAL OF RESIDENTS FROM WHAT CAMPAIGNERS CALL THE FREEDOM ESTATE

Lights go up on Theo in the pirate station. Sebastian appears.

Sebastian.	Theo, this is dad. Don't hang up. I have a right to tell other listeners about my journey too.
Theo.	We know about your journey dad. Walked out on me and mum, and you're still walking…
Sebastion.	Please Theo…(pause).
Theo.	Dad….go on then..(pause)
Sebastian.	I'm here working on the estate; with families, with youths; gangs, old people, mad people, lovely people. You name it, it's here on the estate. And what do those in power care; what do they give! All around you see poverty, but the one bright thing in the lives of the youths is Gun-Boy. He's their hero because they have none; no role models, no nothing. Just a lost and vulnerable little boy with a gun.
Theo.	What d'you know about the estate dad? One minute you're a politician, now you're man of the people.
Sebastian.	It's more complicated than that. I came to find Gun-Boy.

Sebastian.	Might have been until I found him.
Theo.	What? You found Gun-Bwoy. We're live on air!
Sebastian.	Found him in one of the derelict flats; full of rats. Scared, alone, but innocent.
Theo.	(*angry*) then why did you have to find him then?
Sebastian.	(raised voice) Because I'd let down one young boy once and didn't want to do it again.
Theo.	People you listening to this. Gun-Boy has been captured, not by the police, but by my dad. Plus, we've all been fooled by an ex-school cleaner to go on some kind of spiritual journey. And people wonder why the yout's dem get vex. Is pure deceit. There aint no leaders in the community; everyone's for themselves. (*phone rings but Theo slams it down. Another mobile phone rings*)
M. Sankofa.	(speaking on her mobile) Is this how a soldier acts?
Theo.	You're just a cleaner living some mad mad fantasy.
M. Sankofa.	Did you not learn how to defeat your opponent from playing Ayo? Did you not learn to reap what you sow from playing Ayo-oware. Did you not learn how to attack, how to defend, how to bluff, and above all; how to win! Theo, tell all your listeners, and the people from the estate to come to the old school; I will give the assembly, where, we will have the school play that you should have starred in. Tell everyone to come to the service of Sankofa.
Theo.	You're just Aunty Ngosi!
M. Sankofa.	I'm not! I'm a concerned grandma. D'you know what it was like to clean classrooms everyday where Black children or even the white children from poor families never learnt anything about themselves? ..It was June; the children taking exams were about to go on study leave and as they was going through the school gates I met up with five or so of them and I asked them. What have you learnt in school? At first they were puzzled and then they laughed. I shouted at them. What have you learnt? I looked at one and asked 'name me five African leaders?' He couldn't. Looked at another; name me five African heroes? He couldn't? Looked at the other one and said when did African history start? He mumbled something about slavery. There in the playground I screamed at them. 'You have been in school eleven years and you have not learnt anything about yourself. What will you achieve in the world. I stormed back into the school building and in to Ms Maudsley's office and shouted at her. You haven't taught these children anything. She was shocked. Expected me to be the funny little Nigerian cleaner who makes jellof rice for the Christmas party. 'I am the Headteacher and you are the cleaner so will you let me do my job.' She shouted back at me. And on that day I resigned. After I settled back in Nigeria I did what research I could manage and I came to realise that we had a system of education, a system of preparing our children to be adults that was magnificent. (*shaking her head thoughtfully*) No, Madame Sankofa is not just a cleaner. (*pause*)

Theo.	Is this woman for real?
Yvonne.	(*grabbing the phone from M. Sankofa*) Theo, do what she says. What else do we have but ourselves?
M. Sankofa.	(still in her own thoughts) Not just a cleaner. The people are not just car mechanics, secretaries, shop assistants, workers, unemployed people; we have to become mentors, parent-teachers, personal coaches for our children. So come back to school, all of you on the estate; bring your grandparents, bring your cousins, your partners, your husbands, your wives, your children and in-laws….
Theo.	I'm not going anywhere; I'm not setting foot back in that school.
M. Sankofa.	Because you're scared; scared to go on your journey.
Yvonne.	That's why you hide in this little flat, this pirate station talking revolution, but the moment you step out you turn coward..
Theo.	Get over it mum your son dropped out of uni. Accept me for what I am. (*Madame Sankofa has gone to the desk and put on Ms Maudsley's coat and glasses. She now assumes* Ms Maudsley's *character*)
Yvonne.	Our children need you…I know you're still hurting
M. Sankofa.	(as Ms Maudsley) Morning children….I said morning Theo…
Theo.	Don't morning me..I'm a DJ..
M. Sankofa./ Phillipa	..that's better. Before we sing our first hymn, All Things Bright and Beautiful, just to remind some of you that our child psychologist is…
Theo.	Mum, how could you let that man even come near me?..
Yvonne.	(*pointing at* Ms Maudsley/M. Sankofa) I trusted her! (*Enter* Sebastian *holding his mobile*) Sebastian?
M. Sankofa./ Phillipa	..so Theo, see me after lunch; tell your mother to see me after school during parents evening, (*mockingly*) and Theo, tell your father to see me after I've seen mum (*she starts laughing*)
Yvonne.	(*angrily as he was about to put his bottle of whiskey down on the 'shrine'.*) Not again. I'll never trust you.
Sebastian.	(on his mobile and a bittle in his pocket) Came back for you Theo!.. Don't drink as much as…

Theo.	Came back for yourself dad. If it was for me then you'll put it down. (Sebastian *hesitates. He wants to put the bottle on the 'shrine' with the other baggage but he can't. Exit* Sebastian.)
M.Sankofa.	Thought there was going to be a school reunion where we can start our journey? Seems everyone's scared. (M. Sankofa, *now coming out of the* Maudsley *character.*)
Yvonne.	(*determined*) I'm not scared. You hear that Theo! You tell everyone to come down to the school and let's have a real school assembly. You hear me! (pause) …Theo? (*pause*)
Theo.	Hear that people. (in accent) So step forward na. Come everyone; to the old school and let's start our journey by dealing with our miseducation.
Yvonne.	(to the picture) Ms Maudsley, I know that you in middle class retirement in middle class England, but we taking back our children's education. We gone teach them 'bout leadership; about the courage of Olaudah Equiano, the fight of Mary Prince; the tenacity of Queen NZinga, the drive of Ignatious Sancho. Is we who are going to abolish this mental slavery that we're in? Us.. (M. Sankofa *is at the helm. People of the estate are heard coming out of their homes. Sebastian and Monique are seen. Sebastian puts the bottle of drink he has had in his pocket next to Ms Maudsley where the other items are.*)
M. Sankofa.	(*gesturing*) Yvonne? We're back; we've docked
Yvonne.	What?
M. Sankofa.	The school reunion? Deal with their miseducation; start their journey.
Yvonne.	And?
M. Sankofa.	How are people going to come in?
Yvonne.	(*remembering*) The school gates.
M. Sankofa.	The gates of no return have been locked for over five hundred years. How are the people going to come back through? (*shouting*) Open the gates woman!…. (suddenly stopping) No!….As Ms Maudsley.
Yvonne.	Me?
M. Sankofa.	(*pointing*) You. Those gates can only be opened when we stop being afraid.

Yvonne.	(*hesitantly*) But..
M. Sankofa.	…and truly understand the mind that made and created those gates that we were never supposed to come back through..(Yvonne is now putting on Ms Maudsley's coat, and glasses and hat. She now begins to open the gates and take out the items from the school lost property box. She starts to shout)
Yvonne.	Ms Maudsley, I'm not scared of you no more; not you or your world or your education system. (she has now taken off Ms Maudsley clothes and is half stamping on them) (Yvonne runs and starts opening the gates) (now as herself) People..everyone come.. there's nothing to be afraid of….we've got to make the effort…..for our child…we can do it..don't care what baggage you have we can do it….let's believe in ourselves….love ourselves…
M. Sankofa.	(*looking through the binoculars*) They're coming..
Yvonne.	..love ourselves..forgive one another..
M. Sankofa.	Ray-I the Rastaman is coming…
Yvonne.	(*still to herself*) ..with compassion
M. Sankofa.	…and Monique and her child…
Yvonne.	..we all have baggage that we need to deal with but we can return and reclaim our heritage…
M. Sankofa.	..and Dr Tunde. Is he married?
Yvonne.	(*shouting through the gates*) It's time for our school reunion; our family reunion.. so come!
M. Sankofa.	And Sebastian is coming too.
Yvonne.	..(suddenly remembering some of the items on the desk) But we don't need this…or that..or this (*she picks up the wig, the jars of skin lightners, boxes of fast food, fizzy drinks, gangsta rap cds, bottles of alcohol. The people from the estate arrive*)

M. Sankofa.   My people thank you for coming back to school and being brave enough to go back through the gates of no return. May I ask when was the last time you told your children how great they are? May I ask when was the last time you hugged them, praised them, told them how wonderful they are? When was the last time you shouted to the whole world that you love your family? Come on let's shout, WE LOVE OURSELVES! WE LOVE OUR AFRICAN SELVES! My people, Gun-Boy hasn't been caught, he's been saved by our returned soldier Sebastian who has put away another idol that we worshiped. Look at this (*Pointing to Ms Maudsley and the items of skin lighteners, meat, sweets, blonde wigs. There are shouts of amen and hallelujah*) How long are we going to worship things that make us hate ourselves, hate our children, hate our culture! Who is prepared to step forward and bring real education to our children? This is where our journey starts (Theo raises his hand and starts MCing on the microphone.) My people, you have two people here; they were once, man and wife. Should they remain separated? Should they get back together; forgive one another, build back their family life? (*they slowly take up an oar and start rowing in unison*) Madame Sankofa says they must get back together. (*cheering is heard*) My people should we open back this building as a school, with me, the ex-school cleaner as headteacher ?..(*there are loud cheers of yes*). Make some noise. So let's stop feeling down; let's stop complaining and take action; let's bring back the ancestors that we are going to call to attend this school: Lumumba, Biko, Shaka Zulu, Malcolm X, Sobukwe, Toussaint L'Ouverture, Garvey, Bogle, Tubman, Claudia Jones, Queen N'Zinga. Let us be the new revolutionaries and rebuild our family and rebuild our community. (*loud cheering is heard.*)

People of the estate, we are at the school gates; if your mind is ready for revolution then let's continue to march through; let's build our own school, let's learn together as family. This is the place they called the gates of no return, but we have returned, and it's time to reclaim our minds so that we can go forward and create our own future for our families. This is Madame Sankofa, saying God bless you all!

(*Whole cast perform a triumphant song.*)

THE END

Sepo: symbol of freedom of speech

Sepo is the symbol of freedom of speech. In our play, Voices of the Estate, Theo called his radio station Freedom FM because he not only wanted freedom to broadcast and focus on issues that were relevant to the community, but the Sankofa journey made him and his family seek a spiritual freedom.

Ultimately, our inquiry into education and family leads us to freedom, Sepo

We have come to the end of our inquiry into family and education, which has been a mix of so many things but at its centre has been a desire to help families understand what, is going on around them. A desire for self-love to be part of everything we do or we will operate from self-hate which will further destroy family. Theo, who has been looking for his family, now has the African family, which, as we have seen, is wealth, health and a strategy for living and prospering. This is the way that our family tree will grow, it is the way of our ancestors.

Writings of an Educationalist

Africa at the Crossroads: The Message of Yemaya

It is the summer of '08, the rainy season in Nigeria, where, having arrived in Lagos I took a six hour perilous bus journey to Onitsha, in Anambra State, to the east of the country. Onitsha is a commercial centre, and is said to be the largest market town in West Africa. I had important meetings to attend with private school proprietors, headteachers, book distributors and others. I was also keen to visit State schools but I was informed that they were closed due to a prolonged nationwide teacher's strike. Still, there was no anti-climax. Nigeria is too fascinating for any negative posturing, instead, I was excited by the share exuberance of the country, which wasn't diminished by my tiredness or sleep that was eventually disturbed by the cock's crow which announced another morning, another busy market day. So after I awoke and washed, I took a minibus into the main market area. In this market town everything is sold: electrical goods, household goods, watches, jewellery, clothes, food, alcohol, furniture and generators that keep the town lit when the numerous power cuts occur. Simply to observe the melee, you can see that these people are ingenious. There might be no electricity, inadequate employment or problems with pumped water, but they survive; they create things for themselves, and this ingenuity goes back a long way, back to Benin City of 16th century, back to the time when great craft guilds were formed which led to the making of magnificent Benin heads. The history of Onitsha says that they were once of the Benin Empire but, due to trouble in the kingdom of the Oba of Benin, they had to migrate and it was during this migration that they acquired the name Onitsha, which is derived from the Yoruba word orisha, meaning aspect of god. Perhaps this history

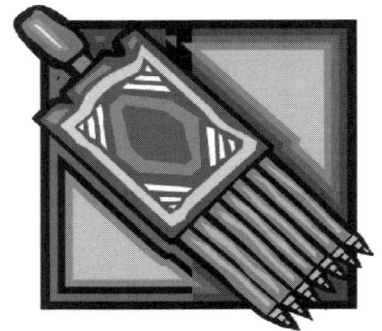

gives us clues about their amazing entrepreneurial spirit, for this migration from the Benin Empire, led by Eze Chima who led his people across the River Niger, and there, then settled on the land having been guided by their great oracle. This was how Onitsha was founded. How did they survive? Perhaps we do not have to look at the history books; perhaps we have to look at the bustling market that is full of Japanese mini buses, motorcyles known as Okadas carrying passengers; cars full of manufactured goods and even livestock. Here people manage in the shadow of neo-colonialism and struggling governments; though there is a new optimism for a new president has been elected which people are positive about. But I am at the crossroads now of the great market town and as I look I see what at first appears to be total chaos. In front of me, beeping away, is a motorcyclist carrying at least six bed mattresses strapped to his bike; at another part of the crossroads riding straight towards this man is another motorcyclist with plumbing pipes that he holds as if they were javelins; and then there is a woman carrying a big pot of water on her head, and she is not alone for there are other women carrying bags of peanuts, fruit, bush meat. People argue, people barter, people laugh and greet one another; mothers walk with sleeping babies tied to their back. Amidst all this there is a man wearing a green and yellow uniform brandishing a whip as if he were a jockey, which he uses to whack or tap the vehicles fighting for road space. He is the lonely policeman, who is totally calm with the occasional vexed moment, but somehow he manages to keep some kind of order. Then, from nowhere, a few characters emerge who completely catch me by surprise. The first is a tall Nigerian man in a black cowboy outfit, cowboy hat and white shirt and black tie. He smokes a big cigar, and walks into the crossroads as if he owns it, as if coming into Dodge City for a shoot out in a Hollywood western. He is oblivious to the cars, the trucks, the goats being carried shoulder high, the market sellers and the policeman. This is his patch, his home. Before my fascination can grow even more, another figure, here at the crossroads, catches my eye. A woman in turquoise, wearing a traditional African clothing, emerges from this chaos, and she serenely carries a large pot of water on her head, and even amidst the heavy car and motorbike fumes I sense that she smells of jasmine, and in my mind I call her *Yemaya of the Sea*, after the Yoruba aspect of god which governs healing, memory and nurturing. I notice that she glances at *The Nigerian Cowboy*, and they in turn glance at *The Policeman with the Stick*, and I sense a relationship between them, as if they are some long lost family. More people come to the crossroad and I have to leave as I make my way into another indoor market, another world full of other characters as I seek out someone to change my pounds into naira.

It would be days like these, when I would talk with ordinary working people that I would find out about Nigeria; hear stories about what happened during the Biafra war (1967 – 1970), here stories about the growing conflict in the Niger Delta where, local people, who have had their fishing and agricultural industries destroyed by oil exploration fight for compensation, development and human rights. Perhaps this is why Yemaya appeared at the crossroads, to tell Nigeria, and all people at the crossroads that we have to heal ourselves, remember our ancestry, but I know that there is more that she wants to tell me but I am lost, like the African Diaspora, at this crossroads and so each time I deliberately look she fails to appear.

A few days later a friend takes me to visit two shrines, the shrine of Otumoye and Iru Ani Onitsha, one of which is guarded by people called *Women of the Shrine*. I ask questions, and the more questions I ask the more I come to realise that these shrines are really family classrooms, community classrooms; that in one instance might hold a mirror up to us so that we can look into ourselves, in another instance, it reminds us of the mission of our family tree; it reminds the community to be respectful, to have high morals and standards; to consider the consequence of certain behaviour patterns which destroy the home, the family and the community. This is systemised family and community learning. Perhaps Yemaya was telling me this; reminding me of a system of learning that involved the whole community. When I began to dwell on her symbolism I find that she is portrayed as the goddess that suckles, a deity that emerges from the sea; a pervading intelligence that requires us, with compassion, to look at our behaviour and forgive ourselves and to forgive others. She is the great foundation. I can remember thinking, 'was my literary imagination over working, or did Yemaya truly have some kind of business in my research.' I was soon to find out.

My next meeting was with a headteacher of a private school, and she, like all the other headteachers that I met were interested in Ebony's teacher training programme. At that time they seemed to think they had no option other than to send hordes of Nigerian teachers to England to have training in subjects like phonics. 'It looks good on their CVs,' she tells me. Of course I am not convinced and by the time I outline the training I could deliver, she not only wants it but offers to act as an agent for me in Nigeria. What also catches my attention is that this teacher mentions the crisis with families attending the school; how they are finding it difficult to pitch their education provision to children coming from homes that have so many issues. She is aware that the provision has to change, and that family has to be included in all educational provisions. What strikes me from listening to the headteachers, school proprietors and all involved in education is that they are keen for a new approach; there is a recognition that teacher training for parents, teachers and the community at large has to be provided. In my view, no African country can go forward if they keep adopting this Eurocentric approach to education; that is, paying large fees for teacher training that is not bespoke in terms of culture, and that does not involve family or a celebration or love of self.

Later on in my visit I am shown classrooms that operate on a teacher ratio of one teacher to one hundred children; classrooms that have leaking roofs, where a black square is painted on the wall and this square is used as the blackboard for these one hundred children, many of whom sit on the floor because some of the older children have taken their stools. There are little resources, but schools manage in spectacular fashion because people care and children desperately want to learn. This glimpse into the education of Nigeria is the same as the one I saw in Ghana, in South Africa, in Grenada and so on. Many governments do not realise that to change a nation, to unlock their genius, is to change the way they think; to provide the people with a diverse and flexible education system that they own and have helped design, and that has family at it centre. I would also meet with a very forward thinking book distributor and we would immediately cut a deal. He is passionate that when Black children open a book that they should learn something that is relevant to them, that represents them positively and that will make them believe that they can achieve something. His passion is infectious.

As I went from meeting to meeting; sometimes as researcher, sometimes as tourist, I kept having strange experiences of seeing beautiful women emerge from crowds, from chaos; emerge supreme, elegant and powerful, whether it was from a modest home, or from clusters of shoppers, or even emerge from the shadows of dark roads. As I kept seeing these women I began to feel that they were signs, (like the Sankofa bird that walks forward but looks back) that Nigeria, like Ghana, like Senegal, like South Africa and Grenada, and the rest of Africa and the African Diaspora has to, with both science and pride, look, appreciate and understand its indigenous knowledge. Africa is at the crossroads, and if it chooses the western family model, the western life, its relationships will end up like that of Yvonne and Sebastian, and there will be no legacy for the children, so, like Theo, they will have to make their way in life the best they can. Africa can choose to keep sending its teachers back to England to learn phonics; it can choose to keep selling goods from brown boxes with *Made In China* stamped on it, or, it can choose, as Yemaya is signalling to me that Africa's beauty, Africa's genius lies within us; something our family tree has shown we spent thousands of years scientifically developing and understanding. We have seen in Theo, how his awakening was inspired by Amma (Amen), that hidden intelligence that we all have. Theo chose to awaken his genius; to adopt a revolutionary approach to his education and understanding of family. As Madame Sankofa tried to tell the people of the estate, only we can bring this system of learning centred on family back; only you can take the action that will restore yourself to your true greatness.

Now that we have come to the end of this brief journey into family and education we should honour our family tree and pour libation to our Ancestors.

African Libation

For all those who have gone before us,
We pour this water and say sacred words, to wet the ground,
In honour of your brave footsteps,
And the kola nuts and prayers that you obeyed;
Yes, we salute your dreams that have become our scriptures.

For all those who have gone before us,
We pour from royal calabash this water and wisdom,
In honour of Nefertari, Nzinga, Asantewa and their sweet sisterhood,
That took bitter counsel from Nature and African cycles,
And so, we offer salutes to these queens that suckled nightly revolution.

For all those who have gone before us,
We pour Yemaya's water so that it might heal wounds,
Of soldiers like, Biko, Bogle and Garvey and their brotherhood,
Who, in death, armed with Ogun's science of battle, still fight,
Even whilst we rest before the next duel with our inner self.

For all those who have gone before us,
We pour carried water on seeds in tiled bloodied soil,
For new trees to grow around almost forgotten graves of martyrs,
To those of you who fell at Adowa, at Sharpeville and in cane fields,
To adorn your courage with medals in this heroic parade from memory.

For all those who have gone before us in uniformed red, gold and green,
We pour this water, cleansed by the earth's mystery and rock,
To those who drew maps of courage in dark sand as shackled minds slept,
That we may again find paths to these Trees on family land,
And pick ripe fruits from our African Tree of Knowledge.

Selected Bibliography

1.   Afrika, O. Llaila. *African Holistic Health*. Sea Island Information Group, 1983.
2.   Agbo, Adolph Hilary. *Values of Adinkra & Agama Symbols*. Bigshy Designs and Publications, 2006.
3.   Amen, Ra Un Nefer. *Tree of Life Meditation System:* Kamit Publications, 1996.
4.   Ampim, Manu. *Towards Black Community Development*. Advancing the Research, 1993.
5.   Bernal, Martin. Black Athena. In "*African Presence in Early Europe*." pp. 66-81. Edited by Ivan Van Sertima. Transaction Books, 1985.
6.   Browder, T. Anthony. *Nile Valley Contributions to Civilisation*. The Institute of Karmic Guidance, 1992.
7.   Diop, Cheikh Anta. *Civilisation or Barbarism*. Lawrence Hiil, 1991; originally published in France by Presence Africaine, 1981.
8.   Dryden, Gordon., Vos, Jeanette. *The Learning Revolution*. Network Educational Press in association with the Learning Web, 2001.
9.   Fanon, Frantz. *The Wretched of the Earth*. Penguin Books, 1967.
10.   Freire, Paulo. *Pedagogy of the Oppressed*, Penguin 1996; originally published in 1970.
11.   Hale E. Janice. *Black Children: Their Roots, Culture and Learning Styles*. John Hopkins University Press, 1986.
12.   Hannaford, Carla. *Smart Moves*. Great Ocean Publishers, 1995.
13.   Henderson, Richard N. *The King in Every Man*. Yale University Press, 1972.
14.   Holford, Patrick. *New Optimum Nutrition for the Mind*. Piatkus Books Ltd, 2007.
15.   Karenga, Maulana. *Introduction to Black Studies*. Kawaida Publications, 1982.
16.   Klein, Naomi. *The Shock Doctrine*. Penguin Books, 2008; originally published by Metropolitan Books, Henry Holt and Co, 2007.
17.   Madhubuti, R. Haki. *Black Men Obsolete, Single, Dangerous?* Third World Press, 1991.
18.   McAdoo, Pipes Harriette (ed.) *Black Families*. Sage Publications, 1988.
19.   McGuinness, Carmen., McGuinness, Geoffrey. *Reading Reflex*. Penguin Books, 1998; originally pub lished by The Free Press, 1998.
20.   Mbiti, John. *Introduction to African Religion*. Heineman, 1991.
21.   Moore, T. Owens. *Dispelling the Myths of Melanin*. Beckham House Publishers, 1995.
22.   Perkins, Useni Eugene. *Harvesting New Generations*. Third World Press, 1986.
23.   Peters T., C. Gilberg. *Autism, Medical and Educational Aspects*. Whurr Publishers, 1999.
24.   Ratey, John. *A User's Guide to the Brain*. Little, Brown and Company, 2001.
25.   Reynolds, Edward. *A History of the Atlantic Slave Trade*. Alison and Busby, 1985.
26.   Rodney, Walter. *How Europe Underdeveloped Africa*. Bogle L'Ouverture, 1972.
27.   Simon, David. *How to Unlock Your Child's Genius*. Ebony Books, 2004.
28.   Walker, Robin. *When We Ruled*. Every Generation Media, 2006.
29.   Wambu, Onyekachi. *Under the Tree of Talking*. Counterpoint, 2007.
30.   Williams, Chancellor. *The Destruction of Black Civilisation*. Third World Press, 1974.
31.   Wilson, N. Amos. *Blueprint for Black Power*. Afrikan World Infosystems, 1998.
32.   Woodson, Carter G. *The Miseducation of the Negro*. Khalif Khalifah's Booksellers and Associates, 2005; originally printed in 1933 by Carter G. Woodson.
33.   Young, O. Robert., *Young, Redford Shelley. The pH Miracle*. Sphere, 2007.
34.   Zaslavsky, Claudia. *Africa Counts*. Lawrence Hill and Company, 1973.